Energize Your Life

Overcoming Fatigue and Stress

Dr Carlson's writings contain invaluable instruction and direction concerning some of the most pressing problems of contemporary life – especially chronic overload and exhaustion. He not only conveys vital medical knowledge, but also a clear and practical wisdom, along with spiritual insight. I believe this book will be very helpful for everyone who is prepared to find their way into a life of practical interaction with the One whose yoke is easy and whose burden is light.

Dallas Willard, Professor of Philosophy, USC, Speaker and Author.

Energize Your Life is a book which makes good on its premise and promise. Written in a readable and practical manner, professionals and laymen alike will benefit and be amazed at the amount of information this book contains. This resource speaks to the heart of the concerns of many who struggle in their daily lives.

H. Norman Wright, Christian Counselor

In this book, Dwight Carlson has combined his psychiatric insights, pastoral care and astute observation of the stress-related challenges of the twenty-first century. Not only has he made an accurate diagnosis of the problem, he has prescribed some approaches to healing that square with the complex realities of contemporary living. What I appreciate most is his holistic wrestling with the multitude of contemporary stressors in a way that acknowledges the importance of integrating biblical truth with his psychiatric observations. This is a most helpful book for those of us dealing with stress and ministering to those who are stressed. I whole-heartedly recommend it!

Rev. John Huffman, Senior Pastor, St. Andrews Presbyterian Church, Newport Beach, California.

Dr Carlson's unique credentials provide a credibility and authenticity unlike most authors in the areas of understanding and experiencing healing of personal stress and fatigue. Drawing on his years as a medical professional, extended time as a psychiatrist, and his extensive personal spiritual insights, you will be enlightened through his clear explanations of stress and fatigue. You will be enriched through his full disclosure of the 'drainers' that contribute to fatigue and 'energizers' that provide strength so you will be able to experience God's full potential for your life. As you read this book, you will be encouraged by Dr. Carlson's very practical counsel for areas in your life in which fatigue can be turned to strength.

Dr. Gordon E. Kirk, Senior Pastor, Lake Avenue Church, Pasadena, California.

Dr. Dwight Carlson's book on energizing your life contains many helpful and practical guidelines as well as much biblical wisdom for overcoming fatigue and stress. I highly recommend it."

Rev. Siang-Yang Tan, Ph.D., Professor of Psychology, Fuller Theological Seminary and Senior Pastor, First Evangelical Church, Glendale, California.

This book is a fountain of sanity and compassionate skill. Let any tired saint drink deeply from its waters and be refreshed, restored and perhaps cured. So if you're tired, read this. If you're under pressure, read this. If you're bewildered by your failures and untouched by your successes, read this. If you want off the Christian treadmill read this. If you've ever wondered how on earth Jesus could have promised rest to those who labour and are heavy laden, but you feel that he must have been meaning you, read this. If you've ever suspected that the promise of abundant life has passed you by, read this. In fact, if you're a human being, read this!

Rarely do we find in one author profound pastoral sensitivity, expert medical opinion, astute biblical awareness and the wisdom of the years. But we certainly find them in Dwight L. Carlson.

Rev. Dominic Smart, Gilcomston South Church of Scotland, Aberdeen, Scotland.

Energize Your Life

Overcoming Fatigue and Stress

Dwight L. Carlson, M.D.

Christian Focus

Sections of this book were originally published under the title: *Run and Not Be Weary*.

ISBN 1-85792-864-4

Published in 2003
by
Christian Focus Publications Ltd.,
Geanies House, Fearn, Tain,
Ross-shire, IV20 1TW, Great Britain.

www.christianfocus.com

Cover Design by Alister MacInnes

Printed and bound by
Mackays of Chatham

CONTENTS

SECTION THREE: THE CAUSE OF ILLNESS

SECTION FOUR: THE ENERGIZERS

Figures: Chapter

Diagrams:

Charts:

I dedicate this book to
Bob Boardman,
who was a significant early
influence in my walk with God.

PREFACE

IN 1972 I was a practicing internist with a busy practice in Southern California. One of the most common complaints that I heard from my patients was that "I am tired" or "exhausted" or "I just don't have the energy that I think I should have." I was taught virtually nothing about the symptom of fatigue in medical school and during seven years of postgraduate training. The medical literature at that time did not shed much more light on the subject. Short sections could be found in medical books or journals on this subject, but where does the layperson turn? So I went to the main branch of our local library and found one book on the subject, one that was published in 1905.

Therefore, as a physician I studied the problem and wrote my initial book on fatigue that was published in 1974 with the title *Run and Not Be Weary*, later it was published in a soft cover with the title *How to Win Over Fatigue*. With the book's publication I changed directions in my medical practice and completed three years of residency training in psychiatry. I have now practiced this specialty for about 25 years, continuing to see patients with stress and fatigue. Since the 1980s much research has been done on the subject of the cause and consequences of stress and fatigue. In addition, I have learned more on the subject through my patients and by an extensive review of the latest literature on the subject. So this is an appropriate time to update and greatly expand the material originally appearing in my first book on fatigue.

Sometimes I feel like an expert on the subject. I have experienced burn out in my late teens, a major depression in midlife, a brother who was martyred as a medical missionary, and a daughter told she was going to die of leukemia. In addition to a busy medical practice with all the daily hassles and stresses inherent in it, I have also experienced as much fatigue – severe, prolonged, and from many different sources – as is possible. In more recent years I have discovered things that I can do to energize my life. At any rate, I do speak from professional and personal experience. I do not claim to have all the answers, but I have learned many lessons along the way. This book is the result of a desire to help the person suffering from stress and fatigue first to understand the problem and its causes, then to present specific solutions available to him or to her. The material in this book will help you gain better control of your life and give you added vitality and serenity. Since I encourage the reader to be open and honest, I have endeavored to practice this openness so that I may relate better to you despite the risks involved.

The topic of fatigue and stress cuts across numerous disciplines: medical, social, psychiatric, nutritional, and spiritual. As an internist and psychiatrist as well as a lifelong student of the Scriptures, I feel uniquely equipped to address this topic.

Some of the examples in this book are taken from my practice of internal medicine and others from my practice of psychiatry. Incidental aspects have been altered enough to preserve the anonymity of the individuals. Where this has been difficult to achieve, permission has been obtained from the persons involved.

I want to thank Dr. Bill Shell for his helpful editing. Last but certainly not least, I want to express my deep gratitude to God for the encouragement, understanding, and patience of my dear wife, Betty.

SECTION ONE

THE PROBLEM

PROLOGUE 1953

THE DOCTOR SAID I was suffering from fatigue and the diagnosis couldn't have been more correct. At the ripe old age of 19 I was utterly exhausted. He encouraged me to develop better eating habits and gave me some iron, vitamins and a B12 shot. But the cause of my fatigue was much deeper than simply not eating properly. Sheer exhaustion had forced me to quit my job altogether and rest.

During the latter part of high school I recommitted my life to God and started to take the Christian life seriously. I was thoroughly convinced that a follower of Christ had to be disciplined. I worked hard to know all that God would teach me about prayer and Bible study; I even tried other disciplines like fasting. Some dynamic Christians that I had met encouraged me to memorize three Bible verses a week. I thought that is three were good, then six must be better, so I began committing to memory six verses per week, month after month. I was convinced that a daily quiet time was crucial so determined to spend 30 minutes each morning with God. Later I discovered a passage in the Bible which says "I have esteemed the words of his mouth more than my necessary food" so I wouldn't have breakfast if I missed my time with God (Job 23:12, KJV). And I love to eat. In fact I had a check chart and checked off some 23 items each day to see if I was living up to my commitments.

I wanted my life to count, so after I graduated from high school I left my job and home and moved near a servicemen's center 100 miles away. I supported myself by working as a mason's tender. After a hard day's work I'd head for the servicemen's center. I spent six nights a week, a half-day Saturday, and all day Sunday at the center talking to Marines heading for the battlefields of Korea about their relationship with God. Someone advised me to take one night off a week, which I did, but instead of relaxing I went to the nearby Marine base where I led a Bible study.

As the months passed it was becoming harder and harder for me to get up in the morning for a quiet time, and putting the alarm clock in a pan across the room was no longer effective. I knew just enough about electricity to be dangerous. So I hooked up a Model T spark coil to a clock and ran two wires under my legs in an effort to jolt myself out of bed at an early hour. The 40,000 volts were effective in getting me out of bed in the morning. However, it is no surprise that I ended up burned-out and utterly exhausted. I literally had to stop all work and let my body recuperate. I was unable to do virtually anything for weeks on end. The year was 1953.

Part One

Stresses
and
Energy Depletion

CHAPTER I

WHAT IS YOUR STRESS LEVEL?

A YOUNG MAN in central Africa was walking to his hut from the river where he had been fishing all afternoon. He sauntered along a path surrounded by tall grass and anthills ten feet tall. Just then, out of the corner of his eye he saw the grass rustling as the stalking lion intensely peered at him. Instantly his heart rate went from 68 to 180, his blood pressure went from 110/75 to 200/110. His respiration increased, blood was immediately shunted away from his internal organs to his muscles, his pupils dilated, and beads of perspiration could be seen on his forehead. The fight-or-flight mechanism was automatically activated to enable him to stand and fight, or to run for his dear life. God gave us this enabling mechanism to handle the stresses of life.[1]

Our bodies are uniquely and wonderfully made. The instant a threat is perceived the entire body goes into action to protect itself against harm and maintain its equilibrium (homeostasis). This is called the *adaptive response*. Hormones are released and the nervous system activated. As adrenalin is pumped into the blood stream, alertness occurs, the metabolic rate is increased, and decreased awareness of pain results. Our blood clots more quickly in case we are injured. This is a marvelous adaptation of our bodies for such emergencies. Our bodies shift into working overtime resulting in *The Classic Stress Syndrome*. This is what happens if a lion is stalking us. Assuming we get away unscathed the body would quickly return to its normal healthy state. But what happens if there are repeated life-threatening occurrences or, for that matter, low level but chronic stresses? Typically, our bodies would shift into *The Sickness Syndrome*. Numerous changes would take place throughout the body with devastating consequences.[2]

The Severe and Widespread Consequences of Stress

Stress, especially when it is chronic, damages virtually every area of our bodies. Stress *causes* or *significantly contributes* to:[3]

- **Fatigue** – Chronic Fatigue Syndrome, Fibromyalgia, and Chemical Sensitivity.
- **Increased sensitivity to pain** – headaches, Rheumatoid Arthritis, and other musculoskeletal disorders.
- **Gastrointestinal disorders** – many are stress related including hyperacidity, Gastroesophageal Reflux Disease (GERD), peptic ulcer disease, constipation, diarrhea, inflammatory bowel disease, and Irritable Bowel Syndrome.
- **Endocrine dysfunction** – manifests itself in Graves Disease, menstrual irregularities, weight change – including obesity, osteoporosis, diabetes, Insulin Resistance Syndrome.
- **Immune system** – causes allergic reactions, autoimmune disease, asthma, an increase in infections including "colds" and other upper respiratory infections, susceptibility to mononucleosis, TB, and yeast infections. It affects the Natural Killer Cells and cytotoxic T cells which play a pivotal role in defending against viral infections, autoimmune and inflammatory disturbances.
- **Cancer** – evidence suggests that stress increases the susceptibility to cancer and exacerbates the metastatic spread of cancer.
- **Cardiovascular diseases** – stress increases blood pressure and arrhythmias, elevates lipids in the blood, including cholesterol, increases insulin production, causes plaque formation (atherosclerosis), increases the coagulability of the blood, all of which greatly increase the likelihood of cardiovascular catastrophes, such as heart attacks and strokes.
- **Dermatological diseases** – most are affected by stress.
- **Psychological illness** – emotional illness is both caused and aggravated by stress, including burn-out, depression, anxiety, panic disorder, compulsive eating, anorexia nervosa, bulimia, and suicide.
- **Chemical abuse** – all types of illicit drug use and abuse of tobacco and alcohol.
- **Sleep disturbances** – especially insomnia.

- **Altered mental functioning** – cognitive impairment occurs, including alterations in memory, attention, concentration, and decision making.
- **Harmed relationships** – adversely affects all relationships, including family and work.
- **Atrophy of the brain** – causes atrophy of the nerve cells; these changes are reversible if of short duration; however, with prolonged stress they become irreversible. Chronic stress can literally lead to a decrease of neurons in the brain and a decrease in the size of specific areas in the brain. In fact, in Post Traumatic Stress Disorder, where an individual undergoes severe stress, one portion of the brain (hippocampal) shows up to a 26 percent reduction in physical size.
- **Tissue aging** – Tissue in our bodies ages more quickly under stress.
- **Decrease in Life satisfaction** – stress decreases overall life satisfaction.
- **Increase of injury rates** – individuals under stress are more prone to accidents and to injure themselves.
- **Spiritual** – fosters emptiness, doubt, loss of meaning, and inability to forgive self and others.
- **Stress aggravates every other illness** – whatever its cause, stress adversely affects all illnesses.
- **Death** – stress has been shown to increase the progression of most illnesses with resultant decrease in overall life expectancy. In other words – death. It has been stated that 50 percent of all deaths are related to lifestyle choices.

Thus the consequences of stress are legion. The above list certainly is not complete, and in a few years more illnesses will be shown to be caused or aggravated by stress.

The Consequences of Stress May Be Permanent and Irreversible

Certain stressors can have permanent consequences on an individual. For instance, early life stresses such as isolation of the infant or altered mother-infant interaction can permanently cause the individual to have an exaggerated hormonal and nervous response to stress throughout the rest of the person's life. Likewise, chronic abuse can leave its lasting scars on the stress response of the individual, making it more difficult to handle future stress. Furthermore, severe lifethreatening stress, such as, rape, a combat situation, or a natural disaster can cause structural changes in the brain that are permanent. It is believed that it actually causes a change in the circuitry of the brain. (But don't stop reading here, as there is much that a person can do to alter this process.)[4]

Cumulative Stress Load

Stress becomes additive whether there are repeated stressful situations of the same or differing types. Our bodies respond to the summation of the stress. It extracts an aggregate toll on the entire body. I will refer to this as "Cumulative Stress Load." This is the big culprit in causing disease.[5]

On top of all of this, many of these problems are both cause and effect. For instance, stress can cause sleep disturbance, which in turn can impair one's subsequent ability to function well the next day. This stress adds to the problem of insomnia, and so the cycle perpetuates itself. Numerous examples could be described of how stress perpetuates a vicious cycle of symptoms and disease which produces more stress with devastating consequences.[6]

Stress Is on the Rise at the Cost of Serenity

Several decades ago we thought that with all the modern conveniences our lives would slow down and there would be increasing free time to enjoy life. Instant e-mail, cell phones, computers, and palm display units were supposed to help us become more efficient. Somehow the opposite has occurred. Our work loads are heavier, our jobs are insecure, and generally a sense of loss of control hangs over our future. Leisure time has significantly decreased. A 45 percent increase in life stresses has occurred in the last 30 years. The industrialized nations have more color TVs, high-speed computers, luxury cars, and brand-name clothes than they did several decades ago; but we are no happier. "Meanwhile, the divorce rate doubled. Teen suicide tripled. Reported violent crime nearly quadrupled . . . [and] depression rates have soared."[7] During the week after the September 11, 2001 terrorist attack on the

World Trade Center 90 percent of adults in the United States experienced some symptoms of stress and 44 percent of all adults experienced symptoms of *substantial* stress. In a recent study in Great Britain it was reported that one in ten believed they would be better off if dead, one in four said they were unhappy in their jobs, while one in three felt exhausted, unappreciated, or underpaid.[8]

With most of the "civilized" world operating under great stress, it is no surprise that serenity is vanishing. "Though census data show that many measures of quality of life have risen since World War II, the number of people who consider themselves happy remains flat."[9] This situation won't improve on its own, so we must take deliberate steps to remedy this plague. Stress is the scourge of our day; it is epidemic.

What Is Stress?

At a conscious level, stress is "a feeling of doubt about being able to cope, a perception that the resources available do not match the demands made."[10] It is our bodies' reaction to anything that threatens the stability of the body (technically this has been called *homeostasis*). Dr. Hans Selye, considered the father of stress research, defines stress as "the nonspecific response of the body to any demand made upon it."[11] In more recent years this has been slightly modified to include the notion that the physiology of the body fluctuates to meet the demands that the stressor places on it (technically referred to as *allostasis*). Dr. Selye further describes three states in the response to stress which he called the *General Adaptation Syndrome*: *The Alarm Stage* which activates the fight or flight response, *The Resistance Stage*, and *The Exhaustion Stage*. We often associate stress with the alarm stage: that is the fight-and-flight response.

The Alarm Stage of Stress

The instant the young man in central Africa sees the stalking lion, the alarm stage is activated. The "Master Gland" was activated directly, stimulating the autonomic (sympathetic) nervous system and causing the release of hormones into the blood that stimulate the adrenal gland to secrete adrenalin and cortisol into the system.

The system was, so to speak, at its battle stations and at maximum alert. This activation of the stress system leads to enhanced alertness, better cognitive function, increased ability to withstand pain, as well as the cardiovascular and other changes described in the introduction to this chapter.[12]

The Resistance and Exhaustion Stage of Stress

The young African has a rifle and decides to stand firm. He drops his catch of fish to the ground, puts his rifle at the shoulder ready to shoot if the lion makes any advance. He is in the midst of the resistance stage of stress, with heart still pounding and all his senses heightened. As the lion saunters off, he drops the rifle to his side, his heart gradually slows, and he feels exhausted as he wanders home to tell his family and relatives of his close encounter. But in the industrialized-computerized world the resistance and exhaustion stage become much more chronic, complex, and hazardous.

Classic Versus Sick Stress Syndrome

With repeated stress our bodies respond in diverse ways. For example, the immune response may increase or decrease, mental capacity may improve or deteriorate, sensitivity to pain may increase or decrease, and so it is for most of the changes in our bodies with ongoing stress. The specifics of these changes have not all been clearly elucidated even though the final devastating results of stress are clear.

It appears that there is a more *Classic Stress Syndrome* closely resembling the changes noted in the fight-or-flight response, such as, increased blood pressure and blood glucose. Then there is what has been called the *Sickness Syndrome,* where chronic stress is more likely to cause nausea, fatigue, depression, somnolence, increased sensitivity to pain, headache, fever, and a feeling of loss of control or defeat. Chronic Fatigue Syndrome and Fibromyalgia (see Chapter 12) may be associated with the Sickness Syndrome.[13]

Stressors

What causes stress? Stressors. None of us would have trouble identifying a lion on the loose as a stressor. But many stressors in modern society are not readily apparent; nevertheless, they can cause all kinds of havoc. A "stressor" is an actual or perceived threat to the stability of the person. The stressors may be acute, chronic, internal or external, physical or psychological, real or imaginary. Furthermore, as we will see in a moment, a stressor may be perceived by our bodies without our conscious awareness.[14]

The Nature of Stress

We often think of stress as being the result of major adverse events in our lives, such as, the loss of a job or the death of a loved one. Yes, these do cause stress, but it's far more complex than that. Hassles, such as breaking a shoe lace, as well as in some instances "good" things that come our way can cause stress. On the other hand, encouraging things, in the literature referred to as "uplifts" – exercise, social support, and other things to be discussed later in the book – can decrease the stress, and its effects in our lives.

Some Sample Stressors[15]

There are innumerable stressors in life. A few representative samples are:
- Major threats to the person:
  - Health problems, such as a heart attack
  - Death of a loved one
  - A major traffic accident
  - Being near "Ground Zero" and seeing jet liners crash into the Trade Center Towers
  - The inability to shut off stress after the stressor is removed
  - Hunger.
  - Psychological factors, such as, anger, anxiety, depression, fear, social defeat, humiliation, and/or disappointment
  - Physical factors, such as overexertion, heat, cold, trauma, infection, inflammation, overload, and/or lack of discretionary time
  - An unhealthy environment, such as, safety threats, poor social ties, or a conflicted, abusive, or violent environment
  - Plus many others (which we will discuss later)

- Hassles:
  Far more common are the "little" stresses, often referred to as *hassles*. Some examples are: traffic jams, e-mails needing a response, noise, isolation and crowding, and many others.
- Any significant change, whether it is perceived as positive or negative. In 1967 Holmes and Rahe published their "Social Readjustment Rating Scale," that was updated by Miller and Rahe in 1997, in which stresses that are generally classified as negative, such as the death of a spouse, and positive stresses, such as marriage, were both weighted as causing adverse stress on an individual. Subsequent researchers have questioned whether positive events should be considered a stressor or an uplifter. It may turn out that our attitude, whether it is pessimistic or optimistic, may determine if a positive event becomes a drainer or an energizer. We will consider this later under "Energizers" (see Section Four).[16]

Anti-stressors

A person can do many things that will reduce or minimize stress. Some samples are uplifts, exercise, and social support. Throughout the rest of the book we will be elaborating on the numerous stressors and anti-stressors.

Our Response to Stress is a Factor in Stress

The specific stressor or uplifter certainly is a big factor in the stress perceived and experienced by an individual. But there is more to the story than that. A given stressor may adversely affect one person significantly more than another person, depending on how the person experiences and responds to the stressor. Our response may have a much greater effect on us than the specific stressor itself. Earlier stressors, what the specific stressor means to us, our attitude towards the stressor, our genetics, and how we choose to respond to the stress, all greatly affect the effects the stressor has on us.

Stress/Productivity/Satisfaction Response Curve

All stress is not bad. In fact, Hans Selye discusses good stress and how each individual may succeed in finding an optimal stress level for himself or herself. He says, "*Stress is not something to be avoided.*" If he does not find the optimal stress level for himself, he will "either suffer the distress of having nothing worthwhile to do or of being constantly overtaxed by excessive activity."[17]

In Figure 1 (below) you will notice on the horizontal axis increasing stimulation or stress from zero to about 175 percent of your "normal." On the vertical axis increasing productivity is displayed. You will note that your productivity starts at zero on the left and only gradually increases at first. However, if you push yourself, productivity can keep increasing until you reach about 125 percent of normal. On the other hand, with further demand or stress, productivity will rapidly fall off. That is, too much demand or stress eventually becomes counter-productive. Then note the dotted line which represents your emotional feelings. You must

Stress/Productivity/Satisfaction Response Curve

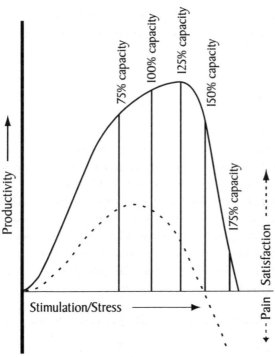

Figure I

have moderate stimulation, or if you will, "stress," for it to start to register satisfaction, enjoyment, or pleasure. But now note what happens as you push yourself. Pleasure plateaus at about 80 percent and starts to decrease at 90 percent normal stimulation/ stress for a given individual. By 125 percent it has fallen off markedly and at 150 percent it crosses the line and our emotional feelings become painful.

This graph illustrates several pivotal points. A certain amount of stimulation/stress is necessary for optimal good feeling and productivity. Though you can push your body beyond its normal 100 percent capacity and eke out some further productivity; it is at a significant cost in your wellbeing, and pushed too much, it becomes counterproductive. The maximum enjoyment comes from life when you function between 70 to 90 percent of your normal capacity.

Awareness of Stress

You might not even be aware that you are under stress, for it can occur without your hardly being cognizant of it. A couple of times a year I may be sitting in my chair at the office and start to notice mild pain and tightness in the back of my neck. If it persists, it can turn into a classic tension headache. As soon as this happens, I know something is bothering me. Prior to the discomfort, I may not be aware that anything is stressing me – but invariably when I ask myself, "What is bothering me?" I know immediately what it is that is making me uptight. However, before that discomfort came, I often wasn't aware that something was bothering me. If I deal with the problem, the pain quickly subsides; if I don't, I suffer the consequences. (I am sure there are other times that I am not as cognizant of this process in my body.)

Research now reveals that we can suffer from stress without being consciously aware of it. With repeated exposure to stress the body tries to adapt so that we become less aware of the stress our bodies are undergoing. Studies have shown that over 71 percent of the time when a stress reaction is going on in our bodies, *we aren't consciously aware of it*. Careful studies reveal that stress hormones increase independently of the person's subjective perception of the stress. In fact, the majority of the "endocrine responses were related to routine events and were not accompanied by [conscious] awareness."[18]

Help Is Available

Help is available to decrease stress and fatigue and increase energy and serenity. If some individuals are able to handle stress better than others, it stands to reason that we can learn ways, numerous ways, to either avoid stressors in the first place, or to handle them with fewer adverse consequences to our bodies. Furthermore, we can learn to put uplifts or anti-stressors into our lives. Research has clearly shown that stress management programs improve immunological function, decrease depression and anxiety, increase empathy, and improve ability to resolve role conflicts, to name a few of the specific benefits. Hans Selye has said, "certain types of activities have a curative effect and actually help to keep the stress mechanism in good shape."[19]

The late Richard Kammann stated in 1983, "Objective life circumstances have a negligible role to play in a theory of happiness. Good and bad events do temporarily influence our moods. . . Yet, in less time than most people suppose, the emotional impact . . . dissipates."[20]

So what makes the difference? If circumstances aren't the primary cause of how we feel and the amount of energy we have – what does make the difference? In the next chapter we will look at the problem of fatigue and then turn our attention to some of the more important stressors in our lives.

CHAPTER 2

WHAT IS YOUR ENERGY LEVEL?

I N THE PROLOGUE I shared with you my personal account of how I went from a robust 18 year old to an utterly exhausted 19 year old. Stress, whether it's demanding too much out of our bodies, adverse events in our lives, or our handling the numerous pressures that face all of us, activates what has been called the General Adaptation Syndrome or the Biological Stress Syndrome. It has three stages: *the alarm reaction, the resistance phase,* and finally *the stage of exhaustion.* I was clearly in the exhaustion stage. In Chapter 1 we looked at an overview of stress and the dire consequences it inflicts on our bodies and interpersonal relationships. In this chapter I want to focus on one significant result of stress – fatigue.[1]

In less than a year my strong energy level had been depleted. Energy Level is illustrated in Figure 2. I find it helpful to think of energy in terms of arbitrary *energy units.* On the left is "0," indicating virtually no energy. This is an individual who is alive, but unable to do anything productive. On the right is "100," indicating maximal energy. The average "normal" individual has about 60 to 90 energy units to use each day. When I started out, I probably had approximately 85 energy units available to me. When total

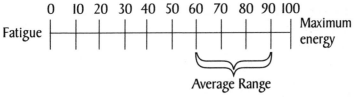

Figure 2

exhaustion set in I was reduced to perhaps 20 units a day. Now it seems quite obvious what caused my utter collapse, but at 19 I did not understand what was going on. I guess I thought that no matter what I did I would always have 85 units available each day to use. How wrong I was. All sorts of things can squander the energy that is available to us each day. The converse is also true, for there are many things we can do to enhance the energy available to us each day.

You might take a moment to consider the energy units you have available each day. Are you in the mid-average range of about 75 units per day, or do you suffer from a moderate degree of fatigue and have about 35 units per day? No matter how many units you now have, this book should help you increase the units available to you each day and to use them more effectively.

The High Cost of Lost Energy

Fatigue not only causes such exhaustion that one may not be able to work or hardly socialize, but its ramifications affect every aspect of our lives – it even kills. Occasionally it does so directly as people fall asleep while driving, or their reflexes are slowed affecting their ability to avoid an accident. New studies show that heart attacks occur twice as often among those who are exhausted. But more commonly stress that can cause fatigue kills more slowly as a result of the many other illnesses either caused or aggravated by stress and fatigue.[2]

Dr. Hans Selye has shown that chronic stress takes its toll on our bodies causing fatigue and numerous other adverse effects that we will soon discuss. He says, "Each period of stress, especially if it results from frustrating, unsuccessful struggles, leaves some irreversible chemical scars which accumulate . . . we might think of exhaustion as largely due to accumulating undesirable by-products of vital chemical reactions."[3]

Then there is the quality of life issue. Fatigue destroys one's happiness, joy, energy, and productivity. The cumulative effect of all of this chronic stress is incalculable in terms of the quality and duration of our lives.

Medical science has shown that numerous illnesses can cause fatigue: we are not sure if Chronic Fatigue Syndrome is one, or a heterogeneous group of illnesses. Furthermore, Fibromyalgia,

Chemical Insensitivities, and Irritable Bowel Syndrome often have fatigue as a significant symptom. More will be said about this later.

Beside the tremendous loss of energy and meaningful life in individuals suffering from these disorders, there is a tremendous cost to society. Family members bear a significant role. The need for health care is greatly increased for those suffering from the loss of energy. In Australia the mean number of appointments of a patient with Chronic Fatigue Syndrome was 21 per year costing about $9,500 per person.[4]

Many individuals with severe fatigue are unable to work, often collecting disability checks. Some workers have suggested that Chronic Fatigue Syndrome in school children is the most common cause of long-term school absenteeism.[5]

Incidence

As a practicing physician in Southern California, I have been repeatedly amazed at the number of patients coming to me whose chief complaint is that of fatigue. Fatigue is one of the most common symptoms for which individuals seek medical attention, accounting for about 20 to 27 percent of visits to a primary-care physician. Studies of the general populations in Great Britain and the United States have shown that significant fatigue affects 14 to 22.5 percent of the population at any given time. Other studies have reported up to half the population complaining of fatigue.[6]

In addition, Fibromyalgia, an illness that is closely related to Chronic Fatigue Syndrome and often has fatigue as a significant symptom, occurs in at least 2 percent of the population and 10 percent of these are disabled by their disease.

Definition

Fatigue can be defined as tiredness or weariness from bodily or mental exertion. It has many synonyms, such as lassitude, lethargy, lack of energy, weakness, and sometimes sleepiness. Patients will often describe it as having no energy, no ambition, no interest, being run down, bushed, pooped, having lack of pep, or just being "all in." It is a subjective feeling that causes a loss of a sense of wellbeing. It drains the vibrant energy right out of our lives. Stating it slightly differently, fatigue can be defined as a deficiency of physical, emotional, or intellectual energy.

Generally, fatigue is divided into two components. *Mental fatigue* manifests itself as lack of motivation or alertness. *Physical fatigue* is a lack of strength or energy involving the muscles. The feeling of fatigue can occur in the absence of significant activity. The term *fatigability* has been used to describe excessive fatigue after exercise. In part this is directly related to the buildup of waste products in the system.[7]

On the other end of the spectrum is energy. This includes a sense that one is able to tackle issues whether mental or physical. In this book we will look at ways to restore or enhance one's energy. A refreshing night of sleep is a good example. Many other enhancers will be discussed later (see Section Four: The Energizers). Just as darkness is the absence of light, so fatigue is the absence of energy.

Fatigue is seldom the result of a single cause in an individual. Often there are multiple factors, so these will be addressed.

Functions That Fatigue Serves

"Is all fatigue destructive?" The obvious answer is no. Fatigue can serve some important functions, many of them good. First, fatigue can be a *friend*. At the end of a good day's work it is normal and a good feeling to be tired and able to sleep soundly. A lack of this kind of fatigue poses a real problem to many individuals with insomnia.

Second, more often in our fast-moving society fatigue is a *warning*. *Harrison's Principles of Internal Medicine* notes, "Psychiatry has postulated that chronic fatigue, like anxiety, is a danger signal that something is wrong: some activity or attitude has been persisted in too intensely or too long. The purpose of fatigue may be regarded as self-preservation."[8] This kind of fatigue is like a fever or pain. It's a warning signal. It doesn't tell us *what* is wrong – like fever or pain the causes are innumerable – but it tells us that *something* is wrong. A specific cause can often be found if we start looking for it. If we don't, irreparable damage may be done.

The Christian Swiss physician Paul Tournier writes, "Each instance of fatigue is a signal. . . It can be the sign that something is not in order in our life, something which we must examine before God. . . Each individual at each instant, each time he is tired . . . must see if God has something to say to him through this fatigue. Our fatigue is, above all, the sign of an estrangement from God and the great fatigue of the modern world expresses its immense need of rediscovering God."[9]

Third, fatigue can be a *trial*. For years in medical school, but especially in internship and residency training, the demands placed on those of us in such training can be overwhelming. We often were required to work 36 hours, then had 12 hours off. The fatigue from lack of sleep and the pressures of making life and death decisions was often staggering. I remember one hectic night when I got to bed at about 2:00 A.M. About 3:00 A.M. one of my two interns woke me up and said that he had just gotten a call from the Emergency Room and that there was *another* patient to evaluate and admit into the hospital. While I was in my almost stuporous state, he told me that he wouldn't be going down to the emergency room to see this patient since he was quitting.

I said, "Quitting what?" He replied, "I am quitting my internship and medicine." With that statement, he walked out of the hospital never to return. So I stumbled out of bed, splashed some cold water in my face, went to the emergency room and evaluated and admitted the patient. During many of those years fatigue was a constant companion and a difficult trial.

Finally, the most serious form that fatigue can take is that of an *enemy*. Medically, certain physiological changes take place in the tired person. His work output is decreased; dissatisfaction and restlessness become apparent. He becomes unable to deal with complex problems and is upset by trivialities. Irritability, a critical attitude, loss of joy, and lack of spontaneity prevail. Reflexes are slowed and he is more prone to accidents.

Spiritually, fatigue encourages doubt and depression. We become extremely susceptible to sin in many forms that otherwise would pose no threat. Elijah is a graphic example of this. After accomplishing a great victory for God his life was threatened resulting in severe fatigue and the wish for death (1 Kings 18; 19:1–4).

Fatigue may also be an indicator of besetting sin in our lives (see Chapters 14 and 15).

Overview of the Causes of Fatigue

As you can see from Figure 3 there are five basic sources which can lead to fatigue. Stressors, whether they be external or internal, can cause all kinds of physical problems and disease including fatigue.

Overview of the Cause of Fatigue

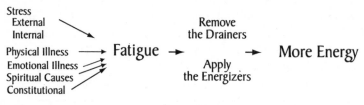

Figure 3

Second, various malfunctions of our bodies can lead to fatigue: anemia or hypothyroidism are examples. Third, various emotional or psychological problems may also result in fatigue: anxiety and depression often cause fatigue. Fourth, spiritual problems, such as guilt and bitterness, are another source of fatigue. Finally, we find constitutional differences in all of us – some people were just born with more energy then others.

The Good News

How to get more energy? That can be seen also in Figure 3. You deal with the various things that are draining you of your energy and you apply energizers. These will be discussed throughout the rest of the book.

Christ put it this way: "Are you tired? Worn out? Burned out on religion? Come to me. Get away with me and you'll recover your life. I'll show you how to take a real rest. Walk with me . . . I won't lay anything heavy or ill-fitting on you. Keep company with me and you'll learn to live freely and lightly" (Matthew 11:28–30, MSG).

If fatigued and stressed individuals made up a large segment of the audience listening to the "Sermon on the Mount," I suspect that Christ's message would have included something like these words, "Blessed, happy, are those who suffer from fatigue, for I will give them my strength," and, "Blessed, happy, are those who are suffering from the consequences of stress, for to them I will give a sound body and my serenity."

SECTION TWO

THE DRAINERS

Part Two

External Stressors

CHAPTER 3

MAJOR LIFE EVENTS AND HASSLES

I WAS VERY depressed and had suicidal thoughts. Now it all seems like a bad dream that occurred over two decades ago. It all started when I assumed the care of a patient who went to the same church as I and with whom I had many common friends. I was feeling great at the time. The patient, whom we'll call Bill, became depressed and sought my help but remained depressed in spite of several different trials of antidepressants. When they failed to help, I admitted him into a psychiatric hospital for more extensive treatment. Despite other consultations and shock treatment, Bill committed suicide in the hospital. I was devastated. I knew that this was an occupational hazard, but that didn't help my sense of failure and grief. I started questioning myself and wondered how the two most important peer groups – my colleagues and my friends at church – judged me. Over the next six months I slipped into a deep depression. I hope I never go through that again.

Major Life Events

What happened? A major event in my life, a *stressor* if you will, hit me and I didn't have or utilize appropriate resources to prevent the depression. All of us have a few abnormal genes which create areas of weakness; I have some genetic loading for depression, so with the impact of a major life event and a weakness, depression developed. If I had a genetic weakness in another area, it might have manifested itself in some other illness.

We have known from antiquity that major stressful events often lead to disease. Researchers Rahe and Holmes were the first investigators to measure the magnitude of various stressors in the mid-1960s and quantitate the likelihood of illness developing. A major updating of this work was done in 1997 by Miller and Rahe. We now find some 74 specific life changes listed in the *Recent Life Changes Questionnaire*. These researchers have found that for most people the greatest life change, or stressor, is the death of a child. This is given an arbitrary Life Change Unit value of 123. A major illness or injury is 74 units; being fired from one's job is 79 units; being jailed is 75 units. We then add up the total score and if a person has had 300 or more units in the previous six months, or 500 or more units in the previous year, it indicates high recent life stress. Some manifestation of that stress is often apparent, including illness.[1]

We can glean several important points from this research. First, that stress is additive. The more recent stressors in your life, the greater the likelihood that it will cause ill effects on your body. Second, the authors talk about "Life Change" rather than stressor. They are committed to the notion that the important characteristic is *change*. Thus divorce, something which we would view as an adverse event, is weighted at 96 Life Change Units, but marriage, something that is viewed as positive, is given 50 units. Other researchers have questioned this approach and would at least qualify and are actually evaluating how the positive events should be viewed and what are the effects they have on people.

Nevertheless, the take home message to us is that significant adverse life changes are stressors and do adversely affect our bodies: and they are cumulative. A vast body of research supports this. These major life events may be illness, trauma, abuse; they can take place at home, work, or for that matter anywhere. Miller and Rahe have seen a 45 percent increase in stresses in the last 30 years. They also found that women react to life stress events at higher levels than men, in fact 17 percent higher. Also, the unmarried have higher scores than those who are married.[2]

These stresses can have all the adverse effects on our lives that were elaborated on in Chapter 1. Fatigue is clearly one of the possible results. Positive events may, in some circumstances, have a negative impact on our lives. More will be said about this later.[3]

Hassles

Every month I noted a significant charge on my business phone bill for an item listed as "Minimum Usage Charge." This was in addition to a "Usage Charge," various taxes which I didn't understand, plus charges for each call made. I could not understand why I should be paying for each call made, plus a "Usage Charge," plus a "Minimum Usage Charge." I had ignored the item for months, but one day I thought, *I'm going to call the phone company and try and understand their charges.* So with bill in hand I called the major telephone company's toll free number. After their phone rang twice, I heard the following message:

"Our options have recently changed, so listen carefully to the following options: If you are calling about a residential or home phone, press number 1; if you are calling about a business phone, press number 2; if you are calling about a local business phone, press number 3."

Not being sure if I was calling about a business phone or a local business phone, I pressed number 2 and heard the following message:

"If you are calling about malfunctioning equipment, press number 1; if you are calling about adding or deleting a phone service, press number 2; if you are calling about a question on your phone bill, press number 3."

I pressed number 3 and got another menu of options; I pressed the appropriate numbers. This happened three or four more times. Finally I heard the following message:

"The minimum usage charge is the minimum amount that we charge for use of the services; thank you for calling. **Click.**"

I was never given the option to talk to a live human being. The only phone number given to call on the bill was the one I called. As I sat there, receiver in hand, I could feel the adrenaline surge through my system. I was aware of the anger I felt at this monster – Corporate America. It wasn't as bad as if I had just noticed a lion stalking me in the open wild, but it was significant, for I felt I had been hassled.

The total time I spent on the phone was probably less than seven minutes. Remember the energy scale in Chapter 2? I suspect I used up 20 of my available energy units for the day. That was probably more units than I would have used counseling three typical patients or would have used doing hard physical work for eight hours. No wonder it has been said, "Even the greatest experts in the field do not know why the stress of frustration is so much more likely than that of excessive muscular work to produce disease."[4]

I sat there in a state of agitation trying to decide what to do next. What are my options? I could make a number of phone calls and find a live person working for this major telephone company, but what is the probability that the answers would be any more satisfying? Was it worth the time and effort? If I spent that much time and continued to get the run around, would I be even more furious? I decided to call another phone company and have them take over the service. How I dealt with my feelings to minimize the toll on my body I will discuss later in the book.

As I write this, I debate with myself whether this is the best example of a hassle? I would love to tell you about several other recent hassles that indelibly stick in my mind – my hassles with Medicare Insurance or getting unsolicited faxes or e-mails. I have a good story about each of these, but I won't bore you with them. I am sure you can give me several excellent aggravating personal examples of hassles you have had to deal with recently.

Then there are the numerous, almost every day, examples of hassles – a traffic jam, getting advertising calls at meal time, misplacing your keys, someone putting a ding in your car while you were shopping, or breaking a shoelace. These all extract their toll as a hassle. They have also been referred to as "micro-stressors." Typically, these are irritants that are not monumental, but nevertheless are significant stressors; irritants that can range from minor annoyances to moderate problems. They can involve areas of work, family, friends, environment, inclement weather, health, and money, to name a few. The most stressful type of hassle is that which involves interpersonal conflicts.[5]

Frequency is a factor in producing disease. Both major life events and hassles are additive. Our assessment and perception of the "hassle" is also an important factor. The adverse effects of hassles last for a long time, sometimes for several months after the hassles are over.[6]

What is some of the evidence that such nuisances cause stress and disease? Hassles cause a decrease in the numbers of T cells and Natural Killer cells that fight disease in a person's body. A hassle can increase the susceptibility to an upper respiratory infection for at least two weeks, and interpersonal conflicts have been shown to affect adversely a person's likelihood to get a cold for the following three months.[7]

We find evidence that Fibromyalgia is associated with both hassles and more major adverse life events. In men with a family history of alcoholism, hassles resulted in greater consumption of alcohol. Hassles are associated with poorer quality of sleep, negative mood, poorer overall health, depression, and a decreased energy level. Hassles increased the number of visits to a doctor and/or hospitalization.[8]

Some studies suggest that hassles are more predictive of major adverse effects on our lives than are "major life events," such as the death of a loved one. In other words, hassles may be more detrimental to our health than are some of the major traumas that we face.[9]

Fortunately, studies have also shown that the ill effects of day-in and day-out major life events and hassles can be reduced by utilizing appropriate coping strategies, which will be discussed in later chapters.

CHAPTER 4

LIFE ON OVERLOAD OR UNDERACTIVITY

"**D**R. CARLSON, DR. CARLSON, please call the operator! Dr. Carlson, please call the operator!" blared the hospital public-address system as I was making evening rounds to see some very sick patients. As I walked to the nearest phone, I wondered who might be calling me now. *I hope it is not an emergency or some other pressure*, I thought as I dialed the operator. I had started work early that morning; it was now 9:00 P.M. and I hadn't been home yet.

"Operator, this is Dr. Carlson," I said.

"Dr. Jackson is on the line," the operator responded. Bob Jackson is a friend and highly respected colleague. I wondered what he wanted.

"Dwight?" It was Bob's voice. "The nominations committee for the hospital met recently and wondered if you would be willing to serve as secretary." Even as he was asking the question, numerous thoughts flashed through my mind. I had been active on the Executive Committee during the last several years and had anticipated the possibility of being asked to become more deeply involved. In fact, I had concluded that I should decline any office if I were asked, because higher priority items were being neglected.

"I . . . I . . . I had already thought about that and had decided to back off this year," I stuttered, as I tried to collect my thoughts and answer in an appropriate way. But before I had even finished my stammering sentence, Bob interrupted.

"Dwight, we want you to know what a fine job you have done the last several years. Your comments at the meetings are always appropriate and have helped immensely in getting the job done," he continued.

"Thanks," I replied, "but I really think I should decline the office this year."

"Dwight, I owe you an apology. We were supposed to get permission from all the candidates nominated but I have been so busy as chairman that I have failed at this point. Ballots were mailed out this afternoon."

"Oh . . . oh . . . oh!" I again stammered as I tried to collect my thoughts and decide what to say next! Then it dawned on me that perhaps I was running against a strong candidate and would not be elected anyway. That should solve my problem. So I asked, "Who am I running against?"

"You are unopposed," he replied. I am sure my mouth was hanging open as he continued, "Thanks, Dwight, I know you will do an excellent job. We really need you and it won't take much of your time."

Still stammering, I managed to say, "Good-bye, Bob," before I heard the click of the receiver on the other end. I was a little stunned as I slowly put the receiver down and went back to my evening rounds, trying to figure out what had just transpired.

In our fast paced society we all face pressure, pressure, and more pressure. The demands leading to overload are widespread. They are not only around us, but as we will see later, they are inside us. And the cost this overload is extracting from us is incalculable.

The Problem of Overload in Society

I know of a soccer mother who has four young children. She is conscientious and wants the best for them, so they each play a musical instrument and need weekly lessons; they are involved in sports — Little League, soccer, ice skating and ballet; in addition, they are in scouting. One child has asthma and extra medical appointments need to be scheduled, another has Attention Defect Hyperactivity Disorder and a learning disability. The mother spends her days as chauffeur and her nights as tutor, all of which adds to her stress. (And woe be to a mother who has to be a wage earner on top of her family responsibilities.) If this soccer mother were to look carefully at her situation, she would observe that not only is she living in a fairly high state of stress, but her children are experiencing it also.

Dad doesn't fare any better. He works a good 50 hours a week, has a long commute to work, and several times a month he has to fly across the country. His stress on the job leaves him with little energy left over for his wife and children.

Not only is there an overload of time and activities, but we also have to face the constant bombardment of soundbites advertising some product on radio and TV, billboards promoting new cars, and even T-shirts trying to communicate some message to us. When one thinks he is finally away from the barrage of advertising, the telephone rings in the middle of dinner, and a telemarketer is on the line – human or machine.

Then we have noise pollution, to say nothing about the exhaust-filled air we breathe all day. All of this overload accumulates causing stress and fatigue for each member of the family. We all live at a frenzied pace. Our lives are filled with hurry and worry.[1]

How did we ever get into such a dreadful state of affairs? We will evaluate this throughout the book in order that we might discover some useful remedies. However, we find two primary causes for this overload: first, pressure from our environment, and second, an internal void. These then feed on each other, quadrupling our cumulative stress load. Consequently, most of us are just trying to survive.

Pressures from Our Environment

Successful advertising works at finding susceptible areas in our lives, then fans the discontentment and tells us how that company's product can remedy the situation. If the advertiser can, he will create a need and tell us that we will only be happy if we have such-and-such a product. Before we know it, we have obligated ourselves or purchased something on credit and now must scramble to pay for it. This process repeats itself in a thousand different ways.

This is much like an interesting laboratory experiment in which frogs when placed directly in hot water would scramble to get out. But frogs placed in cool water, with the water gradually being raised to boiling, are oblivious to their impending fate. In a similar way, we are often insensitive to what is happening to us and we are passing it on to our kids and to our friends.

Overload in the Church

For those of us who have a spiritual bent, it would be nice if we could criticize the secular person for his or her feverish pace and be free of it ourselves; but the fact is that we can't. For the most part we too are as caught up in this harried stride as everyone else. And unfortunately it has infected the church as well.

John Ortberg, teaching pastor at the well-known Willow Creek Community Church, elaborates, "Hurry is the great enemy of spiritual life in our day. Hurry can destroy our souls."[2]

Overwork is probably one of the greatest problem areas for dedicated, sincere Christians today. We have all the same pressures in the world, like making a living and raising a family. But on top of all of that we have the legitimate and sometimes the less legitimate concerns, activities, and pressures of the church. Busyness and uncontrollable activity, all too often, characterize us as well, resulting in fatigue and weariness instead of love, joy, and peace.

Charles E. Hummell, in his classic booklet, *Tyranny of the Urgent,* addressed these concerns in the 1960s. He emphasized the point that so often the urgent immediate task, which seemingly needs to be done right away, keeps us going at a frenetic pace and keeps us from doing the more important task which God wants us to do. Well-meaning Christians may often impose this urgent task on us as we respond to needs rather than the direction of God's Spirit.

About the same time Paul Tournier warned, "We must depart from this atmosphere of the modern world which is completely obsessed with activism, even in the church: do, do, do always more. Let us rather, once again, become inspired and tranquil men."[3] But the momentum of our gait has only increased in the last 40 years.

Curtis and Eldredge in their excellent book, *The Sacred Romance: Drawing Closer to the Heart of God,* have addressed the feeling of many Christians that something is missing:

> We have not been diligent enough in practicing our religion. Our pastor seems to agree with this assessment and exhorts us from the pulpit to be more faithful. We try to silence the voice with outward activity, redoubling our efforts at Christian service. We join a small group and read a book on establishing a more effective prayer life. We train to be part of a church evangelism team. We tell ourselves that the malaise of spirit we feel even as we step up our religious activity is a sign of spiritual immaturity and we scold our heart for its lack of fervor. . . . If the system isn't working, it's because we're not

doing it right. There's always something to work on, with the promise of abundant life just around the corner. Plenty of churches and leaders are ready to show you how to cut a deal. . . . So many of our contemporary churches operate on this same system of guilt. When our people are crying out for communion and rest, we ask them to teach another Sunday school class. When they falter under the load, we admonish them with Scriptures on serving others.[4]

Some Reasons for Overload in the Church

We often operate under the assumption that *the need is the call*. That is, if there is a legitimate need, and no one else is available to meet that need, then it speaks for itself – we should meet that need. Or so the erroneous thinking goes. Christ did not meet every need nor did he teach that his disciples should meet every need. Though there were poor and hungry people around, Christ condoned the "wasting" of the expensive perfume that was used to anoint him (see Luke 7:36–50; John 12:1–7). Often multitudes pressed on him, and he sent them off so that he could be alone with the Father. Many ill people did not get healed during his ministry years. When Mary and Martha summoned him to come and heal their dying brother, Christ delayed two days and Lazarus died (see John 11:1–17). Alice Fryling puts it well in saying that we say "yes" to activities that Christ would have said "no" to and she poses this question: "Are you willing *not* to go where God does not send you?"(Italics added)[5]

In our zeal to get God's message out to the world we often embrace the philosophy that: *the end justifies the means.* Just like the world at large, we address needs, then exert pressure by extracting a commitment from people whether they are the means to meet the need or the final consumer. In this process, Christendom has learned and is applying many of the techniques from godless organizations. In fact, early in my Christian life I had a Christian leader recommend that I buy a secular book on salesmanship and apply the techniques to communicate my faith to others.

My wife had a similar experience. Some years ago several zealous Christian leaders were looking for additional personnel to help "win the entire state for Christ." They had a strategy and went about looking for the right personnel. They needed a young woman to reach the young women, so they called on my wife, then single, to present their plan. Betty arrived at their office before they did and while waiting for them she noticed a little clipping strategically placed on the leader's desk. She was amazed as the caption caught her eye: "How to win men to your way of thinking." As she read the ten points, she somehow felt that for some reason, God had allowed her to read that clipping.

Later, as the interview progressed, she clearly could see the manipulative techniques these men were using to convince her that she was the one for that spot. Yes, she agreed that not all in the state knew Jesus Christ. "Of course, they should all have the opportunity." Yes, she had a desire to reach out to other women. And, "Certainly, if we all put our efforts together in one concentrated area, we could get the job done much more effectively and eventually reach the world." However, for some reason Betty was hesitant. These men's personalities and logic were persuasive. Had she not seen the clipping on the desk she might have erroneously thought this was God's will and failed to hear his "still small voice" beckoning her elsewhere.

Some of these techniques may well be good (see Luke 16:8–9), but that is not the primary issue. The issue is whether or not God is directing *us* in the process. If man is in charge, then what is the price tag on our personal and corporate serenity?

So here we see the technique of judicious pressure and commitment (comparable to closing the sale in selling used by organizing individuals). All kinds of methods are used consciously and unconsciously in an effort to make it difficult for us to say no. This is complicated by the fact that there are so many great spiritual programs being promoted today, most all of them being fully justified and seemingly encouraged from God's Word. Any hesitation on our part causes us to feel guilty and be left with the impression that we are either selfish or just plain lazy. It is exceedingly difficult to say "no" or to voice any negative feelings about the activities of such an organization. To do so makes it seem like we are objecting to the Scriptures or God himself.

We get much positive affirmation by being busy in the Lord's work. Our peer group admires us when we are willing to say "yes" to their requests and effectively censures us when we say "no." And we all like those fuzzy good feelings when people affirm us.

I remember Dawson Trotman, founder of The Navigators, warning us from Proverbs not to love sleep or to be lazy, concluding with the saying that he would rather "burn out than rust out." Dawson was a positive influence in my life, but in retrospect I wonder if my "burning out" at age 19 was, in part, a result of this philosophy.

I remember some of my friends going to the mission field saying that they were going to "burn out for Jesus." This sounds noble — but is it? It is hard for us to use that analogy as we look at the life of Christ. I cannot conjure up the image of him either burning out or rusting out. That analogy just does not fit. He listened to the beckoning of the Father and seemed quite independent from the pressures of the crowds or his disciples. He was aware of need, but virtually was never pressured by those needs.

Henri Nouwen puts his finger on the problem saying, "We simply go along with the many 'musts' and 'oughts' that have been handed on to us, and we live with them as if they were authentic translations of the Gospel of our Lord. People must be motivated to come to church, youth must be entertained, money must be raised, and above all everyone must be happy."[6]

In this process the institution becomes more important than the individual. When we have crossed this threshold, we are in real trouble. Michael Wilkins comments on this saying, "It is a tragedy, then, when our institutions become more important than the individual — when the individual is made to serve the institution. Then supporting the institution becomes the end, and the individual is the means to the end. . . Because my end goal was numbers, not always depth, I considered our church activities more important than the spiritual growth of the people who made up the church."[7]

Eugene Peterson, author of *The Message*, says, "The rise of interest in spiritual direction almost certainly comes from the proliferation of role-defined activism in our culture. We are sick and tired of being slotted into a function and then manipulated with Scripture and prayer to do what someone has decided . . . that we should be doing to bring glory to some religious enterprise or other."[8]

John Eldredge writes in *The Journey of Desire: Searching for the Life We've Only Dreamed Of,* "We don't need more facts, and we certainly don't need more things to do. We need *Life,* and we've been looking for it ever since we lost Paradise . . . [but] . . . we've found a powerful drug — distraction." But he doesn't stop there; he has likened our hectic, pressured, exhausting pace to addiction. He elaborates, "Addiction may seem too strong a term to some of you. The woman who is serving so faithfully at church – surely, there's nothing wrong with that. And who can blame the man who stays long at the office to provide for his family? [then he goes on to warn us] . . . Remember, we will make an idol of anything, especially a good thing."[9]

And all of this seems so normal. We accept it, take it for granted, just like the frogs in hot water, and thus perpetuate it, robbing us of inner peace, tranquillity, and the energy that can liberate us.

Our Internal Void

But the problem is much deeper then that. The fact is that most of us have a significant void and are trying our best to fill it. It's not only not getting met, but the things that we are doing to meet it are only making things much worse.

Over a century ago, G. Campbell Morgan said, "I sometimes think that this is the peculiar sin of the present age, the attempt to make up for lack of character by outside service."[10]

The contempory voice of Dr. Siang-Yang Tan puts it this way:

> We continue to suffer from the disease of "hurry sickness" . . . The enemy of our souls knows full well how hurry sickness or unrest can ultimately destroy us. He will do his best to keep us from God's rest. He entices us to drive ourselves onward, create even more activity, fill our emptiness with external stimuli to avoid the disquiet of our soul. Consequently, we often clutch at people, things, and activities that keep us engaged in the cycle of a hurried and harried life.[11]

So we use distraction focusing on activities, wealth, sports, a new car, or something to try and satisfy the void. It's as if we are rats on a treadmill, working harder and going faster, but getting nowhere, and we are exhausted and depressed in the process. Later we will delve into the depths of what the internal void is all about.

Understimulation

Though the vast majority of individuals in modern society are far more prone to suffer from overwork and overinvolvement, there is a small, but significant, number of people who suffer from the adverse effects of the opposite extreme. Individuals who experience external stimulation as unattractive have been shown to have a higher incidence of fatigue.[12]

How you arrived in such a state of under-stimulation may vary. You may at one time have been excessively busy and gotten weary and fed up with it all. Now you have gone to the other extreme and spend most of your free hours watching the one-eyed monster, or surfing the internet, or in some other unproductive activity. Or perhaps you run from the problems of life and normal struggles because it's just too much effort. You are unwilling to take the normal bruises encountered, so you withdraw into your house and close all the draperies, either literally or figuratively, to prevent contact with the real outside world. Another group of people have had the rug pulled out from under them with an illness that prevented them from doing much, then have gotten stuck there. Individuals with chronic illnesses can easily slip into this mode.

The most vivid example of underactivity and boredom I can remember was while I was in the Navy crossing the Pacific. Individuals who normally got along on six to eight hours of sleep and had plenty of energy now were bored, and not knowing what to do with themselves ended up sleeping 14 or more hours and were tired most of the time.

In 2 Samuel 11, we read that though King David's army was out on the battlefield and usually the king was with them in the campaign, this time he stayed behind. He was living a life of leisure, and one afternoon, arising from his couch, he was tempted, and with seemingly no struggle yielded to the temptations of Bathsheba. The results of his sin affected many lives and his entire future. We can only speculate about how much his underactivity and avoiding the battlefield had contributed to his sin.

Just as the excessively busy person must avoid that extreme of the pendulum's swing, so the inactive person will find his energy and sense of worth vanishing from him. As with so many things in life, there is a beautiful and crucial balance between these extremes. The underactive person may find that energy becomes available to him only as he gets involved in meaningful tasks. He may need to commit himself to a project if he doesn't have the vision to see needs or the ability to motivate himself to follow through on his own. The pace may need to start out slowly, gradually increasing the tempo, but taking deliberate action may be necessary to get things going again.

Our retired senior citizens are especially likely to fall into the trap of inactivity. They cannot expect to keep the pace of years gone by, yet excuses for inactivity often come easily. Some do not appreciate the fact that as long as God gives them breath, he has a plan and purpose for their lives. Along with this plan and purpose, they must realize their worth and value to others and their ability to help meet the needs of those about them. I know one retired businessman who has endeared himself to a small hospital and is now their chaplain, visiting the sick and needy. I have patients in nursing homes who would love to have someone come and extend Christ's love to them. You don't have to look very far if your eyes are open and your feet willing to find someone in need of a cup of cold water given in Christ's name. (I wrote this paragraph 30 years ago when I was in my 30s. It's interesting now as a senior citizen myself, to read this. It remains true today; however, underactivity has never been a problem area for me.)

For some, sleep can be an escape; and an excessive amount of sleep can cause or perpetuate fatigue. Sleep is such an important topic that we will devote an entire chapter to the subject later in the book.

Boredom

Boredom causes fatigue. Boredom is a major factor in producing fatigue. Boredom may manifest itself not only by inactivity but also by disinterest and lack of enthusiasm or spontaneity. There is a clear-cut relationship with the interest one has in activities and fatigue. Individuals that are engaged in activities that they enjoy experience considerably more energy. The reverse is also true. If the activities that one is engaged in are perceived as unattractive, boredom and fatigue tend to be the result.

What happens when a person is continually bored? With decreasing outside interests, an abnormal and distorted self-awareness often develops in the form of fatigue and psychosomatic illnesses. Many bored people turn their attention excessively on themselves, their bodies, and its functions. The tick of a clock is seldom heard in a room where meaningful activities are taking place. But to a bored person sitting alone in the room, the tick may sound like a sledgehammer. So his bodily functions become increasingly noticed and psychosomatic illnesses *may* be the result. An increased need for sleep and withdrawal or drug abuse may ensue.

Other products of boredom are discouragement, disappointment, depression, negativism, and legalism. These may feed the boredom. Thus the vicious cycle perpetuates itself unless the person boldly breaks out of this quagmire.

Other causes of boredom are lack of variety (which is the "spice of life") in all of one's activities — including recreation, physical exertion, and relationships with friends. To be in a rut in any of these areas quickly constricts and limits one's energy.

We find an inverse relationship between fatigue and energy, boredom and interest. To a large degree, boredom is caused by the lack of positive, stimulating, energizing, and exciting factors in life. Also, often we find an excessive amount of unresolved internal conflicts in the individual's life. The energizers which help abolish both fatigue and boredom are spontaneity and vitality toward life in general, obtainable challenging goals, and purpose and meaning in one's life. All of this will be elaborated on later.

The Consequences of Underactivity

Understimulation, boredom, or inactivity due to any reason including severe fatigue or other medical problems has devastating consequences on our bodies. The old adage "use it or lose it" contains a lot of truth. Studies show that prolonged rest affects virtually every system of the body. For example, one week of bed rest results in measurable muscle loss. In four to six weeks it is reported that as much as 40 percent of muscle strength is lost. There are significant changes in the chemistry and adverse effects on the immunological system. After a period of inactivity, reuse of one's muscles causes exhaustion much sooner then otherwise would occur.[13]

Clutter and Poor Organization

Clutter can be a stressor: it often feels like an emotional weight. It breeds inefficiency and the inability to make decisions. Often one is avoiding something. I know individuals who won't have company over because they are embarrassed by the clutter. Sometimes it causes great stress in a marriage. It can be a way to express hostility to another. On occasion it has led to divorce. Clutter can create more housework, make one take more time to locate "lost" items, and it increases losing or misplacing things. It is said that 80 percent of what you keep or file you never look at again. Clutter causes many to feel – anxious, frustrated, overwhelmed, confused, and inefficient, as opposed to calm, productive, confident, and organized.[14]

Compulsive collecting and poor organization inevitably will lead to inefficient use of one's time and all of its consequences of frustration, decreasing sense of worth, and fatigue, to name only a few. Poor organization can be as exhausting as the person who overplans and compulsively must carry out every finite detail. Priorities, proper management of time, and delegation of responsibility are crucial. Anything capable of disorganizing a person is capable of causing fatigue.

Procrastination also has its way of eating away at us. I find that if I have unfinished charts or reports on my desk, they can weigh me down for days until they are completed. Occasionally, it may be necessary to stay up late to complete a burdening task and sense the release and accomplishment it can bring.

Medication and Artificial Stimulants

Other external factors that can cause stress and fatigue are various kinds of medications. Antianxiety pills, sedatives, sleeping aids, and prescribed medications all carry the risk of sedating one and can cause a hangover. Also these medications can accumulate in the system and after extended use produce a significant blood level even days after they are ingested. Many prescribed medications for diverse medical problems can cause significant fatigue. Some of the biggest offenders are antidepressants, B-blockers, antihistamines, and medications to treat an enlarged prostate. There are hundreds of medications that can cause fatigue.

Stimulants, either in the form of medication or caffeine, may give a person a short-term boost of energy but later lead to significant fatigue. Often insomniacs use caffeine to help them through the day, which then may make their sleep disorder worse. Some individuals are very sensitive to caffeine, especially those with panic or anxiety disorders. Caffeine occurs in some medications and many drinks and foods. Coffee, tea, chocolate, and cold drinks are the biggest offenders. Don't forget that some of the cold drinks with the highest concentration of caffeine are crystal clear in appearance.

Conclusion

The Phillips paraphrase on Romans 12:2 says, "Don't let the world around you squeeze you into its own mould, but let God re-mould your minds from within." Unfortunately we have ended up in the predicament about which the Scriptures warned us. Too often the world around us, instead of God, is shaping our lives. It is not God's intention for us to live at a rat-race pace. If we take a close look at our Model – Jesus Christ – we discover that he was never harried or hurried. So who is our model? Are we following Christ or the world?

Time and space do not allow an exhaustive discussion on all the various external stressors that confront us. I have delved into some of the more common ones – as you are aware of your environment, you will notice many other external stressors. In the next section we will continue to look at stressors in our lives, but now we will focus more on internal stressors, that is, stressors that have a lot more to do with what's inside us than what's in the world around us.

Part Three

Internal Stressors

CHAPTER 5

IS YOUR ANGER TOXIC OR HEALTHY?

I WAS 15 years old and had recently gotten my driver's license. Early one Sunday morning I was driving from Los Angeles to the San Fernando Valley on Sepulveda Boulevard. Today it is a freeway but then it was a four-lane winding road over a small mountain pass. No one was on the road at that time and I was going about 40 miles per hour. Out of nowhere a car came up behind me and started tailgating me, at a distance that seemed like five to ten feet away. I became frightened and angry, so I briefly tapped on my brake, then quickly accelerated. This made the tailgater furious and he literally forced my car off the road. Then, in what seemed an instant, he was knocking on my window demanding that I get out of the car and fight him.

He was a big man while I was a frightened, wet-behind-the-ears, 15-year-old boy. My heart was filled with terror. What should I do? No one else was around and my car was pinned in so that I couldn't move. I doubt if a stalking lion would have stirred up any more adrenaline than was surging through my system at this point. Just then a police car pulled up and told the other driver to get in his car and move on. Unnoticed by either of us, the policeman (or was it a guardian angel?) who was on the other side of the road saw the whole incident, quickly made a U-turn, and came to my rescue.

This illustrates how a stressful incident could have become fatal due to the foolish anger of two people. Needless to say, I have never pulled a stunt like that again. Nowadays people have been known to pull guns and kill in such situations.

We are all faced with sundry and repeated stressful situations, and how we handle them may well make a life or death difference. Extreme situations of someone forcing you off the road and wanting to fight, or pulling a gun on you, fortunately, rarely occur in one's life. But we all get upset over people who tailgate or do comparable things, and the anger and fear that these generate can be just as deadly over time. Toxic anger kills.

Kinds of Anger

Discussion as to whether there is any value in anger versus the destructiveness of anger are replete in history, going all the way back to Aristotle. One of the early writers, William of St. Thierry in the 12th century, was most on target. He divided anger into two types: beastly (undesirable) anger and rational anger. Instead of using his terms we will use the terms *Toxic Anger* and *Healthy Anger*.[1]

Toxic Anger

It is said that when you catch a shark and bring it aboard ship, it may be so angry and aggressive that it tries to bite anything in its way. In fact, it can flip around and take a bite out of itself. Unfortunately, what we do to ourselves is often not much better, though not as apparent to ourselves or others. Twenty percent of the general population have a problem with toxic anger that is destructive to them and to others. Let's look at the two categories of toxic anger – Externalized Toxic Anger and Internalized Toxic Anger.[2]

Externalized Toxic Anger

Anger is our response to any actual or perceived threat to us. It is our knee-jerk reaction to frustration or a deed done against us. Externalized toxic anger is emotion that is expressed in inappropriate ways to those about us. It is often impulsive; it is acting aggressively to the world around us; it is hostility that is expressed in a destructive way. This anger is responsible for the rampant abuse in marriages and in homicides. This is the type of anger that has gone awry and put many on death row. The anger literature often refers to this type of anger as "anger out."[3]

But externalized Toxic Anger also exacts a tremendous toll on the seething individual himself: it destroys him. Some years ago it was touted that the type A personality was prone to cardiovascular disease. It is now known that it is competitiveness, impatience, irritability, and the explosive reaction of hostility that is so toxic. It not only causes three to seven times the normal incidence of heart disease, but also is linked to hypertension and virtually all the illnesses listed in Chapter 1. It also causes an increase in mortality. In fact, the greater the anger, the greater the risk of adverse effects. Only about 10 percent of individuals with toxic amounts of anger externalize it; 90 percent internalize it.[4]

Internalized Toxic Anger

You might say that it makes sense that the raging individual is playing with fire and that he and those around him will get burned. But what happens if you have, so it would seem, better control of the anger and you keep it to yourself? You capitulate, give in, acquiesce, accommodate, appease, or surrender. Internalized Toxic Anger is a tendency to suppress the anger rather than appropriately expressing it. But the anger is still alive: it is just buried. You may deny the outrage, blocking it from your mind. In fact, you may even have a smiling face and be known as such a "nice" person. Another form this anger takes is to flee or run from the situation. But the dynamics are still the same. And the smoldering effect of the perceived injustice continues to do its destruction even if the person who is capitulating does not appreciate it. The literature tends to call this "anger in."

Hypertension, cardiovascular disease, and many other illnesses have been reported in the person who internalizes his toxic anger. In fact, with slight variation, virtually all the illnesses and problems of the externalizer of toxic anger can occur with the internalizer. One notable variation in expression is that the externalizer is more prone to abuse others, while the internalizer is more prone to depression.[5]

Toxic Anger

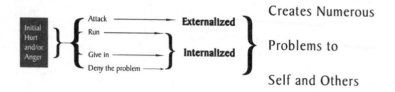

Figure 4

Summary of Toxic Anger

To summarize, whenever we are hurt or angry and the feelings *or* issues are not fully and satisfactory resolved, that energy remains either within us or it spills over on those around us causing all kinds of damage. As illustrated in Figure 4, if in response to hurt or anger we engage in a hostile attack on others, the anger is manifest externally and it "creates numerous problems to self and others." Likewise, if we respond to hurt or anger by running, giving in, or denying that there is a problem at all, we internalize the anger and sooner or later that energy will express itself destructively. Again, it "creates numerous problems to self and others."

Healthy Anger

You might think that if anger causes all these problems, why don't we just figure out a way to rid ourselves of all anger. Christians are often the proponents of this unworkable tenet. Because, for starters, it's impossible to rid ourselves of all anger. We live in a fallen world and injustices will always be done to one another. Others might think that "healthy anger" is an oxymoron, for health and anger are opposites. But anger is a God-given beneficial gift. It is an attribute that God has and he has given it to us as a blessing, for it energizes us and enables us to take appropriate action, when it is needed.

Healthy anger, which is anger that is handled in a healthy way, denotes using methods that are constructive. The literature sometimes refers to this manner of handling anger as "anger-control." It has also been referred to as a "reflective" approach to handling anger. It aims at solving the conflict in a calmer, thoughtful approach. When anger is handled in a healthy way, it doesn't take much out of our system and it adds much to our ability to function.

Inevitably there will be times in our fast paced society that injury or hurt will be perceived by you and *you will either handle it aggressively, capitulate, or handle it in a deliberate and healthy way. You cannot avoid these situations.*

Steps to Handling Anger in a Healthy Way

In a sense it's easy to handle anger *destructively*, that is, it's easy up front. Just bury it or let it all hang out. To handle anger *constructively* takes much more effort initially, but pays gigantic long-term dividends. In trying to deal with my own negative feelings in a healthy way, and in counseling and observing thousands of people, the best way that I can synthesize the process is to explain it with a flow sheet showing its seven steps (see Figure 5, below).

Steps to Handling Anger in a Healthy Way

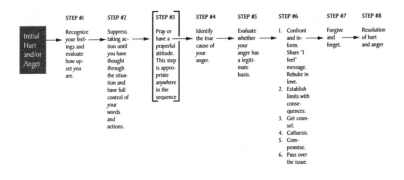

Figure 5

The Initial Injury

In every instance the sequence is started by some act or circumstance in which we feel hurt, a threat, or a misdeed that has been done to us, or someone, or something important to us. It may be actual or imagined; the important thing is that we perceive it as an injustice that in some way affects us personally. The word *hurt* is included here as some individuals don't identify with the word *anger*, but do with the word *hurt;* and the dynamics are the same. We generally don't have much control over the actual injury, but we certainly have control as to how we respond to it.

Step 1: Recognize Your Feelings and Evaluate How Upset You Are.

Most individuals have a pretty good idea when they are hurt, upset, or angry, and for them this step is a "no brainer." But there are individuals who actually don't know when they are angry or have feelings equivalent to anger. I have seen people very depressed or even suicidal without their being aware of the significant role anger is playing in the dynamics. Such a person may have to focus on his or her feelings, that is, to get in touch with this important sixth sense. The second part of this step is to recognize how angry you are. This is important as the greater the issue, the more the hurt or anger, and the more likely you will need to take some deliberate, maybe difficult action to resolve the problem.

Step 2: Suppress Taking Action Until You Have Thought It Through.

So many individuals get into deep trouble in the first few seconds after a perceived injury has been done to them. When I tapped my breaks to get the tailgater off my bumper, I hardly thought about it consciously; and that's just the problem. The old adage, "Count to ten," has much value to it. In other words, stop and think before you react. It is crucial that you *fully think through the situation* before you take any action. If need be, count to 100 or to 1,000!

Furthermore, it is crucial that you don't take any action, including a verbal one, until you have *full control of your words and actions*. You may risk delaying dealing with the issue, but that is far better than an impulsive, poorly thought-through response.

Step 3: Pray.

Pause for a moment and prayerfully consider how God would have you handle the situation; this is always appropriate advice. This may take only a few seconds but it could save you from a great deal of heartache. I have this step in the flow diagram in brackets, as seeking God's help is appropriate anywhere along the way.

Step 4: Identify the True Cause of Your Anger.

It may seem self-evident what is causing your irate feelings, but don't jump to conclusions too quickly. Sometimes you may find more subtle reasons triggering your responses. Occasionally you may need to discuss these feelings with a confidant to clarify what is at stake in causing your reactions.

Step 5: Evaluate Whether Your Anger Has a Legitimate Basis.

Sometimes you may jump to an erroneous conclusion as to the cause of your anger. You need to consider whether you have some responsibility in the conflict with which you are dealing. If so, own it.

Step 6: Take Positive Action.

At any of the previous steps the problem might be clarified and resolved without taking any specific action with the person causing your distressed emotions. But if it is not, especially if the conflict was significant, you will probably have to take one, or several, of the possible courses of action listed below:

* **Confront** – You may need to talk directly and candidly with the individual, getting all the facets of the point of irritation out on the table. When I use the word *confront* I don't mean a harsh accusative dialogue. What I do mean is a kind and forthright listening to the other person and his or her perspective as well as putting forth your own for the person to consider. King Solomon tells us, "A soft answer turneth

away wrath: but grievous words stir up anger" (Proverbs 15:1, KJV).

- **Establish Limits with Consequences** – Many problems develop because clear boundaries are not first of all clarified in our minds and then communicated to the other party. For example, a mother who frequently is angry and yells at her 11-year-old for not doing his homework, may instead need to set the standard that the child may not watch TV until all the homework is done. You will find numerous applications of this concept that can affect most of your relationships.

- **Obtain Counsel** – In the more difficult situations you may need to discuss the situation and get some input from a trusted mature friend, pastor, or on occasion, a professional counselor.

- **Catharsis** – I am not encouraging dumping your *feelings* on another person, but I do encourage talking about the issue and the resultant feelings with another neutral friend. This step sometimes resolves our angry feelings.

- **Compromise** – Seldom in conflict situations is one person 100 percent right and the other person 100 percent wrong. This is especially so when you are living or working with someone, for typically both individuals have contributed to the issue in contention. If you are responsible for some portion of the problem, own up to it. This will set the example and make it far more likely that the other party will admit and own up to his or her part in the conflict.

- **Pass Over the Issue** – This is an important step but it's tricky. As a prerequisite you must have worked through the first five steps in the flow chart. You may or may not have worked through one or more of the sub-steps under Step 6 – such as getting counsel, confronting, or compromise. But when all is said and done, on occasion it is appropriate to "pass over the issue" or to put it in other words, "drop the issue." This means that you will drop completely all ill will and hurt. Yes, it takes a great deal of maturity to be able to do this. The tricky part is that it is extremely easy to confuse this process with the process of "Internalized Toxic Anger," which has a diametric opposite outcome.

Step 7: Forgive and Forget.

If you have worked through the previous steps appropriately, you are ready to forgive. This becomes a choice – a crucial choice for not only the other person but for yourself. If you truly forgive the incident and its accompanying feelings, it will fade with time (see Chapter 9).

Resolution of the Hurt and Anger

The above process should resolve your hurt and anger. However, this is a difficult task for all of us some of the time and some of us most of the time.

Proven Benefits

Studies have shown that individuals with toxic anger who work on their anger problem, learning better coping skills, do decrease their hypertension, the progression of heart disease, and increase their longevity.[6]

More Help is Available

Author's Note: The material in this chapter is a brief overview of dealing with anger. It is a summary of some of the material in my previous book, *Overcoming Hurts and Anger: Finding Freedom from Negative Emotions,* published by Harvest House Publishers, Eugene, Oregon. If you are among the 20 per cent of the population who struggle with Toxic Anger, I would urge you to obtain a copy of my book and carefully study and apply the principles in it.

CHAPTER 6

HOW DO YOU DEAL WITH YOUR FINANCES?

C HUGGING UP A small hill one day in my ten-year-old car, I noticed more than its share of pollution trailing out of the exhaust pipe. *I deserve more than this*, I thought. *After all, I've been out of school seven years. I've worked hard. A man with my training deserves a better car than this.*

It wasn't so much the threat of the car breaking down (although it had been towed away three days in succession for my wife), rather, I simply felt I *deserved* a better car. It's true we could easily have borrowed money for a new car. But with medical-school debts still unpaid and other demands, it didn't seem wise to go farther into debt.

That same week a woman was talking to my wife, criticizing doctors in general for their "high" income and complaining about her own financial status. What she apparently failed to realize is that virtually everyone faces significant financial stress from time to time, at least from his own perspective. Although my salary is certainly adequate, it doesn't minimize the basic urge we all face to want more than we have. I know colleagues of mine who make two and three times what I do, yet they live from paycheck to paycheck.

It's fascinating to read the paragraphs above, written 30 years ago and compare them with my current situation. My wife and I currently have cars that are six and 14 years old. They run very well and are looked after so that they almost look like they have just been driven off the showroom floor. Nevertheless, as I look at all the beautiful new cars that are on the road and that my friends have – many of which are luxury cars – I think to myself, *It would certainly be nice to have a brand new luxury car.*

Most people do not buy new cars because their cars are likely to break down or because it makes financial sense; they buy a new car *as a statement of who they are.* At least this is the case in the United States. The advertising industry and the automobile makers have done a fabulous job of convincing us that we will be happier or be more valued if we drive that new car, SUV, or pickup off the showroom floor for all of our friends and business associates to see. Some European countries even make a celebration over it. The industry doesn't tell you that once it leaves the dealer's lot it has lost 20 percent of its value and its all downhill from there.

Unfortunately, it's not just the car salesman or TV commercial that is urging us to spend more. Sometimes fellow Christians place one more pressure on us instead of helping us with the basic problem. So we are bombarded from all sides.

Our Insatiable Desire for More

One of the richest men on earth in his day, John D. Rockefeller, was once asked, "How much money is enough?" His reported answer was, "Just a little bit more." If we are going to try to satisfy our internal needs with wealth and what it will buy, we will always want "a little bit more."

Living beyond one's means is epidemic in the United States today. An article in the *Los Angeles Times* stated:

> American society is acquisitive. It is one of possession, competition, and change that generally is called progress. We are forever seeking new levels. Our appetites are insatiable. We live in a high pressure society. New images are placed before us by advertising. Desires are aroused. Competition is encouraged. Ambition is acclaimed, success admired and easy credit pays the way. If you remain unaware of the commercial world's methods you cannot deal with it on its own level. The person who remains unaware, who doesn't set his own goals and standards, loses his options by default. He will be buffeted about. Instead of pursuing a straight course, he will react frantically to a million stimuli directed his way. He will wonder where the money has gone.[1]

You would think that was written today. It was written 30 years ago, but its appraisal is just as apropos today as it was then. The problem has gotten much worse. College students were recently asked on a survey about what was important to them in life. Three decades ago 43 percent of them said, "Making more money was very important to them." In a recent survey 75 percent said it was very important to them. In the same period of time the choice, "Developing a meaningful philosophy in life" dropped from 83 percent to 40 percent![2]

It's not just college students who are affected by this change, but virtually all of us. Money – whether you have it or don't – for the average person, occupies much of his, or her thinking – how to gain it, how to preserve it, where to invest it, and when to use it. With so much credit card indebtedness today, it's often how to meet the next payment.

Undue concern about finances and possessions is just as great a problem for the middle class and rich as it is for the poor, for the average Christian as for the non-Christian. In one evangelical church 45 percent of those responding to a questionnaire said that personal or family finances occupied a prominent segment of time in their thinking. Christ addressed the issue of money as much as any other single topic in the Gospels. It is no wonder the Scriptures record this strong statement: "The love of money is the root of all evil" (1 Timothy 6:10, KJV).

Money and Things Do Not Bring Happiness

Virtually all this striving leaves people empty. An article in the *American Psychologist* says:

> In the United States, Canada, and Europe, the correlation between income and personal happiness . . . is . . . virtually negligible . . . people who go to work in their overalls and on the bus are just as happy, on the average, as those in suits who drive to work in their own Mercedes . . . The more people strive for extrinsic goals such as money, the more numerous their problems and the less robust their wellbeing . . . our becoming much better off over the last four decades has not been accompanied by one iota of increased subjective wellbeing.[3]

Solomon said virtually the same thing 3,000 years ago, "He who loves money will not be satisfied with money; nor he who loves wealth, with gain" (Ecclesiastes 5:10, RSV). That person will also discover that striving to achieve these overextended self-made goals will produce weariness and anxiety of body and soul. This striving causes stress and fatigue.

The Stress Money Creates

We do need enough money for our basic needs, for without that we will have stress. But beyond basic subsistence, a striving after "a little bit more" quickly adds stress to our cumulative stress load and leads to all the problems that excess stress can cause.

I frequently see individuals whose financial problems, especially their commitments or debts, are creating tremendous internal turmoil resulting in anxiety, depression, resentment, bitterness, and fatigue.

One example of how financial stress can lead to emotional symptoms is illustrated by the closure of a bank. In 1985 the First Colonial Bank of the Marshall Islands had to close its doors due to fraud. A careful study was made of a group of 72 of these individuals who lost all of their savings. Within 20 months 30 percent had developed major depression and 27 percent diagnosable anxiety disorders. This demonstrates the tremendous effects our finances have on our wellbeing.[4]

The Solution

First, you must commit this entire area of your life to God. Yielding every area of your life to God except the area of finances and possessions will lead to sorrow as you miss the true riches of the life which God has for you. The rich young ruler apparently kept all of God's commandments except that he was unwilling to yield his possessions. He missed the kingdom of God (see Luke 18).

Remember Abraham? He had to be willing to yield his most precious possession, his son Isaac, without knowing whether God would give him back or not. Only when his yieldedness was obvious did God return Isaac to him (see Genesis 22). Job lost all of his riches during the time of his trial. But later they were returned double "when he had prayed for his [accusing] friends" (Job 42:10). God may or may not choose to take our possessions away from us. The important thing is for us to be willing to let him do with them as he chooses.

We must hold on to material things loosely. No matter what we have, the title must always rest in God's hand. Everything is safe when he holds the title; nothing is safe when we hold it. Our prime concern before money, possessions, and all other things must be to seek first the kingdom of God and his will for our lives (see Matthew 6:19–34).

Second, you must decide firmly that your standards are going to be different from the world's, including possibly many in the "Christian world." If your standards are going to be set under God's guidance, then you will have to tune the world out and God in. This doesn't just happen, for it must be planned, executed, and repeatedly re-evaluated.

Remember Paul's statement, "Don't let the world around you squeeze you into its own mould" (Romans 12:2, PH). This certainly is appropriate in the arena of finances. This means you must not only crucify the onslaught of pressures and standards from the world around you but also those from within. Do not compare yourselves with others, which is a tough job for us all. Your standard of living may have to be set several notches lower than your peers or even your Christian friends.

Continually be on guard to avoid the high-pressure salesmanship techniques, which can coax you into buying things you really do not need and may not even want. Regarding pressures to give to the many worthy opportunities for the "Lord's work," even here we must get careful direction from God.

Third, decide that you will be content with what you have. The Scriptures remind us, "Keep your life free from love of money, and be content with what you have; for he has said, 'I will never fail you nor forsake you'" (Hebrews 13:5, RSV). And, "There is great gain in godliness with contentment" (1 Timothy 6:6–12, RSV).

The *Fourth* step is a practical one. You can do a number of specific things if there are just too many bills due before the next paycheck:

- Reduce Expenses: take a careful inventory of where your money is going and, seeking God's guidance, look for places where you can reduce or eliminate expenditures.
- Consider living on a budget; determine ahead of time where you will be spending your money.
- Consider living on a "cash" basis. People who have trouble with credit-buying may literally need to cut up their credit cards and buy on a "cash only" basis. Some advisors have suggested that when you get your paycheck, cash it and put money in envelopes, marking each envelope according to your budget, then spend that money only as predetermined.
- Plan your buying carefully. Shop for bargains, but don't go bargain shopping. That is, if you truly need something, try and buy it at the lowest price possible; but just because the paper or TV advertises "bargains," don't go shopping. It is not unusual for people to buy bargains they don't need: these are not bargains no matter how little you pay for them.
- If you have a number of debts on which you are paying interest, pay off the accounts that charge the highest interest rate first.
- Don't go into debt if at all possible. The only exception is in buying a house and perhaps educational or unexpected medical expenses. If you use credit cards, pay them off completely each month. Having lived many years with the debts of medical school and in recent decades living without debt, I can attest that it is a great reliever of stress not to feel the burden of debt.
- If all else is not enough, you may need to find ways to increase your earning ability temporarily through additional education or promotions. Occasionally, overtime or an additional job has its place, particularly under times of stress, such as during educational years.
- If the above steps are not enough, consider seeing a qualified financial counselor. My only caution here is for you to be very careful, especially if he or she is trying to sell you something.

Fifth, you must be willing to ruthlessly follow through on God's direction regarding your finances and possessions. If you have certain weaknesses in the area of follow-through, identify them and take the necessary steps to avoid making serious mistakes. Many years ago, I determined under God's guidance to limit my practice so that I would have time to do many other things that I felt my life should include. Despite this resolve I became aware of the subtle tendency to allow *my* practice to increase for financial reasons, which, of course, decreased available time. To help me curb this, for several years my wife and I determined to give four times our usual percentage to God's work if a certain base income was surpassed. This, along with taxes, removed the incentive to work more hours for personal financial gain and so helped me obtain my basic goals.

So how does my buying a new car fit into all of this? A new car, even a luxury car, is not wrong or sinful. But it is incumbent on my wife and me to consider the appropriateness of such an expenditure in light of our entire financial picture. We must also consider how this fits with the needs around the world and our personal future needs. I must ruthlessly be careful to keep this area yielded to God's will lest the pressures of the world squeeze me.

Finally, be assured that God, our loving heavenly Father, knows your needs and will meet them as you are yielded to him. When you turn your deep yearnings over to him, he will refine them and give you what is consistent with his will and often what you really want. He may even choose to give something back that you had to sacrifice earlier in life. Paul shared with us a valuable lesson, "I have learned, in whatever state I am, to be content; I know how to be abased, and I know how to abound; in any and all circumstances I have learned the secret of facing plenty and hunger, abundance and want. I can do all things in Him who strengthens me . . . [Paul went on and encouraged the church at Philippi , saying] my God will supply every need of yours according to his riches in glory in Christ Jesus" (Philippians 4:11–13, 19, RSV).

CHAPTER 7

WHAT WILL OTHER PEOPLE THINK?

W<small>E ALL SUFFER</small> from a tremendous desire and inborn urge to be liked and admired by others. Even those who would protest and say they are the exception have their group of people by whom they want to be thought of highly. This is true if you are a member of a motorcycle group, an elite academic hierarchy, or a Christian. Henri Nouwen says, "Whether I am a pianist, a businessman, or a minister, what matters is how I am perceived by my world."[1]

To have people's admiration and praise typically means that we have to please them. And the more we say "yes" to their requests, the more affirmation we get from them; that's what it's all about for many of us. To some extent every one of us suffers from this malady. Some have a major problem here, and the religious person is especially susceptible to this difficulty.

This is normal in many situations. Certainly, as we learn to love people in Christ, an outgrowth of activities will develop that will be pleasing to others. But for the vast majority of us it goes far beyond normal and appropriate limits. Alice Fryling in *Too Busy?* makes this troubling observation, "If we are honest, we must admit that much of what we do in God's name is motivated by our desire to look good."[2]

On the surface, being a people-pleaser might seem to have the best interests of the person we are trying to please, but just the opposite is true. The person who is the typical people-pleaser is doing it so that he, the people-pleaser, will be admired, valued, and praised. The motivation for his behavior is based on self-love, not primarily on love for others. The external appearance of his activities may be that of self-sacrificing concern for another; however, his real motive is to gain favor, praise, understanding, acceptance, approval, and love for himself. Contrary to how it might appear, this individual is self-centered. "People-pleasers" ultimately must have the approval and praise of others, regardless of the cost to themselves or to anyone else.

Many of our social obligations fall under the category of people-pleasing. We attend certain meetings and functions, not because we really want to or because our presence will be of help to anyone. We go because we have been asked, and are afraid we will offend someone if we don't go. We accept an assignment on various committees or auxiliaries for the same reason.

Certainly we should not be rude to people. As Christians we must have a high degree of sensitivity to the needs of those around us. At times we certainly need to give of ourselves and of our substance to others. However, some people are overly sensitive to the needs and opinions of others to the point of being pathological. They spend a lot of time thinking, *What does so-and-so think of me? What does he expect of me? How can I please him?* Soon these thoughts may become so automatic, even unconscious, that the person doesn't even realize the extent to which he has become a people-pleaser.

The Problem – The High Cost of People-Pleasing

We find many examples of people-pleasing in the Scriptures. Balaam is a good illustration of this: he was a prophet who communicated with God and was advised by the Lord not to return with King Balak's honored men and do what they wanted him to do. But the Moabites pressed him with the allurement of personal gain and he finally yielded. The result was a trouble-filled trip with both God and King Balak angry at him. His acts ultimately cost him his life (see Numbers 22–24, 31).

King Saul is another vivid and pathetic case of being a people-pleaser. Even when confronted by the Prophet Samuel for his sin of disobedience to God, he tacitly said, "I have sinned . . . ," but without taking a breath continued, "[but] I feared the people and listened to their voice. . . Please honor me now before the elders of my people" (1 Samuel 15:24, 30). God was severely displeased with Saul and eventually took away his entire kingdom from him, giving it to David (see 1 Samuel 15:28; 16:13–14).

The religious leaders of Christ's day also had a major problem with people-pleasing. They went to great efforts to be sure others knew of their religious deeds, such as praying and fasting (note Matthew 6:16; Luke 18:9–14). Jesus' conclusion was, "How on earth can you believe [have faith] while you are for ever looking for each other's approval and not for the glory [honor] that comes from the one God?" (John 5:44, PH).

So what are some of the costs of people-pleasing?

- People-pleasing is a wearisome task. It leads to tremendous internal conflict with the inevitable result of stress and fatigue. The uncertainty of wondering what people really think of us produces anxiety and even depression if we think we have lost another person's esteem – which sooner or later will occur.
- The people-pleaser has a hard time saying "no" and ultimately ends up being overloaded.
- Often, legitimate family needs and even his own needs will go ignored as he frantically tries to impress his more distant audience. I know of a situation where a person is highly regarded by his church friends for his self-sacrifice. He is readily available to help anyone in need, but his spouse at home experiences him as a tyrant with whom she has great difficulty living.
- The people-pleaser does not know his own mind, wishes, or needs because he is focused on what other people want him to do and be, or what he thinks others want him to do.
- Once pleasing people becomes a high priority, that person will not know God's will and potential for him.
- Ultimately the people-pleaser may end up losing everything – God's approval, his family, and all his coveted admirers.

The Solution – Live to Seek God's Approval Only

Each of us must be willing to die to the people around us and follow God alone – the *Living* God. Henri Nouwen cuts to the core of the issue saying, "We have to give up measuring our meaning and value with the yardstick of others."[3] If we are unwilling to do this, we will suffer great loss. A people-pleaser is licked before he gets started; he can never please one person all of the time or all of the people part of the time. And certainly he never pleases God or himself. So he must choose: will he serve God or man? More accurately stated, "will he serve God or himself?"

The focal point of our approval has to move from ourselves or others, to God. We need consciously to seek the honor that comes from God alone (see the latter part of John 5:44). As we do this, we will be able to say with Jesus, "I always do what is pleasing to him [God]" (John 8:29, RSV), and with the Apostle Paul, "So we speak, not to please men, but to please God who tests our hearts" (1 Thessalonians 2:4; see also Galatians 1:10; Matthew 6:1– 6).

Brother Lawrence, in *The Practice of the Presence of God,* puts us on the right track in dealing with this problem. He exhorts, "I began to live as if there was none but He [God] and I in the world." Elsewhere he says, "[I am] seeking Him only, and nothing else, not even His gifts."[4]

At first glance, such statements may seem like he was totally inconsiderate of the needs of those around him; however, nothing could be farther from the truth. Brother Lawrence simply knew how to put first things first. So we must be willing to sacrifice every good thought people have about us in order to seek God's favor. This will mean saying "no" to certain requests and at times being misunderstood. God will occasionally test us to see just who has first place in our hearts.

Several years ago I was very busy in leadership at church, probably investing at least ten hours a week on meetings and other related activities. Some things occurred that greatly troubled me, and verbally addressing the issues got me nowhere. It seemed that resigning was my only option. I normally don't resign from anything, and usually stick with my commitments to the very end. If I did resign, I felt it would be misunderstood and I might be censured. I would lose the esteem of the most important peer group to me and possibly forfeit the opportunity of speaking and being involved in other leadership activities. All these things are very important to me. Thus resignation could prove to be quite a loss to me. It would be the diametric opposite of being a people-pleaser. After much prayer and consultation with my wife and trusted friends, I did resign. Initially there was internal turmoil and disapproval ensued when I made known my decision, but shortly after I had wonderful relief and peace. I felt I did what God wanted. I felt free from needing to please people, and on top of it all I regained many hours to invest in other ways. It was not only a freeing experience, but it energized me and gave me a tremendous sense of serenity.

CHAPTER 8

ARE YOU HIDING BEHIND THE MASK?

H OW MANY PEOPLE really know you? Does anyone really know you – your aspirations, insecurities, fears, misdeeds, or sins? Do you want people, or any one person for that matter, to really know you in depth? If you don't – and most people don't – it forces you to wear a mask, that is, to communicate an image that is different from the "you" that you know down deep inside. It is a deliberate mechanism to keep other people at an arm's distance. Its aim is to have admirers – at a distance – because of fears that closeness will expose you. This is a variation of being a people-pleaser – you want others to be pleased by what they see in you, even if it is phoney. People in the world may "let it all hang out," that is, they may not care as much what others know about them. Thus this problem inherently is greater with those who are religious. They have a standard to live up to, an image to protect.

Speaking to the religious leaders of his day, Christ said, "Alas for you, you hypocritical Scribes and Pharisees! You are like white-washed tombs, which look fine on the outside but inside are full of dead men's bones and all kinds of rottenness. In the same way you appear like good men on the outside – but inside you are a mass of pretense and wickedness" (Matthew 23:27– 28, PH).

Definition and Cause

A mask is a covering to conceal or disguise your true identity. It is a pretense, a false claim or profession, a façade or front usually concealing something perceived by the wearer of the mask as inferior.

The Bible gives us a graphic portrayal of the mask and how it started (see Genesis 3). At first, Adam and Eve walked with God unashamedly; then they sinned. In their sin they became aware of their nakedness and what they had done and wanted to run and hide. Sin, guilt, self-centeredness, and pride lead people to putting on and wearing masks – putting their best foot forward to the point of hiding their true selves from others.

The Costs of Wearing the Masks

Hiding from God and others leads to hiding your true inner person from yourself, and the tendency to flee from God. You may become a stranger to yourself, God, and others without realizing what is happening. Consciously or unconsciously, this leads to a fear of being found out. And so the mask becomes a shield to protect you from what others might say or think about you if they really knew what you were like. Consequently you begin to feel like a deceiver. This entire pretense robs you of close relationships with others, because the closer people get to you the more likely they just might be able to see behind your mask.

This internal and external deception has a significant price tag. It requires a great deal of energy and leads to a host of problems, including fear, irritability, excusing yourself, blaming others, and, not infrequently, deceit and frank lying.

Furthermore, as I have talked with and observed numerous individuals in the office, church, or society, I am convinced that the mask causes internal stress potentially resulting in all the various symptoms and diseases discussed in Chapter 1. For many it may be only a minute contributing factor, but for others it can become a gigantic load.

Another consequence of wearing a mask is that it fosters the tendency for those about you to wear a mask as well; this is especially true of those in leadership positions.

Removing the Mask

Masks tend to stick on your face, especially if they have been worn for a long time and if there is a great disparity between what you portray to others and what is really you. There is the fear of exposing yourself. You become frightened about what you might see and the repercussions when others see you as you really are.

How do you take off your mask? It is not just a simple matter of slipping the rubber bands off from behind your ears and dropping the mask to the ground. There will be a lot of internal resistance. In order to remove your mask, you have to be honest with yourself, admitting who you really are. This is very difficult for many people because they have even disguised themselves from themselves. So you may want to start with the biblical prayer, "Search me, O Lord, and show me if I am hiding something from you, myself, or others" (author's paraphrase of Psalm 139:23-24). Once you admit to yourself that you are wearing a mask, then you must be willing to admit its presence to God. Wearing a mask is deceitful, therefore it is sin. It's really a matter of surrendering this area of your life to God, including whatever consequences might result.

It will necessitate a willingness to deal with some areas of your life that you have avoided for a long time, and in accepting and allowing others to accept or reject those areas we cannot change.

Truly realizing the devastating effects the mask is having on you and those around you also helps you to remove the mask. When you finally realize that it need not remain, you catch a glimpse of the possible you, without a mask. Sometimes the fear of what people might think is much worse then what they actually will think.

Having admitted to yourself and God the presence of a mask, the next step is to find a friend or small group with whom you feel safe. Decide that at the appropriate time you will start exposing your real self. Soon you will be more comfortable with your new true self, and the honest transparent relationship will spread. Removing your mask may bring to light some other areas on which you will need to work, such as, guilt, bitterness, or people-pleasing. You must be willing to work on these areas as God directs if you want to keep the mask off.

A word of caution: taking the mask off does not mean you should purposefully expose every aspect of your life to everyone around you. At times, this may not only serve no useful function, but may be damaging and unloving to others or yourself. It does, however, mean that you *must be willing* to expose any area God should indicate needs exposing; and what you do reveal is an accurate representation of the authentic you. You must never be phoney.

There is a real risk with removing the mask. Some people will use your willful exposure against you. I have had this happen to me in the past and am aware as I write certain paragraphs in this book that I am running that risk. But in an effort to model what I teach, I have chosen to take that risk.

Misconceptions

Two significant misconceptions foster maintaining the mask: Fear that the truth about you will hurt your testimony and thus the gospel and the Lord, and the misconception that the abundant life means a life without problems.

To those of you who would say that exposing yourself might hurt your testimony, please note what the Apostle Peter has to say: "For the time is come that judgment must begin at the house of God: and if it first begin at us, what shall the end be of them that obey not the gospel of God?" (1 Peter 4:17, KJV).

If a Christian leader is living a life of pretense, it is most likely (despite the seeming results to which he may proudly point) his life is accomplishing very little of eternal value. It may even be hindering God's work in the lives of people around him. God's plan and desire is that we honestly and openly recognize who and what we are — imperfect vessels of clay. Then we must actively rely on and follow him, as he gives strength to help us work on our imperfections. Only in this way will our lives have eternal significance and glorify God and further the gospel. This is often the means God uses to start revival in his church.

A big factor in promoting the mask in the Christian community is because, for the most part, Christian leaders have not been willing to remove their own masks. This not only sets a bad example, but it encourages others, so to speak, under him or her to keep their masks on very tightly. Furthermore, if one person in the Christian community should work at being transparent, others at all levels in the Christian leadership would typically criticize that person who is trying to be honest and give him all kinds of clichés, Bible verses, and judgments. Before long that individual, in one way or another, will be ostracized. If there is ever going to be any widespread transparency in the Christian community, it will have to start at the top and trickle down.

The second misconception is that the abundant life means one free of problems. If not resolved, this misconception can cause internal problems and lead to pretense, doubt, despair, and even rejection of the Christian life. Some people have the mistaken idea that once they have received Christ, they will have a happy life that is free of all struggles. From the eternal perspective, God promises to give every believer life that is abundant. But we live in a world that is hostile to God and his people, and God doesn't always intervene to protect us from that.

Positive Benefits of Removing the Masks

If we would only stop pretending and accept God's evaluation of us that we are nothing apart from him but have everything with him, then we can start to bring harmony to the person inside and the personage that people see. Now the energy – once used to maintain a mask – can be distributed in useful tasks. Transparency in the body of Christ would transform the church and cause radical positive changes for the kingdom of God for all to see.

The Apostle Paul put it well: "We refuse to wear masks and play games. We don't maneuver and manipulate behind the scenes. . . Rather, we keep everything we do and say out in the open, the whole truth on display so that those who want to can see and judge for themselves in the presence of God" (2 Corinthians 4:2-3, MSG).

CHAPTER 9

HOW DO YOU HANDLE BITTERNESS AND RESENTMENT?

EVERY TIME I saw a certain elder at church I would get a sick feeling in the pit of my stomach. Fortunately, he went to a different service than I did, so that I didn't see him very often. Finally, after about the fifth time this happened, over a three-year period, I determined to take some action. This whole thing started with the only phone call I ever received from him, one that came about ten o'clock one night. In that conversation he wanted to know my stance on some doctrinal issues. In fact, I initially felt interrogated and, after a few minutes, judged by him. We had no other contact before or after this incident – except for the upset feeling in the pit of my stomach when I saw him.

So I called him and asked him out for breakfast or lunch. When we met, his curiosity peaked; he immediately asked why I wanted to meet with him. I related to him the incident three years earlier and my feelings immediately after the conversation and subsequently every time I saw him. He scratched his head and said he didn't remember the conversation but apologized for his hurting me. I immediately accepted his apology and now when I see him, there are no longer any ill feelings toward him.

Then there was the minister whom I was treating for both fatigue and depression. One day he came to the office and told me he had just gone to his father's grave and "gotten rid of a belly full of resentments." This significantly helped restore a joyful attitude and energy, for he had finally dealt with bitterness toward his dad.

It is no wonder that Abraham Lincoln, while overhearing Civil War enemies denouncing the opposition, said, "Insane as it may seem,

I hold malice toward none of them. I have neither the time nor the energy in this life to hold that kind of resentment."[1]

I am convinced that resentment, bitterness, and the resultant unforgivingness are great internal drainers of energy and often lead to depression and a host of other emotional, physical, and interpersonal problems.

Earlier in the book we talked about anger (Chapter 5). Anger is typically the feeling close to an injury. If that is not dealt with properly at the time, it typically turns into a cauldron of bitterness and resentment. It is this fermenting internalized toxic anger that we now want to address.

Manifestations

I frequently see bitterness and resentment overflowing from my patients. Sometimes bitterness and resentment exude from the person and it is obvious to all; but many others disguise or bury it so well that no one knows it is there, sometimes, not even the person himself.

And once we have given in to bitterness and resentment, it can spread easily. The writer to the Hebrews admonishes his readers with the plea "that no root of bitterness . . . [should be part of our lives causing] trouble, and by it many be defiled" (Hebrews 12:15). Bitterness can grow like a cancer affecting our entire being and may infect whole families and even an entire church or society. In fact, most of the current strife around the world can be directly attributed to bitterness and resentment toward another group of people – whether they be Palestinians or Israelis, Catholics or Protestants, Christians or Muslims, black or white, and the list goes on and on.

But why does this "cancer" affect some and apparently not others? I am reminded of two individuals. Both lost their daughters as a direct result of a negligent drunk driver. One was in the same car, literally seeing her daughter die. The other arrived on the scene minutes after the accident, helping to pull his dying daughter out of the car. But from there, the similarity changes totally.

One immediately forgave the drunk, and was freed from the consequences of unforgivingness. The other individual remains hateful and unforgiving. He has said, "I remember condemning the drunk to a life in hell for eternity. Certain things are unforgivable." He continued, "I have never felt such rage and hate . . . it destroys you." His whole life centers around this hate. He says he can't come to God as long as he so tenaciously holds on to his vengeance. It's no wonder he has suicidal depression, fatigue, and carnage in his interpersonal relationships. Both of these individuals had sustained a horrendous, unjustified loss. But one person's life goes on, while the other is stuck in a quagmire of self-destruction. What makes the difference?

The Cost of Unforgivingness

Jesus Christ once told a parable about a benevolent king who was owed an insurmountable debt—in today's currency probably millions of dollars (Matthew 18:21–35). His servant "did not have the means to repay," so he said, "Have patience with me, and I will repay you everything" (verses 25–26). He asked for mercy—an extension of time, a delay; this was the servant's misconception of forgiveness. The king, however, offered the servant "compassion and released him and forgave him the debt" (verse 27).

Shortly thereafter the servant found a fellow servant who owed him the equivalent of a few dollars and demanded payment; when it was not forthcoming, he threw him into a debtor's prison. When the king heard of this, he threw the first servant into prison, allowing him to be tortured until his debt was paid in full.[2]

In fact, the verb *to torment* comes from the term *torturers*, which is the same word used earlier by Christ to describe "great [physical] pain" (Matthew 8:6) and by Peter to depict mental pain (2 Peter 2:8). It is also used by Christ to describe the misery of a man "in agony" of hell (Luke 16:23–24). The unforgiving servant ended up with a tormented imprisoned life. One of the points of this parable is that if we don't forgive others the injustices they have done to us, we will live out our days in an imprisoned, tormented state. The price of unforgivingness is horrendous.

It is important to understand the neurochemistry of the brain. In such a destructive means of reacting to injury the mind repeatedly replays thoughts and images with their resultant feelings over and over again. Each time that occurs, with the desire to retaliate, it is more deeply imprinted in the mind. The torment within the prison of our minds is repeated again. It is somewhat like memorizing something—with repetition, it's etched more deeply into our minds.

Like Toxic Internalized Anger discussed earlier, studies have shown that people who have "resentments," those who "brood" or have "restrained retaliation" or "experience marital conflict and keep it to themselves" have evidence of great stress on their bodies.[3]

The scientific community is just now beginning to study the effects of unforgiveness in a systematic manner. Already there is evidence that unforgiveness is associated with more psychopathology; forgiveness on the other hand is associated with lower blood pressure, less depression and anxiety, fewer negative emotions and a more healthy appraisal of oneself.[4]

Definitions and Source

The term *bitterness* means a sharp disagreeable taste, discomfort, or pain. *Resentment* means a feeling of being injured or offended; literally it means to sense or feel again. Many people knowingly harbor resentment and are acutely aware of a hostile, angry feeling springing up from within. This feeling may even cause their heart rates to speed up and moisture to appear on their brows and hands; their entire fight-or-flight mechanism may go into action with its resultant use of precious energy. But for some, bitterness and resentment are deeply repressed. The only manifestation may be that when a person or event periodically crosses their minds, they feel slightly hurt, disappointed, neglected, or have some other negative reaction.

Life is full of joys, successes and delights. But also inherent in life are sorrows, failures, and disappointments. Thus we have many opportunities to develop anger. When we don't handle anger properly, it becomes deep-seated, ensnaring the individual as it turns into bitterness and resentment.

Other people most commonly incite our resentments: husbands may resent wives, children their parents, youth the establishment, middle-aged people the changes of the youth, the worker his employer, and parishioners their pastor. We are particularly vulnerable when a person or group of people has authority over us. Even ministers have to deal with the problem of resentment toward their parishioners. Forty percent of the people in an active and growing evangelical church said, on an anonymous questionnaire, that they, too, were often bitter or resentful. Not infrequently, the resentment is really toward God, whether conscious or unconscious, for not giving us all we "deserve" or allowing "this" to happen to us. In every such situation we feel a "right" of ours has been violated.[5]

But in our high-tech age there is no end to the causative factors: senior citizens may resent the low interest rate or inflation, and the taxpayer his government. Resentment can develop toward anything with which we come in contact, including inanimate objects such as a computer which crashes or a new car that is a lemon.

The Difficult Process of Forgiveness

But it is difficult to forgive. It is not natural for us. It is a godly activity. Forgiveness takes hard work and much grace, but all too often pastors and Christian leaders tell us, "Just forgive," implying that it is a simple act of the will like turning off a light switch; we should just instantly turn off bitterness and resentment.

I recently listened to a tape of an outstanding pastor, whom most Christians would instantly recognize, talk with admiration of King David's forgiving Shimei, a Benjamite who had cursed him when he was fleeing from Absalom (see 2 Samuel 16:5–8). In his talk he discussed the first two episodes (2 Samuel 16:5–13; 19:16–23) of David's encounter with Shimei, but failed entirely to mention the third and fourth episodes (1 Kings 2:8–9 and 2:36–46), in which David suggested to Solomon that he punish Shimei and that ultimately Solomon had him killed.

One workbook on forgiveness, which discusses how Joseph responded to injustices, has you look up all the injustices done to him, then asks, "What was Joseph's attitude during his lifetime?" Then it gives only one reference, Genesis 50:15–21, which is the positive final conclusion. This glosses over the difficult process that Joseph had to work through to come to the place of forgiving his brothers.

It is true that Joseph was ill-treated over a period of years by his brothers and the rulers in Egypt (see Genesis 37–41). But it is also true that when Joseph's brothers went to Egypt to buy food during the famine, Joseph treated them pretty badly. He speaks harshly to them, accusing them of being spies, puts them in prison, keeps Simeon as a hostage, and frames them threatening to keep Benjamin as a slave (Genesis 42–45). Joseph behaved like a scoundrel in his first meetings with his brothers, but this was his way of working through his hurt feelings and eventually coming to the place of completely forgiving them. Only then was he able to say, "You meant evil against me, but God meant it for good . . . [and] he comforted them and spoke kindly to them" (Genesis 50:20–21). In the deeper hurts of life forgiveness is a process, sometimes a difficult but necessary process.

Steps to Forgiveness

In the chart that follows (Figure 6) I have summarized the six steps necessary to come to the place of being able to forgive and

When an Injustice is Done

Injustice Done to (Offended): Person A	Injustice Done by (Offender): Person B
1. Prerequisite: acceptance of the person, desire to reconcile	
2. Responsible to initiate dialogue if aware of hurt or altered relationship Matthew 18:15–17; Luke 17:1–4	2. Responsible to initiate dialogue if aware of injury or altered relationship Matthew 5:23–24
3. Full appreciation of injury done and effects	
	4. Must repent (own injury); Matthew 18:15-17; Luke 17:3 The Process: a: Have a contrite heart b: Confess (acknowledge to the one hurt); 1 John 1:9; James 5:16. Must be willing to apologize. c: Be willing to make restitution (rectify) where indicated. d: Purpose not to repeat the "injury".
5. Forgive (accepting what the other has communicated). Luke 17:3 – let go of claims	
6. Be willing to actively restore/rebuild the relationship. Must work at trusting.	6. Be willing to rebuild the relationship on the basis of developing trust by not repeating the injury
7. Reconciliation	
8. Forget	

Figure 6

to work towards reconciliation. Please study the chart carefully, then I will elaborate on each step in some detail.

Steps to Forgiveness – The Details

Step 1. Value the Other Person

To start with, it is crucial to see the other party (the offender) as a valuable person, one whom the Lord loves even if you are struggling with your feelings toward that person. The Scriptures command us to love our neighbor as ourselves (see Leviticus 19:15–18 and Mark 12:31a), but Christ adds to this admonition that we should love even our enemies (Matthew 5:43–48). We need to see the other party as equally precious in God's eyes.

Step 2. Initiate Dialogue (Confrontation)

It is very interesting to note that the Scriptures require both parties, the offended and the offender, whoever is aware of the apparent injustice or rift in the relationship, to initiate the dialogue. To say that "he hurt me, therefore I will wait for him to initiate the discussion" violates this principle. If you are aware that you *might* have hurt someone, it is up to you to go to that person and ask if what you have said or done was offensive. If you are aware that you feel hurt and have any unforgivingness present, you need to go to that person and initiate dialogue (with the exception of rare occasions which will be mentioned later). The elder referred to at the beginning of this chapter would have never come to me. If I was to resolve my hurt and lack of forgiveness, I had to go to him.

Talking to the other party is actually a confrontation – a face-to- face encounter bringing the issue to the other person's awareness. It involves clearly putting into words, usually verbally, but it could be written, the issue causing the conflict. *It is not attacking and it should be done as lovingly as possible.* The aim is not to get even or even get it off your chest; it is to bring the issue up to the conscious awareness of both parties, to put the issue on "the table," so to speak. An important passage on this step is Ephesians 4:15–32.

What are the issues on which you should initiate a dialogue? That is an important question. Generally it is any issue that causes bitterness, resentment, unforgivingness, or any other ill feelings. Generally, bitterness and resentment bespeak a smoldering ill-feeling that has been present for some time, possibly even many years. But please note some other factors that should be considered. When any of the following situations are present, the appropriateness of confrontation is increased. They are:

- The bigger the offense, the more important it is to confront.
- The closer the relationship, the greater is the need for confrontation.
- The greater the continued contact with the person, the more necessary is the confrontation.
- When the problem is liable to keep recurring.
- When forgiveness cannot be achieved without confronting.
- When the other person is likely to receive confrontation constructively.
- When our leadership role requires that we confront a person or issue.
- When it is needful for the offender (such as, for growth, so it won't hurt others).
- When the offender is hurting defenseless individuals (such as, molesting, beating, and similar issues).
- When you have discussed the situation with a mature friend or counselor and he/she concurs that a confrontation is necessary.

In some other situations confrontation is probably ill-advised. They include:

- You have tried to confront in the past and the person wasn't receptive (Matthew 7:6).
- The problem was primarily between two other people (for example, if the conflict is between two co-workers).
- The problem is greatly aggravated by unresolved hurts from people other than the one you are considering confronting. For example, if you have bitterness toward your boss when the major unresolved problem is with your father.

In yet other situations it is almost always ill-advised to confront. They are:

- The problem is largely your distortion of reality. All of us distort reality from time to time. This is exemplified with the proverbial illustration of two people witnessing the same auto accident and describing differently what happened. This often occurs in close relationships that have conflicts. But sometimes it goes further than that. Sometimes your mind can actually distort the truth. Sometimes it helps to consider if other people saw what this person did to you, would they unequivocally conclude that the person did you a significant injustice? If not, you probably shouldn't confront.
- If it would do great damage to the other party with scant probability of benefit.
- When the other party might retaliate physically.
- When a mature counselor concurs that there be no confrontation.

Here are some practical suggestions regarding confrontation:

- Of course it is always wise to ask God for his help (as you read in James 1:5).
- When confronting, stick to observable facts and your feelings. Avoid judgments, affixing motives, put-downs, and reading into the situation more than would be *observable* by a third party, if he or she had witnessed the situation.
- Try to be as open as you can to consider the other party's perspective.
- Own up to any fault or responsibility you have in the situation. However, do not confess responsibility for something you definitely do not believe you are responsible. I have heard Christian leaders suggest going to the other person and confessing that you have done wrong even if you believe it's all the other person's fault. These leaders believed that this would open up the conversation. The confession might open up the conversation, but you are lying if you admit to something that you don't believe you did. Furthermore, I have seen situations in which individuals have done this; and at this point the other party jumped on the erroneous confession and would not admit

any personal responsibility. This really compounds the problem.

- Generally discuss an offense privately, especially when it was done in private (Matthew 18:15–16).

- If the offense happened in front of others – it can be appropriate to confront in front of *the same individuals*. In fact, in some situations this is preferable. For example, in a situation where a husband chronically puts down his wife in front of others and private discussion has not corrected the problem. Typically, the observing friends think less of both parties. In that situation, if the wife kindly but firmly confronts the husband in front of the friends, they will think more of the wife, and the husband is more likely to stop this inappropriate behavior.

- If it is probable that the other party would be verbally or physically abusive, or might distort what is said, it is best to have a third party present even if the offense occurred in private. Alternately, a written confrontation might be preferable.

Step 3. Have a Full Appreciation of the Injury Done and Its Effects

Generally the person injured will be acutely aware of the injury before confronting the offending party. On the other hand, often the offender will be minimally or totally unaware of the pain prior to the confrontation. It is crucial that both parties be fully aware of the pain and resultant effects of the injury done. If either party minimizes the offense, the process toward forgiveness and reconciliation will be affected irreparably. Genuine forgiveness demands full understanding of the offense being forgiven.

Lewis Smedes says, "It is not enough to admit that they hurt you; they must feel the very hurt they hurt you with."[6]

Step 4. The Offender Must Repent

Repentance is owning the responsibility for what has taken place that has hurt the other person. Repentance means "to turn around."

- Sometimes debatable offenses may be resolved by empathic listening to the injured parties' feelings and hurt. A tremendous amount of help can be given by compassionate listening and getting in touch with the other's pain.

- An apology or acknowledging that the other person was hurt may be all that is necessary for some offenses.

- When you have offended someone, own up to it as quickly as you can. Not doing this can wreck your life as much as King Saul's was destroyed in ancient Israel. We read how in one situation Saul was defensive and had alibis to explain his disobedience to God (1 Samuel 15:13–30). Only when the Prophet Samuel strongly confronted him with his wrong behavior did Saul say, "I have sinned; I have indeed transgressed the command of the LORD and your words" (verse 24). But he followed this with more excuses and his major concern was how he was viewed by others. He said some of the right words but he was not repentant. In contrast to this, King David sinned, but when confronted by the Prophet Nathan, he completely and fully repented and is heralded as a man after God's heart (see 2 Samuel 12:1–13; Psalm 51; Acts 13:22).

- Repentance includes *a contrite heart*, one that is sincerely remorseful (see Psalm 51:17). Dallas Willard speaking about the necessity of remorse says: "There is little hope for genuine change in one who is without remorse, without the *anguish* of regret."[7]

- Repentance involves *confession,* both to God and to men, "If we confess our sins, He is faithful and righteous to forgive us our sins and to cleanse us from all unrighteousness," and, "Confess your sins to one another . . . so that you may be healed" (1 John 1:9; James 5:16).

  - Confession means "to name it the same, or to agree with." In other words, to call the act what God calls it — no more, but certainly no less.

  - Confession generally should be as public as the knowledge of the act.

  - Some Christian leaders suggest a specific phrase that you should say. One such "right approach" is, "I realize I have been wrong in _____ [basic offense], will you please forgive me?"[8] This is a good model to follow; however, you do not need to use any magic words or set formula. For example, in the Scriptures we see the man on the cross with Christ, the prodigal son, and Zaccheus – they all said something different but all were clearly repentant and verbalized it. On the other hand, King Saul at one point said the "right words," but it is clear he was neither repentant nor forgiven. However, if there are some words that you can't, won't, or find difficult to say, you need to understand what that is all about. For many, the words, "I'm sorry, I was wrong, will you please forgive me," are the hardest words to say in any language.

The reasons for this typically go back into one's childhood. Sometimes a child was forced to say, "I'm sorry," when he or she didn't even do the deed in question. Unfortunately, later in life many of these individuals find it extremely difficult to say, "I'm sorry," when it is totally appropriate. Bringing home a dozen long stemmed roses or baking a cherry pie will never take the place of verbally admitting wrong, when you have injured another person. If you are wrong – and we all are from time to time – a sign of maturity is that you can quickly and clearly verbalize it. Sometimes it is appropriate to ask the other party for a response to your asking forgiveness; it can help to clarify and seal the transaction for both of you.

- Repentance may sometimes include *restitution*:

  - The Old Testament teaches restitution; for example, the Israelites were told to pay full restitution plus 20 percent (Leviticus 6:5).

  - The New Testament is not as clear in prescribing restitution. The tax collector Zacchaeus volunteered restitution (Luke 19:1–10). Paul sent the runaway slave, Onesimus, back to his master (Philemon 10–20). Matthew was a tax collector and may well have over-taxed people, yet Christ just said "follow me"; nothing was said about restitution (Mark 2:14). Finally, Paul wrote, "Let him who steals steal no longer; but rather let him labor, performing with his own hands what is good" (Ephesians 4:28). The passage says nothing about restitution.

- Having said all of this, if our behavior has caused material loss to another person, we should prayfully consider making full compensation, when it is feasible.
- Resolve not to repeat the offense:
  - "He who conceals his transgressions will not prosper, but he who confesses and *forsakes* them will find compassion" (Proverbs 28:13, *italics* added).
  - "Therefore bring forth fruits in keeping with your repentance" (Luke 3:8).
  - To the woman forgiven of adultery Christ said, "Go your way. From now on sin no more" (John 8:11).
  - Paul speaks about those Gentiles to whom he preached "that they should repent and turn to God, performing deeds appropriate to repentance" (Acts 26:20).
  - Lewis Smedes writes, "Those who hurt you must return to you with a promise that they will not hurt you again; and you need to believe that they intend to keep the promise they make. . . You should not ask for a lot more; but you should ask for no less. They cannot offer you a guarantee."[9]
  - Can the offender guarantee that he or she will not repeat the injury?
    - In some situations you cannot totally guarantee that you will not repeat an offense. For example, you cannot promise you will never be late for supper again or possibly that you won't ever lose your temper. It is appropriate to promise to make a concerted effort to change such behavior and such change can and should be expected.
    - There are other situations in which you should promise never to repeat the wrong behavior again. For example: "I will never hit you again," or, "I will never have another affair." Furthermore, in these more onerous injuries, it is appropriate for the offender to be willing to be more accountable. For example, the husband who has had an affair should account for all significant periods of time when he is not with his wife. This decreases his temptation as well as his wife's wondering "where is he now?"

Penance is not appropriate. Penance is "an act of self-abasement, mortification, or devotion performed to show sorrow or repentance for sin." We do not have to go through a grieving process making ourselves unhappy for a period of time before we deserve to be happy again. I occasionally see in solid Bible-based Christians a sense that they need to go through this process, though they will never call it penance. I think of a woman whose mother told her repeatedly when she was growing up that she must reap seven times what she sowed. Unfortunately, this has become a self-fulfilling prophecy, that is, she continually feels guilty and has a hard time enjoying life because "of the life style I lived in college."

Step 5. The Offended Must Forgive

Forgiveness is dropping the indictment that I am holding onto against the other person. It is giving up my personal right to hurt back – to get even or try to get revenge (Ephesians 4:26–32).

- The person who is very deeply hurt, such as in a rape or homicide, especially if not a Christian, may find the notion of forgiveness repulsive. When I am working with people like this, I don't initially talk about forgiveness. Instead I start by allowing them to ventilate their anger. Later I will discuss with them the adverse effects that their anger is having on them and how to drop the anger that is destroying them. Ultimately, they will need God's help in pursuing this process.
- With true forgiveness the emotional charge will start to diminish.
- Forgiveness releases the offended person.
- Once all these steps are fully discussed and worked through, the offended party should seldom, if ever, mention the painful event again to the offender.
- Repentance, forgiveness, and reconciliation are ultimately an act of the will.
- Individuals who have trouble in this process often have some of their own deep earlier hurts with which they have to deal. The details of this process are beyond the scope of this book.

Step 6. Purpose to Rebuild the Relationship

- If true repentance by the offender and true forgiveness by the offended have taken place, then both should work at trying to rebuild the relationship. This may need to start out with small steps.
- As mentioned above, there may be a need for increased accountability and a willingness to work toward rebuilding trust.

Step 7. Reconciliation

To reconcile means to bring together that which belongs together, but is apart (Mattthew 5:24).

- If the previous six steps are taken, reconciliation should be the natural next step.
- If both the offended and the offender follow this process, they should be at least as close after the offense as they were before the offense occurred. In fact, in most cases the relationship will be closer.

Forgiveness Always – Reconciliation Sometimes

Some might ask should we as Christians always be reconciled with others? The answer to this is "no." It takes both parties to reconcile. The Apostle Paul writes about blessing those who persecute you, never paying back your offenders, then concludes with, "If possible, so far as it depends on you, be at peace with all men" (Romans 12:14–18). Think of the parallel in God's relationship with men and women. God has fully forgiven us, but if we don't repent we are not reconciled to God.

Do Negative Feelings Disappear with True Forgiveness?

What will happen to our feelings with true forgivenesss. Authors differ on this point. Some say negative feelings may not disappear even though one has truly forgiven. Lewis Smedes, who went through some very difficult trauma as a youngster says:

> Is there anger after forgiving? Yes, often. It can't be helped.
> Some people believe that they should not feel anger in their

hearts once they forgive. I do not agree. I think that anger and forgiving can live together in the same heart. You are not a failure at forgiving just because you are still angry that a painful wrong was done to you. . . . When you are wronged, that wrong becomes an indestructible reality of your life. When you forgive, you heal your hate for the person who created that reality. But you do not change the facts. And you do not undo all of their consequences. . . A man does not forget that his father abused him as a child. . . Can you look back on the painful moment – or painful years – without a passionate, furious, aching longing that what hurt you so much had never happened? Some people probably can. But I don't think you should expect such placid escape from terrible memories. You can be angry still, and you can have your anger without hate. Once you start on your forgiving journey, you will begin to lose the passion of malice.[10]

But other capable authors take the opposite position: that anger, resentment, and bitterness *will* disappear when true forgiveness takes place. Goldie Bristol in dealing with forgiveness of a man who murdered her daughter says, "Forgiveness means our emotional response to our offender has changed from negative to positive."[11] Some would go on to say that forgetting occurs when our negative feelings disappear.

Does Forgiveness Always Lead to Forgetting?

Periodically I hear the statement, "I can forgive but I can't forget." On the surface this sounds legitimate. After all, the offended did forgive the offender. And since we are all creatures with memories and have no way of obliterating something from our minds, the person who "can't forget" is seemingly merely making a statement of fact. Forgiving is not forgetting, but once we truly forgive we have a new freedom to forget.

David Augsburger has written:

To say, "I can forgive but I can't forget" is really saying, "I know how to overlook a wrong but not to forgive it." Now, let's be clear, forgetful forgiveness is not a case of holy amnesia

106

which erases the past. No, instead it is the experience of healing which draws the poison from the wound. You may recall the hurt, but you will not relive it! No constant reviewing, no rehashing of the old hurt, no going back to sit on the old gravestones where past grievances lie buried. True, the hornet of memory may fly again, but forgiveness has drawn its sting. . . Not that the past is changed. The past is the past. Nothing can alter the facts. What has happened has happened forever. But the meaning can be changed. That is forgiveness. Forgiveness restores the present, heals for the future, and releases us from the past.[12]

It is true that wounds leave permanent scars and some things are never exactly the same after an injustice has occurred. However, in every situation with which I have been familiar, the person *emphasizing* that he can't forget, in reality has never truly forgiven or has been unwilling to do all in his power to forget. Neither of these just happens. Forgiving and forgetting both involve the will.

In most cases with true forgiveness, the emotional pain will disappear almost immediately after forgiveness. In some instances where the injury has been monumental, it may take time. However, with time the emotional charge will progressively decrease and very likely one day when you are reminded of the injury, you will become aware that there is no pain with it.

Mutual Forgiveness

In the above discussion, for simplicity sake, I have referred to one person as the offended and the other as the offender. However, in everyday interpersonal relationships the issues of life are seldom all black or white. This is so especially in this area of bitterness and resentment where we usually find shades of gray. Each person has his own areas of right and wrong. We need not – should not – either whitewash or justify inappropriately another person when giving up resentments. If another person has a large or small part of the responsibility, that is his problem. Ours is to delineate carefully what part is our fault and responsibility – whether it is 5 percent or 95 percent – and to deal with it appropriately.

Take into account that we all have some emotional myopia, that is, we acutely see our hurts and often the other person's hurts are somewhat out of focus. If a wrong deed was done to us by someone else, we would perceive the wrong done to us as more heinous than if we did the same deed to someone else. This is why two individuals or two nations who are trying to "get even" will never have peace nor will they ever reconcile. To feel that they have gotten "even" will necessitate that they retaliate with interest; then the other party will have to do the same — retaliate with interest.

Earlier we discussed Joseph. It is easy to see the wrong that Joseph's ten brothers did to him. In their jealous rage they put Joseph in a pit, debated killing him, and finally sold him into a life of slavery. But in reality his father bore some responsibility as well in showering special attention and gifts on Joseph. Furthermore, Joseph was unwise in telling his brothers of his dreams that they would be subservient to him. Each party bore some responsibility for the subsequent actions.

A practical suggestion along this line is to take a piece of paper and divide it into quarters. List areas where the other person was right and wrong and where you have been right and wrong. Also it is sometimes helpful to include factors in the other person's present and past life which may have been a contributing factor in how he or she acted. But be careful not to linger at this step too long. In the final analysis you must accept *full* responsibility for *any* aspects for which you *may* be responsible. You must then deal with your part of the responsibility, regardless of how the other party handles his part of the responsibility. Our aim should be to have a conscience void of offense toward every man, group, organization, and God (see Acts 24:16). We must forgive and have a clear conscience toward others even if they are unwilling to do the same toward us.

Further Help in Forgiving

* Try to determine why the person acted in the way he or she did. Try to reconstruct and determine what the person's childhood was like: the injuries he might be carrying that distort and make it difficult for him to appreciate fully his hurt to you. This doesn't justify his inappropriate behavior toward you, but it can help soften your attitude toward him.

- If you don't forgive, you have placed yourself on God's throne and are passing judgment on the offending person. I remember one patient who was complaining of an injustice his wife did to him. She did not want to continue the heavy responsibility of caring for his invalid mother. He judged this as an "inhuman act. . . . I can't imagine forgiving something like this; it would be comparable to forgiving Hitler." This patient went on to say, "I have a file of offenses. . . I constantly use it as a justification of my feelings." He also said, "I am not willing to forgive." No wonder he was contemplating suicide, living a miserable life, and soon found himself divorced.

- If you could put all your bitterness and resentment in a box and give it to Christ, would you? If you wouldn't, you are holding on to it and you need to examine why you are doing so.

- A life of faith and a willingness to actively fill your mind and heart with wholesome, positive thoughts facilitates forgiveness. These and many other points that will assist in dealing with forgiveness will be covered in later chapters.

Do We Need to Forgive if the Other Party Is Not Repentant?

Sometimes the offender is unwilling to recognize the injury he or she has done to you, sometimes even in a defiant attitude. Do you still have to forgive? The ultimate answer is an emphatic "yes"!

A compelling statement by Jesus declares, "But if you do not forgive others their trespasses – their reckless and wilful sins, leaving them, letting them go and giving up resentment – neither will your Father forgive you your trespasses" (Matthew 6:15, AMP). If we don't forgive others, God won't forgive us. We *must* forgive even another's "reckless and wilful sins." This is sometimes very hard and may take some time.

Remember, too, that the perfect Son of God came voluntarily to this earth for you and me, was rejected by his own people, ridiculed, beaten, and killed on a painful cross. Yet he bore all this without resentment or bitterness. Such knowledge should help us resolve our petty grudges. *But forgiving another in such a situation does not mean that we reconcile with him or her.* Depending on the situation, it might mean no further dealings or contact with that person.

Benefits of Forgiving

Forgiveness liberates us, freeing us from all kinds of internal stress and turmoil, reducing our cumulative stress load. It allows us to use the emotional energy that is destroying us for better pursuits.

In some parts of the world hunters capture monkeys by drilling a hole in a tree that is just the size of a monkey's paw; they hollow it out so that it is a little larger inside the hole and place a peanut there. An unsuspecting monkey will come along, spot the peanut in the hole, reach out and grab the nut, but with the nut in its closed paw it is unable to remove the paw from the hole in the tree. It now has a choice – drop the nut, leaving it behind, and be free; or hold on to the nut and be shackled to the tree and captured. Most of the time the monkeys do not let go of the nut.

When we hold on to our bitterness and resentment, we are imprisoned and tortured by our own unforgivingness. When we let them go, we are freed, releasing energy, serenity, and joy that affect us and all those around us.

Conclusion of Part 3

We have now discussed some internal and external causes of stress. Clearly this is not an exhaustive list, for that would make the book voluminous. However, the ones that I have covered are amongst the more important ones that we face in the 21st century. If you have these under control you will be off to an excellent start and, as you are open, God will reveal others to you, should they need attention. Now let's turn our attention to the biological causes of illness.

Part Four

Biological Illnesses

CHAPTER 10

MEDICAL ILLNESSES CAUSE FATIGUE

INFIRMITIES THAT CAN cause fatigue are legion. Sooner or later almost every conceivable disease causes fatigue. The table of contents of a several-thousand-page medical book would be an incomplete listing. It is no wonder that the complaint of fatigue is so common. Obviously we can only deal with a smattering of the illnesses here. However, a few more common medical disorders have fatigue as a prominent early symptom. A panoramic view of these medical conditions follows. In subsequent chapters we will address Chronic Fatigue Syndrome, Viruses, Chemical Sensitivity, Fibromyalgia, sleep disorders, and emotional illnesses.

Biological Causes of Fatigue

Organic, biological, or physical are virtually synonyms indicating that there is a tangible, identifiable illness. Stress may contribute to these, but regardless of that, these illnesses have a physical component to them. Medicine can identify some specific physical or chemical abnormality.

Endocrine

Thyroid Disease. Endocrine disorders are often implicated as the cause for fatigue. Hypothyroidism (low thyroid) heads the list. Typically the individual feels lethargic, speech may be slower, and his skin will be coarse; he may experience cold intolerance and weight gain; these are but a few of the more typical symptoms. Sometimes he has constipation and depression. When I first started the practice of medicine, the laboratory tests that were used to diagnose this disorder were somewhat crude. As a result, this was an over-diagnosed disease and many individuals who were on thyroid medication didn't need it. Now laboratory tests are reliable so that an accurate diagnosis can be made and treatment is readily available.

Hyperthyroidism (overactive thyroid) may present itself in a dramatic way or be very subtle. The symptoms of excessive thyroid commonly are weight loss, irritability, nervousness, heart palpitations, an enlarged thyroid gland, insomnia, diarrhea, and sweating. Though we sometimes think of the person with an overactive thyroid as having more energy, he or she may complain of fatigue. Here again, treatment is usually quite successful.

Insulin Resistance Syndrome. Disorders in insulin metabolism and consequently blood sugar are becoming increasingly common and are a public health concern. Insulin Resistance Syndrome is also known as Syndrome X or Metabolic Syndrome. It consists of elevated levels of insulin in the system, glucose intolerance, elevated lipids (fats), high blood pressure, abdominal obesity, and an increased tendency to coagulation of one's blood. Often individuals with this disorder have significant amounts of toxic anger and excessive tiredness. Stress, genetics, and a sedentary lifestyle are significant factors in the development of this disease. This condition readily leads to frank diabetes, increased cardiovascular disease, and increased mortality.

No single test makes the diagnosis of this malady. However, waist circumference, weight, blood pressure, cholesterol and glucose measurment can assist in the diagnosis. Determining a blood sugar over 140 mg two hours after drinking 75 grams of sugar is one of the better means to determine the disease. Men with a waistline over 40 inches or women with a waistline over 35 inches are at an increased risk for this disorder. Recently, experts in endocrinology called a special meeting to address their concerns about this specific illness. Alarming them was the fact that the prevalence of Insulin Resistance Syndrome had increased by 61 percent in the last decade and children are starting to develop the disorder. It was estimated that up to one-third of Americans suffer from this disorder. The physician who coined the term *Syndrome X* believes that individuals with this affliction are "sitting on a powder keg." Furthermore, it is his opinion that most physicians are not familiar with this disease. Treatment addresses the specific symptoms of the disorder in addition to stress and weight reduction; exercise is also part of the treatment.[1]

Reactive Hypoglycemia is a related disorder that can cause troubling symptoms. When a susceptible person eats a large amount of carbohydrates (that is, starches or sugars), at a fairly predictable time after eating these foods – usually two to five hours – he will experience nervousness, pounding of the heart, sweating, irritability, and hunger. Also, he may experience fatigue. Usually these symptoms will last for only five to fifteen minutes, then the body will compensate through reserve mechanisms by overcoming the drop in blood sugar which has resulted. These symptoms occur when carbohydrates are eaten and the amount of insulin secreted by the pancreas overshoots, so to speak, the amount of sugar in the system, and hypoglycemia, that is low blood sugar, is the result. Thirty years ago this was a popular and over-diagnosed condition.

Nonetheless this disorder, on occasion, does occur. A diagnosis is suggested if an individual develops the symptoms at a fairly predictable time – two to five hours after eating a large amount of carbohydrates without any protein. Determining the blood sugar level when people believe they are experiencing the symptoms described can make a diagnosis. The treatment is rather simple. A diet high in protein content and low in carbohydrates is usually all that is necessary. Most of these people have no further problem with hypoglycemia as long as they follow their diet. However, we do find the rare person who will later develop diabetes, so blood sugars should be checked periodically.

Adrenal Disease. The adrenal glands have a very important function in stress. However, when they cease to function, Adrenal Insufficiency, which is also called Addison's Disease develops. This is a fairly uncommon illness that is characterized by fatigue, weakness, lightheadedness on standing, darkening of the skin, and rarely can be fatal. Again treatment is readily available provided the disorder is recognized.[2]

Infections

Virtually any infection can cause fatigue. If the infection is acute with fever and other symptoms, it is quite clear what the problem is. In low grade chronic infections like Tuberculosis, diagnostic tests like a chest X-ray will clarify the diagnosis. One specific infectious disease that warrants further discussion is Lyme Disease.

Lyme Disease is named after the town of Old Lyme in Connecticut and is caused by an infecting agent called a *spirochete* that is transmitted by a tick. It occurs primarily in some parts of the United States and less commonly in Europe, Asia, and Australia. The diagnosis is made by a history of a tick bite; in fact, the tick typically has to feed for at least 24 hours to transmit the disease. At the site of the bite there is a flat or slightly raised red lesion on the skin and as it expands, it clears in the center and the infected person develops flu-like symptoms. Later the patient often develops fatigue, a stiff neck or headache, alterations in heart rhythm, arthritis, and aching limbs. Blood studies can help confirm the diagnosis. However, over-diagnosis is also a problem. Antibiotics are appropriate in accurately diagnosed individuals and, when given early, can cure the infection and prevent the later manifestations of the disease.[3]

Other Illnesses

Anemia of any origin causes fatigue. Menstruating women are more prone to anemia. A laboratory test can easily check for this. Some reports suggest that some women who do not have anemia but who have decreased iron storage in the bone marrow actually feel better taking small amounts of iron. If this is necessary, the inexpensive ferrous sulphate form of iron is almost always adequate.

Nutritional Causes. Nutritional health in the western world leaves something to be desired. Our diets tend to be filled with fats, carbohydrates, sugars, excessive calories, and stimulants. These take their toll on our bodies. For example, drinking the equivalent of the caffeine in four cups of coffee produces an increase in stress hormone, and individuals feel more stressed.[4]

Nutritional inadequacies are often blamed for fatigue, especially by individuals and companies profiting from this philosophy, sometimes by doctors or patients who are looking for something tangible to blame for their fatigue. Dietary recommendations are common at the checkout counter of the typical grocery store, the news-stand or from books on fatigue and stress.

There are many proponents of various herbs and nutritional supplements. The place for these has yet to be determined. But it is exceedingly difficult to study the validity of any of these dietary recommendations on a scientific basis; therefore, most of the hype is based on testimonials.

Seldom is malnutrition or vitamin deficiency a problem in the industrialized world if we have any regular intake of the basic food classes, which include cereals, fruits, vegetables, meat, fish, poultry, and dairy products. Only if there is some coexistent disease will a person be malnourished even though he eats from these various classes regularly.

I generally encourage a multivitamin. Though additional vitamins seldom hurt, they usually provide an excess of the basic needs of the body and are excreted in the waste products. It is possible, however, to take too much of some vitamins. Excessive amounts of vitamins A and D can cause, in part, irritability, headaches, loss of hair, decalcification of bone, loss of appetite, an elevated calcium, and other toxic effects on the system.

Probably the greatest nutritional problem in our modem society in the west is too much food. *Obesity* has reached epidemic proportions. It takes a tremendous toll in morbidity and mortality – it decreases the quality and length of life for untold millions. Many diseases are either caused by or adversely affected by it. A partial list includes heart disease, hypertension, diabetes, hyperlipedemia (elevated fats), and arthritis, to say nothing of the tremendous emotional disability affecting every thought and act of the overweight person.

Obesity also causes fatigue. Part of this fatigue is "postprandial fatigue," which to some extent occurs in all of us after we eat. This is due to blood going to the gastrointestinal tract for the chemical processes of digestion and metabolism. The Spanish and Latin Americans take advantage of this during the heat of the day and have a siesta. College students sometimes yield to the temptation to nap during their one o'clock classes, especially if the room is dark and a movie is being shown or the lecturer is boring. The point is that we all experience some of this, but the obese person experiences more. Also he finds that it is a much bigger job to move around numerous pounds of extra adipose (fat) to say nothing of the emotional drain. At any rate, obesity is a definite cause of stress and fatigue.

This is not even a primer on the diseases that can cause fatigue. However, the illnesses that we don't discuss, though many, account for a very small percentage of the total individuals that complain of fatigue. Put another way, in this book we will discuss the causes of fatigue in the vast majority of individuals complaining of this malady.

Constitutional Causes of Fatigue

Normal variations occur in almost every aspect of life. We have blondes and brunettes in our society, tall people and short people, varying IQs, and different physiques. This difference is certainly true relative to a person's innate energy level. So we need to be honest and realistic about ourselves. A person with an IQ of 80 will never be able to keep up educationally with someone whose IQ is 140. Also, some people will never be able to keep up the energetic pace of others about them. Fortunately, God knows better than we do about our energy capacity and never requires of us more than he knows that we are capable of achieving. We, then, must accept ourselves as God has made us — with varying capabilities. We must be careful about comparing ourselves with others (see 2 Corinthians 10:12).

The wise person with less innate energy will know it and accept it. He (or she) will know that God accepts it. He will pace himself to maximize the energy that he does have.

But please don't stop reading here. Many who might quickly assume there is a constitutional cause for their fatigue may find the real cause to be discussed in the next few chapters.

CHAPTER 11

"OH, FOR A REFRESHING NIGHT'S SLEEP"

I WAS UTTERLY exhausted and would go to bed at 11 o'clock only to lie wide awake, unable to sleep. After tossing and turning for an hour I might sleep for an hour, awaking at one in the morning still feeling drained; but at the same time my mind was aroused – I knew I wasn't going to be able to sleep for a long time. I would get up for an hour and read as best I could, considering that my concentration was almost nonexistent. I'd go back to bed at 2 o'clock, and repeat the whole process again. Finally at 5:30AM I was awake again, feeling stimulated as though I had drunk ten cups of coffee, yet still exhausted. I knew I wasn't going to sleep any more; so I'd get up feeling worse than when I went to bed the night before. This was a typical night during the months I was struggling with depression. Oh, how I wished for a decent night's sleep, but it eluded me. This is a somewhat extreme, yet true story of how sleep can be adversely affected by another illness.

An article appearing in the *British Medical Journal* on sleeplessness says:

> The subject of sleeplessness is once more under public discussion. The hurry and excitement of modern life is quite correctly held to be responsible for much of the insomnia of which we hear; and most of the articles and letters are full of good advice to live more quietly and of platitudes concerning the harmfulness of rush and worry. The pity of it is that so many people are unable to follow this good advice and are obliged to lead a life of anxiety.[1]

This evaluation of society is certainly as appropriate for us today as it was when it was written in 1894! We not only learn slowly, but I suspect the problem of insomnia and hurry and worry is much worse today then it was over a century ago.

Good sleep can be so refreshing, whereas bad sleep will not only increase your stress and weariness the next day, but actually can kill. Untold millions sacrifice their quality of life due to a sleep disorder. They have trouble concentrating, maintaining vigilance, have mood changes, irritability, and general impairment in overall functioning. In addition, people, while driving, fall asleep at the wheel due to disturbed nighttime sleep. An article noted that missing one night of sleep affects one's performance as much as an alcohol blood level above the legal limit. Sleep apnea can cause depression, fatal cardiac arrhythmias, strokes, and death. It may also contribute to obesity and diabetes. [2]

This is not an isolated problem. It is reported that up to half of the population have some sort of sleep difficulty. Either they have trouble falling asleep, staying asleep, waking too early, or not feeling refreshed after sleep. Ten to 37 percent of adults have a chronic sleep problem which interferes with their activities several days a week. Excessive daytime sleepiness is a concern for 4 to 12 percent of adults. The problem increases with age and is more common in women. Children are not immune to this problem. Those 3-14 years of age have been found to have over a 16 percent incidence of insomnia and 4 percent have excessive daytime sleepiness. One half of the individuals who have chronic insomnia have never discussed it with their physician. [3]

Insomnia is experiencing either inadequate or poor quality sleep. It is considered "acute insomnia" if the insomnia lasts less than a couple of weeks. "Chronic insomnia" is when one has trouble sleeping a least three nights a week for a month or more.

In 1995 it was estimated that insomnia cost France two billion and the United States 13.9 billion dollars as a direct result of visits to physicians and medications, both prescription and over-the-counter sleep remedies. [4]

During all my medical school training and seven years of postgraduate training I don't remember any instruction about sleep or lack of it. I do remember a situation where a patient complained that she was only getting two to three hours of sleep a night and the staff physician responded with "lack of sleep won't kill you." The only problem with that is that lack of sleep does, in fact, kill. A recent article said, "We need to elevate sleep in the public consciousness to an equal footing with nutrition and exercise."[5] Even now medical schools generally devote less then four hours of formal training to sleep medicine.

Earlier in the book we discussed both external stressors in our environment and internal stresses within ourselves that drain us. In this section of the book we are focusing on biological causes of stress and fatigue. Insomnia is caused by numerous factors in each of these categories. We know of over 80 recognized conditions that can adversely affect sleep. Generally sleep disturbances are categorized as either primary or secondary. Primary sleep disorders are illnesses that affect one's sleep directly and specifically. Secondary sleep disturbances are the numerous situations that secondarily affect one's sleep.

Secondary Sleep Disturbances

The things that can adversely affect one's sleep are innumerable. Some examples of things that will secondarily affect sleep include the following:[6]

- *Stress and Hassles* of all types adversely alter sleep.

- *Environmental Disturbances* such as noise, light, and inappropriate temperatures all significantly affect our sleep. In addition, many people work evening or night shifts and this greatly upsets sleep patterns. This is especially true if one works varying shifts. Shift work or other disruptions of one's circadian rhythm (or biological clock) create havoc with one's sleep and general feeling of wellbeing.

- *Foods and Chemicals.* Caffeine, especially later in the day or evening interferes with sleep. Alcohol can seem to help a person sleep initially, but it, in fact, adversely affects the quality of sleep and is strongly discouraged as a treatment for a sleep disorder. Medications can interfere with sleep. Some examples are steroids, decongestants, beta blockers, and stimulating antidepressants.

- **Chronic Illnesses.** Many physical problems disturb our sleep. Pain from any cause interrupts sleep. Esophageal reflux, asthma, pregnancy, menopause, and the list can become endless.[7]

- **Emotional Problems.** This is an important and common cause of sleep disturbance. Most emotional or mental problems adversely affect sleep. This is especially true of anxiety, panic disorder, post-traumatic stress disorder, obsessive-compulsive disorder, depression, seasonal affective disorder, bipolar depression, eating disorders, and alcoholism. Sometimes depression is caused by or exacerbated by sleep problems, especially sleep apnea.

Primary Sleep Disorders

Certain conditions primarily affect sleep. Some of the more important ones are discussed below:

- **Circadian Rhythm Sleep Disorders.** This is where the body's awake-sleep cycle is disturbed. The most classical example is jet lag. You fly from San Francisco to London and find that your body wants to sleep when the clock and sun tell you it is time to be awake. Typically it takes four to seven days of staying up during normally awake hours to "force" your circadian rhythm to adjust to the new time zone.

- **Delayed Sleep Phase Syndrome** is where one's biological clock is slower than actual time. I fall into that category and would be happy with a 25-hour day; however, with appropriate discipline I can nudge my biological clock to coincide with the clock on the wall. Those with an "advanced sleep phase syndrome" have the opposite problem and must struggle to stay awake until the clock on the wall tells them it is bedtime. Many older people who don't have a schedule to which they need to adhere, start going to bed earlier and earlier and mess up their circadian rhythm. I have seen older individuals move their circadian rhythm so that they are up most of the night and sleep on and off virtually all day. Bright light has been used successfully to treat this disturbance.

- **Periodic Limb Movement Disorder.** Some people have repeated rhythmic twitching of their legs and occasionally their arms. These movements which may be twitches or sometimes forceful jerking movements of the extremities occur about every 20–90 seconds and can disturb the quality of sleep even though the person may not be aware he or she has these muscle contractions. The bed partner is the best reporter of this disorder. This is more likely to occur as we get older.

- **Restless Legs Syndrome.** Six percent of the adult population has what is called the Restless Legs Syndrome. Older individuals suffer more from this disorder with some reports indicating that up to 28 percent of adults over 65 are afflicted with this ailment. Such individuals experience uncomfortable sensations in their legs with inactivity. The uncomfortable feelings can be distressing and the sufferer is relieved of these sensations by moving the limbs. This becomes worse as the day progresses, especially at bedtime. Such individuals not only suffer from insomnia, but daytime fatigue as well. A variety of medications have been used to treat this disorder with moderate success. [8]

- **Obstructive Sleep Apnea.** This is an important and potentially deadly disorder that just recently has been given the attention it is due. This illness typically occurs in middle age and is characterized by loud snoring, gasping, or struggling for air. Sometimes the person stops breathing altogether for a brief period of time. The bed partner is the best observer of this disorder. Such a sufferer typically has a drop in the oxygen saturation of his or her blood. This disease has many serious consequences – hypertension, fatigue, daytime sleepiness, impotence, depression, or other emotional problems. In addition, it can lead to cardiac arrhythmias, heart attacks, strokes, and cause death. Individuals with sleep apnea are three times more likely to be involved in a car accident as compared to those without it. [9]

This disorder is more common in middle-aged men. Reports on the frequency of this illness vary tremendously. One recent study noted that apneic events occur in 24 percent of middle-aged men referred for sleep studies. The author states that this disorder is undiagnosed in 80 percent of affected men.[10]

Polysomnography is the definitive means of diagnosing this disorder. Polysomnography is usually performed in the hospital and the procedure is to hook up the individual to a machine with numerous wires that will determine throughout the night the oxygen level, EKG of the heart rhythm, EEG of brain waves, and respirations.

Treatment consists of weight loss and Continuous Positive Airway Pressure (CPAP). In CPAP therapy the individual wears a nasal mask producing positive pressure during the night that keeps the passages of the nose and throat open. Surgery sometimes is recommended to open up the passage allowing air to flow more freely. Occasionally, in less severe cases, sewing a tennis ball in the back of one's pajamas helps keep the individual sleeping on his side, which may decrease the snoring and sleep apnea.

- *Narcolepsy.* This name comes from the Greek words for "somnolence" and "to seize." It is a fairly rare disorder characterized by disrupted sleep, excessive daytime drowsiness, and brief episodes of muscle weakness. Medications can be helpful for this disease.

- *Primary Insomnia.* When all other factors causing sleep disturbance are excluded, it is labeled primary insomnia. In reality, very few individuals fit into this diagnostic category.

Enhancers of Sleep

If you have a primary sleep disorder, it is crucial that you get medical treatment for the disorder. On the other hand, if your disturbed sleep is secondary to some other specific problem or illness, then that specific disorder needs to be addressed and treated. Deal with any specific external and internal stressors. In Chapter 1 we discussed our stress response and that stressors raised the stress hormone cortisol. It is not surprising that insomniacs have a significantly higher stress hormone level not only when they try to sleep at night, but they have an elevated hormone level all day long. Thus anything that helps one deal with these stresses more constructively will help reduce the hormone level and facilitate more restful sleep.

Following are some additional suggestions that will often help a person have restorative sleep. We sometimes call this "sleep hygiene."

- *Slow down several hours before bedtime.* Avoid exercise or anything stimulating at least two to four hours before your bedtime. Stimulants like caffeine should be avoided at least six to eight hours before bedtime and large amounts any time in the 24 hours may disturb sleep. Large meals late in the evening can disrupt sleep. Nicotine and alcohol are also known to interfere with sleep.

- *Restrict fluid intake.* Some physicians advise avoiding fluid intake several hours before bedtime to reduce the need to get up and urinate at night.

- *Exercise.* Good physical exercise, getting your heart rate up, preferably daily for 30 minutes can enhance your sense of well-being and improve sleep. It is best not to exercise within a few hours of bedtime.

- *Drink warm milk.* Some people find a glass of warm milk or other light snack before bed helpful. Others find a warm tub bath before bed a benefit.

- *Keep regular hours.* Go to bed and get up at the same time every day. Most important is getting up at the same time each day. I can have trouble sleeping, so I discipline myself to get up at 6 o'clock every morning. This includes weekends and vacations. I probably manage this 29 out of 30 days a month. I often just get going at 9 o'clock in the evening and hate to stop. Left to myself I would stay up. If I don't get to bed by 11 o'clock in the evening at the latest, I pay the price the next day. This is especially true if I stay up a couple of nights in a row.

- *Sleep in a room conducive for sleep.* As far as possible, eliminate extraneous noises and light. Sometimes earplugs may be necessary. Most people sleep best in a cool room about 65 degrees Fahrenheit.

- *Use the bedroom only for sleep.* Most people find that they sleep better if the bedroom is reserved for sleep and sex. Many recommend that activities such as watching TV and reading should be done in other rooms.

- *Suggestions when you can't sleep.* If you are in bed and know you aren't going to go to sleep or back to sleep in 15 to 20 minutes, get up and go into another room. Keep the light toward the low side and listen to some soothing music or read something relaxing. Quoting Bible verses or reading the Psalms are excellent at a time like this. Some people find praying and meditating on the wonders of God and his creation helpful in quieting their hearts before God, enabling them to exclude the external pressures of the day. A wonderful verse on this is Psalm 63:6 "If I'm sleepless at midnight, I spend the hours in grateful reflection" (MSG).

  Others focus their minds on something boring, like thinking about the side of a red barn, or counting sheep to quiet their minds. Avoid TV or anything stimulating – either in a positive or negative way. This includes thinking about stimulating past, present or future events. Usually in 20 to 30 minutes you will feel sleepy and can go back to bed and sleep.

- *Write pressing thoughts down on paper, then forget them.* If you are in bed and think of something that you want to be sure you remember the next day, write it down, forget it, then go back to sleep.

- *Forget the clock.* It's often best not to have a clock in plain view from the bed as some insomniacs tend to focus too much on it.

- *Remember a satisfying day's work.* A satisfying day's work, especially if it includes some physical activity, helps you sleep better at night.

- *Be very careful of naps.* Some people, especially older individuals, find that if they take a nap in the late afternoon, say for a half hour, they can stay up a full extra hour in the evening. If that is the case for you, naps may be appropriate. However, for many with problematic sleep, naps can adversely affect sleep even though they may feel so good at the time. For anyone with difficulty sleeping, napping in the daytime is strongly discouraged. By the way, this includes "resting your eyes" in a chair.

- *Don't spend too much time in bed.* If your sleep is fragmented, you don't feel rested in the daytime; and if you are in bed more than about eight hours out of 24, you may be spending too much time in bed. Contrary to how it might feel, you may need to discipline yourself to spend less time in bed to improve the quality of your sleep. You may feel worse the first week in which you limit your time in bed (just like with jet lag), but for many this discipline can improve sleep quality over the long haul.

How Much Should You Sleep?

For a long time medical science has debated about how much a person should sleep. No doubt there are significant individual variations in the amount of sleep that a person needs. To some degree this may be altered. I find that though I enjoy eight hours of sleep a night, I usually can function quite well if I get seven hours. However, if I consistently get much below that, the warning signs develop before many days pass.

Some books suggest that the more sleep the better. This is now being seriously questioned. In an impressive study of 1.1 million men and women 30 to 102 years of age, those who slept about seven hours had the lowest mortality. If a person slept less then 6.5 hours a night or more than 7.4 hours, the study found that these individuals had an increase in mortality rate. In an earlier study it was found that long sleepers reported less energy.[11]

In all of this remember that the Lord wants to give us refreshing sleep. The psalmist says, "It is senseless for you to work so hard from early morning until late at night, fearing you will starve to death; for God wants his loved ones to get their proper rest" (Psalm 127:2, TLB).

CHAPTER 12

CHRONIC FATIGUE SYNDROME, FIBROMYALGIA, IMMUNE DYSFUNCTION, VIRUSES AND CHEMICALS

IN THE LATE 1800s George Beard's *Practical Treatise on Nervous Exhaustion* describes Neurasthenia, as "the Central Africa of medicine, an unexplored territory into which few men enter, and those few have been compelled to bring reports that have been neither credited or comprehended."[1] This description is as apropos today as it was then. We don't know much about these diseases and what we do know remains controversial. Neurologist George Beard used the term *neurasthenia* to describe individuals who suffered from severe fatigue; the word means "loss of nerve strength." It was believed to be due to "nervous exhaustion." It was probably first described in the 1700s.

Historically there have been outbreaks of significant fatigue reported in clusters in many different locations and countries. In 1934 an outbreak was reported in the Los Angeles area; in 1948 in Akureyri, Iceland; in 1955 at the Royal Free Hospital of London, and in 1985 in Incline Village, Nevada, to name a few of many such outbreaks. Such clusters of outbreaks suggested a common infectious or environmental cause.

Over the years various names have been given to chronic fatigue. A sampling includes: Effort Syndrome, Chemical Sensitivity Syndrome, Chronic Mononucleosis-like Syndrome, Postviral Syndrome, and Epstein-Barr-Virus Syndrome. Their names suggest the various causes implicated.

The name currently used in the medical literature is Chronic Fatigue Syndrome (CFS), although it is also called Myalgic Encephalomyelitis(ME) and Chronic Fatigue Immune Dysfunction Syndrome (CFIDS). Ongoing discussions continue about what this illness should be called.

To qualify for the diagnosis of CFS, significant unexplained fatigue must have lasted for at least six months. Furthermore, no other medical or psychological illness can be present to explain the fatigue. In addition, at least four of the following eight symptoms must also be present:

- Difficulty remembering new things
- A sore throat
- Tender lymph nodes in the neck or under the arms
- Muscle pain
- Pain in several joints without associated swelling or redness
- Headaches of a new type, pattern, or severity
- Not feeling refreshed after a night's sleep
- Exercise producing excessive fatigue lasting more than 24 hours

Additional symptoms that often are seen in this disorder include mild fever or chills, generalized muscle weakness, enlarged lymph nodes in the neck or under the arms, and gastrointestinal symptoms. Typically, this illness develops abruptly.

Studies vary greatly as to the prevalence of Chronic Fatigue Syndrome. As we discussed in Chapter 2 the incidence of fatigue due to all causes is very high. However, using *strict criteria* the incidence of CFS has been reported as low as 1 percent and as high as 9 percent of the general population. Chronic Fatigue Syndrome accounts for 3 percent of the visits to a primary care physician. Women are twice as likely to have this disorder than men. Its peak incidence is between 25 and 45 years of age. About 2 percent of children and adolescents have CFS.[2]

Fibromyalgia (FM)

Fibromyalgia has been described in the literature since the early 1800s and given various names, such as, fibrositis, fibromyositis, myofibrositis, and myofascial pain syndrome. In 1976 it was given the name "fibromyalgia" and in 1990 diagnostic criteria were established. Fibromyalgia is a commonly encountered disorder that has many similarities with Chronic Fatigue Syndrome, and the two disorders overlap with musculoskeletal pain being most pronounced in FM, while fatigue dominates CFS.[3]

To make a diagnosis of Fibromyalgia the patient must have a three-month history of pain involving muscles and some of the deeper structures with widespread pain to moderate pressure. Specifically, a physician looks for at least 11 areas of tenderness (trigger points) out of 18 possible tender point sites. Often chronic fatigue, a sleep disturbance, depression, headaches, numbness, irritable bowel, cold sensitivity, tingling of the extremities, intolerance to exercise are present, but these symptoms are not necessary for the diagnosis. About one-third of the patients have a history of trauma prior to the onset of the illness, and another one-third seem to develop the disorder after a viral infection.[4]

Women are eight times more likely to have this disorder than men and it becomes more prevalent with age. On the average it occurs in about 2 percent of the population. In women it affects 3.5 percent but that figure jumps up to 7.5 percent by age 80. It has been reported that 6-15 percent of individuals seeking medical attention have FM and 20 percent of patients seeing a Rheumatologist have FM. Ten percent of these patients are disabled by their illness. Up to 70 percent of patients with either CFS or FM actually meet the diagnostic criteria for both disorders.[5]

Another illness that seems to be closely related to CFS and FM is called Multiple Chemical Sensitivities (MCS). No agreement exists on diagnostic criteria for this disorder, but generally the sufferer complains of irritation of the skin or mucous membranes, fatigue, aches and pains, fevers, trouble with memory, and mood changes, many of which are symptoms similar to CFS. The patient experiences these after exposure to small amounts of pollutants, such as, cigarette smoke, solvent fumes, or perfumes.[6]

The Cause of These Illnesses

At this point in time the cause of these illnesses is still unknown. Many theories exist as to the cause of CFS. Infectious and immune disorders have been postulated. Frequently CFS seems to occur immediately after a viral infection. The Epstein-Barr-Virus, enteroviruses, retroviruses, and even the herpes virus have been suggested, but the proof of a persisting infectious agent perpetuating the disease is lacking, and some theories have been disproved. These illnesses may be a heterogenous manifestation of the same disorder. On the other hand, it is possible that there are a number of causes producing one or more of these diseases. One hundred percent of patients with CFS have fatigue, while 93 percent of FM patients and 90 percent of MCS patients have significant fatigue.[7]

One thing is clear: the evidence of individuals who were once the picture of health and then become virtually incapacitated by these illnesses is impressive. These individuals *suffer real physical symptoms*. Despite this, these illnesses have been punctuated with controversies with some critics saying they were manifestations of a psychological illness. It is true that up to two-thirds of individuals have coexistent significant depression. But there is no proof that the illnesses are caused by psychological factors. In addition, the person attributing this entirely to psychological causes needs to remember that throughout history there have been illnesses that the medical profession hasn't been able to explain; so the illness has either been dismissed or passed off as all psychological – that is, until the real pathogen was discovered. Examples of this are Syphilis and Lyme Disease.[8]

It is now quite clear that there are several definite biological abnormalities in the majority of patients with the disorders we are discussing. At the onset there is typically an infection associated with external stresses and psychological distress. Either at the onset, or as a result of the symptoms, there is a disturbance in the neuroendocrine system involving the hypothalamic-pituitary-adrenal (glands) axis with a decrease in hormone production and a dysfunction of the immune response. Preliminary evidence is emerging that suggests a familial or genetic predisposition to CFS.

Dr. Komaroff of the Department of Medicine at Harvard concludes, "In summary, there is now considerable evidence of an underlying biological process in most patients who meet the [diagnosis] . . . of chronic fatigue syndrome." To those that would view Chronic Fatigue Syndrome as being psychological with no biological basis this author adds, "It is time to put that hypothesis to rest and to pursue biological clues."[9]

Response of Professionals and Families

Since the etiology of these illnesses is uncertain and treatment leaves something to be desired, it puts everyone in a quandary. Frequently physicians and family members fall into one of two extremes. One extreme tends to have little patience with the sufferer, writing the whole thing off as psychological or by implying that the patient is making too much of the illness.

So the individual must turn to the few professionals who usually specialize in these illnesses and who sympathize with these patients. Many of these physicians are excellent. However, some professionals perform numerous tests of dubious value and recommend treatments that are not much better and, on occasion, may reinforce the sick role.

All of these things put the patients in a horrible bind and they understandably become defensive. They often will form lay support groups typically emphasizing the physical basis of their illness; in addition they often develop feelings of anger toward the established medical community. These patients are extremely appreciative of anyone who does not judge them and understands their pain.

An understanding physician is important, one who will consider and treat all aspects of the disease. The exceedingly difficult position, whether physician, family member, or for that matter the patient, is to avoid either of these extremes. Patients with CFS, FM, and MCS have a legitimate and often debilitating illness. They need understanding and acceptance. Likewise, they need gentle encouragement to do all that they are able to do.

Diagnostic Evaluation

Despite the strong suggestion of a biological basis, to date we have no specific laboratory tests that are characteristic of these disorders or that help in their diagnoses. Thus diagnosis is based on symptoms and some physical findings. Therefore, most authorities urge a limited medical evaluation.[10]

Why a limited evaluation? A detailed history, general physical exam, and basic laboratory tests are essential. The major reason for the laboratory tests is to be sure there is not another treatable illness masquerading as CFS, FM, or MCS. But beyond this, further testing is usually of little value and carries some risks. For example, viral tests are often performed. However, most of the general population have positive findings for these tests – so they don't mean much even when they are positive. Likewise, if they are negative and one otherwise meets the diagnostic criteria for CFS or FM the negative test doesn't change the diagnoses, or for that matter the treatment. In Chapter 16 I will make a case for, at times, pressing the medical community to perform appropriate testing. But the opposite is also true. Recently I had a physician wanting to perform a procedure on me that involved a minor risk. I asked him, "What will we learn that we don't already know and how will its findings alter treatment?" He said, "Let's skip the test." The biggest risk with CFS, FM, and MCS is that unnecessary testing keeps the patient focused on the disease instead of what he or she can personally do to get better.

Treatment

Not being able to pinpoint the exact cause and specific treatment to remedy these diseases, we are forced to do the next best thing – empirically seeing what helps treat the symptoms with well designed scientific protocols, then recommending what works. In fact, all the specifics listed in this book have their place – addressing each symptom and doing all we can to alleviate it, eliminating what might drain the patient's energy, applying good health habits, and utilizing the "energizers."

Most symptoms in these disorders are physical, thus it is understandable that the perception by the sufferers is that they have a physical condition and are disinclined to accept that psychological factors may have a contributing role. But the sufferer needs to understand and accept that there are both physical and emotional aspects to these diseases. Every chronic illness will invariably have a secondary psychological component. If you have a degenerated vertebra and chronic back pain or MS, though your initial illness is 100 percent physical, before long you *will have* an emotional response to that illness. That secondary emotional response may be minimal, moderate, or severe, *but it will be there.*

Having an emotional reaction to any chronic distressing problem does not mean the disease is caused by an emotional problem. Acceptance of this fact and an honest and open evaluation of the multiple influences of these diseases is the first step to a comprehensive approach that will lead to improving the patient's situation. Your openness to these matters is crucial for treatment to be effective.

A co-operative effort between patient and physician is important for optimal treatment. The sufferer and his or her physician should evaluate each symptom and determine the best approach in dealing with that symptom.

The following modalities **have been** shown to be helpful for *some* individuals:[11]

- Cognitive behavioral therapy.
- Graded exercise.
- Stress management.
- Judicious use of medications have yielded a 30–50 percent improvement when directed toward the specific symptoms.
- Antidepressant medications, including the tricyclic (such as nortriptyline, amitriptyline, and others) and selective serotonin re-uptake inhibitors, such as, fluoxetine (Prozac), paroxetine (Paxil), sertraline (Zoloft), and possibly some of the newer antidepressants. These can be helpful whether the individual has depression or not. Often one can use lower doses if depression is not present.
- The muscle relaxant cyclobenzaprine HCL (Flexeril).
- Antihistamines may be helpful for allergic rhinitis and sinusitis.
- Analgesics sometimes are helpful for pain.
- Sometimes antianxiety and/or sleep medications.

Generally, the medical profession agrees that the following modalities have **not** been effective:[12]

- The antiviral medication acyclovir (Zovirax) and immunoglobulin.
- Corticosteroids (these may result in limited improvement, but the side effects are substantial, which make steroids generally inappropriate for use in these disorders).
- Intramuscular liver extract.
- Food elimination diets, various herbs, and dietary supplements.

Cognitive Behavioral Therapy

The medical profession has found Cognitive Behavioral Therapy (CBT) to be helpful. This is therapy that focuses on (1) our thought processes (how we view things) and also on (2) our actual behavior including graded exercises. In fact, 69 to 73 percent of patients who completed CBT therapy, reported a satisfactory outcome; whereas only 6 to 27 percent reported a satisfactory outcome by receiving only standard medical treatment. Furthermore, individuals who were resistive to these interventions did poorly.[13]

CBT Patients' Shift in Thinking

Their approach about the illness from:	To the following healthy ways to think and change behavior to:
catastrophic thinking, reducing excessive perfectionism, and self - criticism	realistic to optimistic viewpoint
focusing on bodily symptoms	a positive perspective about life
thinking about it as a simple disease	consider any possible contributing role of psychological and social factors
dependence on physicians prescribing treatments or medications	take more active control of one's life; improvement of coping strategies; taking an active approach to interpersonal and occupational difficulties
a general negative outlook	a positive attitude towards rehabilitation
avoiding activity and exercise	gradually increasing the level of physical activity and exercise

Figure 7

Furthermore, it is important to understand that inactivity for any reason causes both physical and psychological effects of physical deconditioning, including alterations in the circadian rhythm, and even changes in the neuroendocrine system involving the hypothalamic-pituitary-adrenal system. Excessive inactivity only aggravates this problem. Remember the robust astronaut who goes into space, but after a period of time must be carried off the shuttle on a stretcher due to the effects of deconditioning. He must gradually increase his physical activities in an environment that includes the effects of gravity to regain his strength and stamina. As we discussed in Chapter 4, just four to six weeks of inactivity can cause the loss of 40 percent of muscle strength and the inactivity alone causes increased fatigue of the muscles if one tries to use them.

A recent review article combining 44 different studies involving 2,801 patients evaluating all the various modalities of treatment came to the conclusion that graded exercise therapy and cognitive behavioral therapy are currently the most effective treatments to date.[14]

When patients were educated to the role of deconditioning and they undertook a program of gradually increasing their activities and exercise, they not only improved significantly, but their perception of the illness changed as well.[15]

Those who undertook CBT reported the following change in perception . . .

Results from CBT Treatment Shifts

Perception:	Before Treatment:	After Treatment:
Believed their condition was caused by a persistent virus:	81%	23%
Believed their condition was related to physical deconditioning:	15%	81%
Avoided physical activity and exercise:	82%	6%

Figure 8

Furthermore, the understanding of deconditioning and taking part in graded exercise convinced 94 percent of the patients to continue the graded exercise.

Though evidence looks fairly strong for the above recommendations, in all fairness it should be stated that some workers in this field believe that the graded exercise program is an overly simplified recommendation. They propose that more research is needed before CBT is accepted as the most helpful approach to the majority of patients with CFS.[16]

Since these illnesses can be waxing and waning in their manifestation, and some have more limitations than others, activities and exercise must be individualized. I like the analogy of catching a fish. If you pull too hard, you break the line and lose the fish. If you don't assert some pressure, you will never reel in the fish. The fisherman knows when to give slack and when to apply gentle pressure to achieve his goal of bringing in the fish. The same is true in applying the above principles of therapy. Some gentle pressure needs to be applied to move to healing, but every person is different. Some patients may have to slack off for a while. But the goal of moving toward normal activities should be kept in mind and, as they are able, they should move forward.

In a disease process like this one every aspect is often challenged and prognosis is no exception; nevertheless, it is encouraging to note that patients "should be reassured that full recovery is eventually possible in most cases."[17]

CHAPTER 13

MENTAL ILLNESS AND ITS CAUSES

W HEN I FIRST started practicing Internal Medicine, a general practitioner referred a young woman to me who was complaining of fatigue and weakness to the point that she could hardly speak or keep her eyes open. The family brought her to my office in a wheelchair because she could not walk. I remember vividly several of us attempting to help her up on the examining table – an experience that seemed like trying to move 125 pounds of jelly without a container. She slept almost continually and actually *felt* exhausted though her problem proved to be psychiatric in origin. With appropriate treatment she regained her normal energy level in a matter of weeks.

As we will see in Chapter 15, we potentially have four main causes of illness. However, in this chapter we want to address several facets of mental illness. Medicine is in the process of rediscovering the "mind-body connection." That is the important connection and interaction the mind has on the body, and likewise the body on the mind. In this chapter we will look at this in three different ways: (1) the role of stress in causing emotional illness, (2) the relationship of emotional illness and fatigue, and (3) psychosomatic fatigue.

The Role of Stress

Stress is a significant factor in causing mental illness. When the Federal Building in Oklahoma City was bombed in 1995, 182 individuals were killed and 684 were injured. Six months later individuals who had direct exposure to the situation were interviewed and 45 percent met diagnostic criteria for a major psychiatric disorder. Thus stressful life events often precipitate, cause, or aggravate mental illness. Here are some facts on this important subject:[1]

- Internalized toxic anger is often a factor in causing depression. Furthermore, recent losses, especially if multiple, cause or aggravate depression. Depressive psychosis often is preceded by a stressful life event one to two months before the onset of the depression.
- In Bipolar Disorders there is often a higher incidence of stressful life events just prior to developing the illness and likewise stress often precipitates a relapse.
- Early traumatic events in a person's life, especially the separation of parents, recent stresses, especially if they involve that person's performance, are all related to an increase of agoraphobia or panic attacks. Almost all patients with this disorder report a stressful life event occurring within two months of the first panic attack.
- Schizophrenia has a physical and often genetic basis, in addition it is frequently precipitated by stress.

This is by no means an exhaustive review of the literature on the role of stress in causing mental illness, but it does give you a picture of the important role it plays. Stress, in fact, plays a role in essentially every emotional illness.

Emotional Illness and Fatigue

Most emotional illnesses can and often do have fatigue as a prominent symptom. A sampling of some of them would be:[2]

- Major Depression: this is where a person feels very down, often can't sleep, has no energy, has difficulty in concentrating, and often loses weight.
- Dysthymia: this is a milder form of chronic depression; these individuals often will have fatigue.
- Bipolar Affective Disorder: this is an illness in which the individual often feels energetic, only to be followed by 180° turnaround, marked with all the symptoms of depression – including lack of energy.
- Seasonal Affective Disorder (SAD): this is depression in the dark winter months. A cardinal symptom of SAD is fatigue and often excessive sleep (hypersomnia). Its incidence close to the equator is less than 1 percent, but as you go to a northern

latitude such as North Wales or New York it is 2.4 to 5 percent, and in the arctic it is 6 to 9 percent. In the Arctic it is often called "cabin fever" and almost 50 percent of the population experience some symptoms of depression during the long winters. Bright light therapy is the treatment of choice. Individuals with a combination of both SAD and Chronic Fatigue Syndrome (CFS) often are helped by light therapy.

• Other illnesses include schizophrenia, anorexia nervosa, bulimia, and substance abuse.

Psychologically induced fatigue as opposed to organic fatigue is generally worse in the morning and may improve throughout the day. Very often it is activity related. The tiredness is worse when the individual is bored and improves when the individual becomes involved in interesting activities. Fatigue from emotional causes is just as real and incapacitating to the person experiencing it as fatigue produced by a severe organic cause. It is not "all in his head," for the sufferer actually *feels* it.

Why are we including these mental illnesses under the heading of "Biological Illnesses"? The simple answer is that in each of these we find a significant biological or organic cause; or to put it another way, we have a chemical basis for these diseases. Note again the incidence and symptoms of SAD. Individuals living closer to the North Pole have a much higher incidence, whereas those who live closer to the equator, where its inhabitants have adequate light the year around, have virtually no SAD. On top of that, exposure to bright light treats the depression. All of this is convincing evidence of a physical basis causing SAD.

For anyone who questions the biological basis of most of our emotional illnesses, please refer to my book *Why Do Christians Shoot Their Wounded? Helping (Not Hurting) Those with Emotional Difficulties*.[3] That book deals extensively with the biological basis of mental illness.

Psychosomatic Fatigue

A debate continues as to the cause of symptoms in individuals who have Chronic Fatigue Syndrome, Fibromyalgia, or related disorders. Could there be *some* in whom it is psychological in origin? What might be called Psychosomatic Fatigue. (A psychosomatic illness is a condition that is virtually 100 percent caused by a person's mind and does not have a physical or chemical basis even though it *feels* totally physical.) At this point in time, no one can answer that question unequivocally. However, on the basis of treating many patients and carefully reviewing the medical literature, the overwhelming evidence, in *most* instances, makes it clear that these illnesses are **not** psychosomatic in origin.

Having said that, let's make a few qualifying remarks. It is quite possible that CFS may have several different causes. In a small percentage of patients it **may be** psychosomatic in origin. The patient I told you about in the introduction to this chapter had incapacitating fatigue but with several weeks of psychological assistance her stamina returned to normal. In *her specific situation* the cause of her fatigue seemed psychosomatic in origin.

Some people have significant stresses in their lives and unresolved internal conflicts of such a magnitude that the emotional stress will express itself in some way, for the body will always find a way to manifest this internal unsettled discord. For some it may express itself in backaches, or gastrointestinal symptoms, others headaches, and still others fatigue, to name a few of the innumerable possible manifestations. What complicates the picture is that the person with a tension headache may have more physical pain than a person with a headache caused by a brain tumor. Likewise, a person with fatigue caused by psychological reasons may be more tired than the cancer patient with severe anemia.

In other words, regardless of the cause, the symptoms are physical. So often the sufferer *hears* from others, "You don't have bonafide physical feelings," or, "It's just in your head," or, "It's just that you think you are fatigued." In reality, no matter what the cause might be, the feelings *are* physical – the sufferer *feels* and *is* exhausted. Moreover, the person thinks that he is being accused of malingering and that he or she just needs "to knock it off" and the fatigue will be gone. But that's not true. Even if that were true he would not have the foggiest idea of how to go about doing that. The sufferer remains exhausted, feels totally misunderstood, judged, and therefore is defensive.

Another complicating factor is that there unfortunately is still so much prejudice against emotional illness; this is especially true in the religious community. I remember a patient telling me, "Don't tell me my illness is emotional. If it is, I don't want to hear it."

More often, people will use nonverbal communication to imply the same message to a physician or family member. Not infrequently in situations like this the patient will communicate non-verbally, "I'm going to be angry at you if you tell me my problem is psychological." This tends to reinforce the physician's impression that it is psychological, *even when the physician is wrong*. This is the kind of bind that patients and doctors find themselves in with an illness like chronic fatigue. But on the opposite end of the spectrum is the physician who tells the patient exactly what he or she wants to hear. It takes a skillful physician and a thinking but open patient to navigate these difficult waters.

Open to Truth

Not facing the truth, whatever that might be, does everyone a disservice. When our daughter, then 21, had an abnormal white count and enlarged lymph nodes, I took her to a local hematologist/ oncologist. For a month he temporized, doing tests and prescribing iron. It is my opinion, that he either consciously or unconsciously didn't want to be the bearer of bad news; she had acute leukemia and most likely would soon die. But he didn't do any of us a service, as we spent a month of anguish and uncertainty while delaying proper treatment. It could have cost us her life.

The point of my telling you this story is that truth, though sometimes painful, is ultimately in our best interest and often is a necessary ingredient for proper solutions to difficult problems.

Open to Where Truth Takes You

Naaman, a commander of the Syrian army and a leper, had to learn to be willing to seek help on the terms available rather than on his own terms. He was willing to seek help from his king, but God's plan for him was not to be found through pomp, but through a lowly man of God. The Prophet Elisha would not even talk to Naaman face-to-face, but sent a messenger instead. Naaman was told to do something that not only did not make sense, but he could think of better ways of meeting the need. His pride almost got in the way, preventing God's deliverance. But a lowly servant girl persuaded him to obey Elisha and wash himself in the muddy Jordan River to receive his healing (see 2 Kings 5).

Conclusion

If we really want help for a problem, we must be willing to seek it any way that God would provide it. We have a choice as to whether we will be open to truth — even if that is different than what our preconceived ideas might be.

Having said this, let me reiterate what I said earlier, *I do not think most chronic fatigue is all psychological,* but I am urging you to keep an open mind to whatever truth might be in your situation.

The psalmist prayed, "Search me, O God, and know my heart; test me and know my thoughts. Point out anything in me that offends you" (Psalm139:23-24, NLT). If we want to know the truth, we must be open to whatever that truth is. Jesus, speaking on a different issue, does point out that a willingness to know whatever the truth is, is essential to being able to know the truth (John 7:17). In other words, if we go into a situation with our minds made up, we won't be open to truth.

Part Five

Spiritual Illness

CHAPTER 14

OUR SPIRITUAL VOID

IN 1974 DR. KARL Menninger, one of the founders of the world-renowned psychiatric center in Topeka, Kansas, which carries the family name, wrote a book about a very unlikely and unpopular subject. This was about the time when the world was enamored with Sigmund Freud's view that religious people were "neurotic"; Karl Marx's view that "religion is the opiate of the people" was widely believed, and America was debating the philosophy of whether "God Is Dead."

The Best Kept Secret

The book Dr. Menninger published that year was *Whatever Became of Sin?* Yes, he resurrected a subject that most of the world was trying to bury – that there is such a thing as sin. The forces of evil had tried and, for the most part, had done a marvelous job of keeping secret that sin exists. "Evil" had succeeded in keeping out of our collective consciousness that we humans are responsible for our sins and that sin has its consequences. Our frantic pace was a ploy to keep us from thinking or doing anything about this ancient problem.

Jesus Christ told us centuries ago that Satan, the thief, "comes only to steal, and kill, and destroy," in contrast to the Son of God who came that we "might have life and might have it abundantly" (John 10:10). The battle we really face is not the obvious external one with which we are confronted day by day, but it is against strong, unseen spiritual forces of evil (see Ephesians 6:11–12).

Satan is alive and well on Planet Earth and will do everything in his power to sabotage our experiencing what God has for us.

The Consequences of Sin

Moses in the Old Testament warns all generations: "Be sure your sin will find you out" (Numbers 32:23). We can ignore the fact of sin in our world, but we will nevertheless suffer its repercussions. We can choose to ignore the consequences of speeding on the highway or the law of gravity, but if we violate these laws, we will pay the price. It is better for us if we look at the implications, then decide what to do about this "avoid at all costs" subject.

Humanity's first contact with Satan is described in Genesis 3. He is characterized as the most crafty of beings and he plants seeds of suspicion about the goodness and motives of God in both Eve and Adam. Tragically, Eve yields to the temptation, which sets in motion a whole series of consequences that we face every day. Let's look at some of the ramifications.

Alienation from God and Each Other

Sin caused Adam and Eve to flee and hide from God's presence even though God was actively seeking them. Furthermore, their sin caused guilt, lying, blaming, and alienation between them and future generations.

Death

God had warned that the result of disobedience would be death. This death involved both our spiritual lives as well as our physical bodies. For the most part death was not immediate, but the process was started and continues to this day. Occasionally, we do find examples in the Bible of death occurring as a prompt and direct result of an individual's sin. Some examples are Er (Genesis 38:7), Achan (Joshua 7:16–25), and Ananias and Sapphira (Acts 5:1–11).

Illness

More often our fallen nature manifests itself in the *process* of death. The Apostle Paul tells us that our sin can cause not only death but weakness and illness. He writes, "That is why many of you are weak and sick, and some have even died" (1 Corinthians 11:30, TLB). A clear example of this is King Nebuchadnezzar who developed a psychosis as a direct result of his sin (Daniel 4:28–33).

Anywhere we look we can see the process of illness manifesting itself and ultimately leading to death. It doesn't take the Bible or medical literature to convince us that, drug abuse, alcoholism, or sexual promiscuity, for example, lead to illnesses and an early demise.

Aristotle, in the 4th century BC made an interesting and valid observation: "The soul sympathizes with the diseased and traumatized body and the body suffers when the soul is ailing."[1]

A. W. Tozer spoke of this more recently, "All of our heartaches and a great many of our physical ills spring directly from our sins. Pride, arrogance, resentfulness, evil imaginations, malice, greed: these are the sources of more human pain than all the diseases that ever afflicted mortal flesh. . . . The burden borne by mankind is a heavy and a crushing thing. . . . Let us examine our burden. It is altogether an interior one."[2]

Even science is beginning to recognize the adverse effects of a life void of God. Sigmund Freud did not do any true scientific research, but from his armchair concluded that religion caused neurosis. Now that hundreds of well-documented research studies have been completed on the effects of religion and faith on our lives, it has become clear that he was wrong. Over 80 percent of the studies conclude that spiritual wellbeing has a positive effect on our lives. For example, it has been clearly demonstrated that those with a strong faith have better mental health, less depression, more stable immune systems, lower blood pressure, and, in fact, live longer. We will elaborate on this in more detail later.[3]

Internal Void

We are all troubled by the condition of the world: bloodshed, hunger, homelessness, illnesses, and death. We would all like to conquer these, and if that's not possible, at least minimize their effects.

But there is a bigger albatross hanging around the neck of humanity – an internal void. Saint Augustine said, "Our hearts are restless until they find their rest in Thee."[4] The French philosopher and physicist Pascal said, "There is a God-shaped vacuum in the heart of every man which only God can fill through His Son, Jesus Christ."[5] These quotes are generally and appropriately used to suggest that those who have not trusted Christ have an internal spiritual need that only God can fill. But the fact is that there is a God-shaped vacuum and a restless heart in the innermost being of the vast majority of people, certainly in the world at large; but it is also true, that it often exists within those who believe in God and name the Name of Christ. Unless we somehow experience that "Living Water" continuously flowing through us – we will be thirsty (see John 7:37–39). Thus, in our world today the atheist, the Muslim, the Jew, the Hindu, and for that matter many Christians – remain thirsty and weary.

As thirsty individuals we try and fill the void ourselves instead of going to God to fill that emptiness. Satan, the deceiver, has sent out all kinds of decoys to lead us away from God. In warfare, if a missile is fired at a target, it stands a chance of being shot down by the opposing side's missile. To prevent this from happening, the military fires, along with the original missile, a number of objects that are capable of reflecting radar waves. Now the enemy's rocket has to try and decipher which of the 20 objects in the sky reflecting the radar beam is the real missile and which are the 19 meaningless decoys; it must do it instantaneously or the day is lost.

Likewise, each one of us has an internal void that only a genuine relationship with God can fill. Our enemy doesn't want us to have this relationship with God, so he fires off all kinds of decoys. What does he use? Money, business, bigger houses, toys, knowledge, control, power, sex, and pleasure, to name just a few. Thus we are sitting ducks for the advertisers and all the allurements of the world. The whirlwind pace and all its consequences are an inevitable result. This is an illness, and at the deepest level, ultimately a spiritual illness. It is an infectious illness, as it insidiously spreads to every part of our lives, and then to others. All the stresses discussed in the previous chapters ultimately have their roots in spiritual issues.

Most of us are desperately searching for satisfaction and looking in the wrong places, which is only making our problem worse. Dallas Willard has recently stated, "That harassing, hovering feeling of 'have to' largely comes from the vacuum in your soul."[6] And so the Christian can get caught up in this same whirlwind, even with good Christian service.

This is, in fact, often the cause of a frantic pace, overextension, allowing ourselves to be inundated with pressures that stress us, as well as unresolved internal problems. A case could be made that all the items that we talked about in Parts 2 and 3 of this book are actually the result of our spiritual void. A life that is not fully satisfied by God or filled with his peace will try to fill that emptiness with the "stuff" of the world; unfortunately, sometimes some of the same ingredients are in our churches. We will need to make a quantum shift in our emphases if we are going to avoid being squeezed into the world's mold.

A Qualifier

Please note one big word of caution. Readers might erroneously conclude from what has just been said that all our griefs and illnesses are a direct and immediate result of our personal sins. And the often suggested easy answer is, "Just confess your sin and all your illnesses and problems will go away." That is not the case. This simplistic counsel at the wrong time can play havoc, especially with a sensitive and sincere individual. All sin and the ravishes it causes is the direct result of someone's sin at some point in time. Adam and Eve in the Fall set into motion the numerous changes in our genes that led to illnesses generations later. Also, the sin of abusing parents adversely affects their children to the 3rd and 4th generation. The alcoholic can kill and maim another. In each of these situations someone's sin caused the problem, but not the sufferer. In these and in many situations, the illness, suffering, or death is not the result of the immediate personal sin of the sufferer. In psychiatry we often see Christians accusing the person suffering from an emotional illness of causing their own illness. Occasionally that may be the case, but in the vast majority of situations it is *not* the case.

Remedy for Spiritual Illness

I am reminded of Mr. and Mrs. R. who sought my help as an internist. They had little use for God until Mr. R. developed cancer. Then they became interested in hearing about God's love and plan for their lives.

I remember vividly the night I talked with them, because I didn't get out of the office till after 8 o'clock. I was tired, but believed that God wanted me to go to their home and share God's plan of salvation with them. Mrs. R. said later that she knew before I rang their doorbell that something special was going to happen that night – and it did! They both put their trust in the finished work of Christ.

Mr. R.'s illness and subsequent death were hard on his wife, but she bravely faced it, has eagerly grown in Christ, and is concerned about sharing her testimony with those who don't know her Lord. She was doing quite well until just recently when she started developing several physical symptoms, one of which was severe insomnia which was not relieved with typical medical management.

After re-evaluating her for any diseases which might be causing her symptoms, I became quite certain that something emotional or spiritual was underneath it all. We discussed this, but despite a frank and honest exchange, the problem eluded us both. Shortly thereafter, she spent an evening of spiritual sharing with my wife. Through this time of honest discussion it dawned on Mrs. R. that she had set up in her mind's eye the image of what a "good Christian" should be. Although she was trying hard and had grown a tremendous amount, she was still falling short of her self-imposed image. She called me a few days later to report that since that night with my wife she realized that God accepted her just as she was, and she thus accepted herself. Since that night she has been "sleeping like a baby."

I tell you this story about Mr. and Mrs. R. to illustrate several points. The first step in dealing with the sin problem is to put your trust in Christ. This is important relative to your eternal destiny. This comes about as you put your trust in his completed work on your behalf (see John 3:16; Romans 10:9–10).

In step two, as a follower of Jesus, if you sin, you need to deal with that sin by confessing and forsaking it. The Apostle John encourages you by stating, "If we confess our sins, he [God] is faithful and just to forgive us our sins, and to cleanse us from all unrighteousness" (1 John 1:9, KJV).

The third step is to remain in relationship with Christ. The Lord uses the metaphor of the vine and the branches, in which he is the vine, and we are the branches. We must remain in contact with and dependent on the vine for the sustenance of our lives. In his conversation with the woman in Samaria, Christ uses the analogy of water, telling us that he wants to give us continuous internal refreshment. He says, "Anyone who drinks the water I give will never thirst – not ever. The water I give will be an artesian spring within, gushing fountains of endless life" (John 4:14, MSG). The word *drinks* indicates a continuing process of drinking from the eternal fountain – Christ. Our remaining in communion with Christ is the antidote to the frantic whirlwind pace with which the world, and sometimes the church, is constantly enticing us.

Another teaching of his which addresses the same issue in a slightly different way is this: "Come to Me all who are weary and heavy-laden, and I will give you rest. Take My yoke upon you, and learn from Me, for I am gentle and humble in heart; and you shall find rest for your souls. For My yoke is easy, and My burden is light" (Matthew 11:28–30). The "weary and heavy-laden" are invited to come to him initially and have "rest." But then we are encouraged to take the second step – obediently to learn of him, in order to have "soul rest." This does *not* mean a great deal of the head knowledge of the Scriptures or busy Christian activity, it is something much deeper than that. The Old Testament nation of Israel failed at this point despite a great deal of head knowledge and many works of righteousness. They failed to enter into God's rest (see Hebrews 4:1–11). God has a rest for us, but we must be "diligent" to enter into it – resting, abiding, trusting, communing with him – and we must "cease from our own works" in trying to do it all ourselves.

SECTION THREE

THE CAUSE OF ILLNESS

Part Six

The Multifactorial Model

of Illness

CHAPTER 15

MAKING SENSE OUT OF THE CAUSES OF ILLNESS

ILLNESS IS SELDOM the result of one causative factor (mono-etiology). When we think about *the cause of an illness*, we tend to think about it and verbalize it as if there is one causative factor. For example, when we think of someone coming down with a cold or the flu, it almost goes without saying that a virus caused that illness. If someone was in an accident, it is logical to think that someone was negligent. For years it was believed that if a person had a stomach ulcer, then stress was the cause.

If you want to go back to Adam and Eve and original sin, then maybe you can make a case for a single cause; that is, sin, and only sin, caused all of man's infirmities. Yes, it is true that some illnesses, especially the genetic ones that have full penetrance, such as Down's Syndrome (mongolism), are the result of one cause – an abnormal gene. A number of illnesses like this exist; however, most illnesses are the end result of multiple causative factors. When that is the case, we do ourselves and those we influence a great injustice if we think in a mono-factorial approach.

Most illnesses are caused by several significant factors. Let's go back to the stomach ulcer. Clearly stress *is* a factor; however, elevated steroid hormones, drugs such as aspirin, individuals with 0+ blood type, and a specific bacteria – Helicobacter pylori – are all contributing factors in leading to an ulcer. A given individual may have several, but not all, of these factors, and still develop an ulcer. It is readily apparent why knowing what the determining variables are is essential in treating this illness. The person can work at reducing stress; he or she can stop taking offending medications and take a course of antibiotics to eradicate the bacteria. But that individual can't do anything about his or her blood type.

What about the common cold and other upper respiratory tract infections? Certainly there is a viral pathogen that causes the "cold." But susceptibility can be altered by stress, anxiety, depression, positive or negative experiences in one's life, status of one's immune system, social connectedness, a sedentary lifestyle, and allergic disorders. Thus you can have three individuals equally exposed to the same virus; one comes down with severe and prolonged symptoms, the second comes down with mild symptoms, and the third has no symptoms.[1]

In some illnesses the medical profession has come a long way in thinking about them in a multifactorial manner. One example is heart attacks (Myocardial Infarction). We know that genetics, abnormal lipids in the blood, diabetes, stress, toxic anger, obesity, sedentary lifestyle, smoking, and depression all play a role in the development of heart attacks. Knowing this puts us on the right track for prevention, that is, addressing each factor and reducing it as much as possible.

Many people tend to view the cause of mental illness as due to one factor. This is a gross disservice to the sufferer. Numerous people think it is due to the sufferer's poor choices; many religious people view it as due to sin. Some see it as a weakness. The fact is that the vast majority of these illnesses are multifactorial. For example, panic attacks are often seen in individuals where there is: (1) a genetic tendency, (2) early childhood traumas, such as loss or abandonment of a parent, (3) a precipitating crisis event, (4) avoidance behavior, and (5) unhelpful thinking patterns tend to perpetrate the panic episodes. In Schizophrenia we know that genetics plays a role, as does infections of the mother during the second trimester and complications during delivery; all may contribute to the development of this disorder. Fortunately, we are no longer blaming it on the poor parenting of the mother, labeling her a "schizophrenogenic mother," as we did in the mid 20th century.[2]

The Multifactorial Model of Illness

In previous chapters we have discussed that illness is not due to only physical or biological causes but that there is a "Mind/Body Connection," that the mind plays an important role in illness. More recently the importance of the social has been emphasized in the medical literature so it has been referred to as the biopsychosocial cause of illness. However, considering all the material that has and will be presented in this book I believe a strong case can be made for multiple causes in illness: they include genetic, biological, developmental, social, environmental, psychological, nutritional, spiritual, and personal choices. There are many ways that one might group these various causative factors. I believe it is utilitarian to combine these under the following four groups (see Diagram 1).

1.　Biological. This includes the genetic, physical, organic, or chemical factors causing the illness. Examples would be Down's Syndrome or Tuberculosis.

2.　Environmental. This includes environmental factors, whether it is exposure to toxic substances, abusive parenting, or stresses in our environment. It also includes social interaction (see Chapter 21).

3.　Spiritual. This would be conscious disobedience to God and his commands (see Chapter 14).

4.　Personal Choice includes: ignorance and unwise decisions. (An example of ignorance might be an individual who knows he snores loudly, his wife knows that he seems to struggle for air at times, but neither of them realize the seriousness of the problem in his situation. Likewise, they have never discussed it with a health professional. So this could be an unrecognized, potentially life-threatening illness that is not receiving proper and available treatment.)

Sometimes these causes are clear-cut and perceived by all; at other times the etiology is murky and one causative factor may lead to another. For example, if a person is exposed to excessive radiation from his environment, initially the diagnosis would fall under Category 2 – Environmental. But if the radiation was sufficient and it started mutation of that person's cells, it would now fall into Category 1 – Biological.

Diagram 1 illustrates the four causative factors. In this example each of the contributing factors is listed equally – 25 percent to the overall illness, symptom, or problem.

Now let's look at an actual illness. I will take a hypothetical, but true to life, situation of depression. Four individuals may come to me complaining of severe depression.

The first individual with depression gives a history of several family members also having had depression, one being a Manic Depressive. In his situation the literature records that 70 to 85 percent of the cause of his depression may be inherited. Thus the major cause of his depression is Biological. The cause of his illness is illustrated with Diagram 2 (Person "A").[3]

A second person comes in, again complaining of significant depression. She gives a history of repeatedly being sexually abused as a child by her stepfather. The major cause of her depression is Environmental. I illustrate this with Person "B" in Diagram 3.

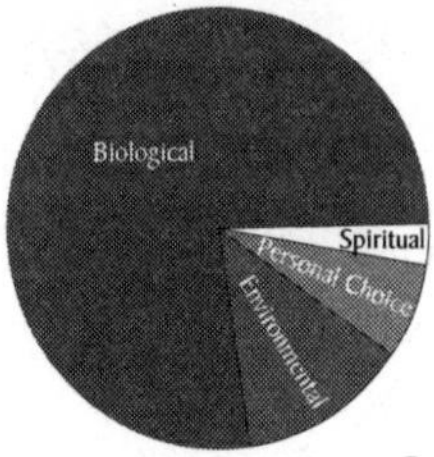

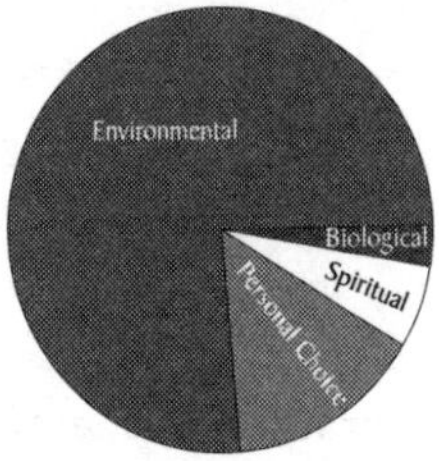

Another person comes in who has repeatedly made bad choices with two failed marriages; he recently told his boss off at work and was fired without another job available; and he is on the verge of bankruptcy. The majority of his depression is a direct result of awful Personal Choices. This is illustrated in Diagram 4 as Person "C."

The General Cause of Illness

Diagram 1

Person "A"

Diagram 2

Person "B"

Diagram 3

Person "C"

Diagram 4

The fourth person is furious at God for the untimely loss of a child and blames God for the many problems in his life. He is Person "D," whose major problem is a spiritual one. See Diagram 5.

Person "D"

Diagram 5

Admittedly, this is somewhat over-simplified as life is seldom this clear-cut. Nevertheless, the message it conveys is accurate. Here we have four equally depressed individuals. But the cause is different in each situation. To put them all on an antidepressant and send them on their way is not the answer. I need to address each person's unique cause of depression and try and help him or her deal with it in a constructive way.

Now let's turn our attention to fatigue and how we can profitably view all illnesses. As indicated in Chapter 12 no one knows the cause of Chronic Fatigue Syndrome, Fibromyalgia, Multiple Chemical Sensitivities, and related disorders. But when you study large groups of people with these ailments, four factors often emerge. At the time that a majority of these individuals initially came down with symptoms, (1) they were under significant stress, (2) they were exposed to some sort of infection, usually viral, (3) and they were struggling with some emotional difficulties. The relationship of these is largely conjecture. Not all individuals with these disorders have all of these factors present. It has been suggested that these factors working in consonance lead to the development of these illnesses. Another frequent finding in these patients is (4) an alteration in the Hypothalamic-Pituitary-Adrenal Axis. It is not clear whether the altered functioning is present at the onset of the illness or if it develops later. Regardless, this is biological in nature.

Person "E" at Time of Onset of Chronic Fatigue

With this information let us go back to the pie illustrations of the causes of illnesses. In Diagram 6, I am illustrating a hypothetical person ("E") who has recently developed Chronic Fatigue Syndrome. For ease we will call the person "Jan."

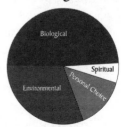

Diagram 6

As you can see from the diagram, the major cause of her illness is Biological (Category 1) due to a viral infection. The second major contributor to the illness is Environmental (Category 2). Jan has just been laid off from work due to closure of the plant and is faced with a major financial deficit. Furthermore, she has a strained relationship with her family that has caused emotional turmoil for some time (Category 2 & 4).

Now let's look at Jan six months later. The viral infection has run its course and the remaining biological sequela is probably an altered Hypothalamic-Pituitary-Adrenal Axis and immune system. With regard to the Environmental factors, she has gotten another job, though it doesn't pay as well, and her family and her physician are critical of her choices and illness. With regard to Personal Choices, she is blaming others for her predicament and allowing anger to churn within her, both at others and at God. She is not exercising, living a very sedentary life. The cause of her current symptoms is illustrated in Diagram 7.

Let's be very clear. Diagrams 6 and 7 are hypothetical possibilities that are realistic and true to life. But there are numerous possibilities. Every person will have a slightly different make-up of either factors originally causing or contributing to the disease, and likewise every person will have a different combination of factors if the disease is chronic.

Person "E" 6 Months After Onset of Fatigue

Diagram 7

Now for some observations:

- Typically there are several factors that contribute to the development of any illness.
- Though a number of individuals may have the same illness, the contributing factors to it might be different in each of these individuals.
- In any chronic illness the factors contributing to the symptoms an individual has, may change with time.

- Though there may be some factors you can't change, usually there are several that you can change. These may make a significant difference not only in how you feel but in the final outcome of the illness. Sometimes when you change the areas that are under your volitional control, your body discovers ways to improve the areas that are not under your direct control.

Let us now consider Jan in a little more detail and the things that are currently contributing to her symptoms six months after the onset of her fatigue. She would consider the four general causes of illnesses – Biological, Environmental, Personal Choice, and Spiritual. If we were to ask Jan on the basis of her knowledge of herself what factors in her symptoms might fall under each category, she might list them as noted below in Chart 1. In the last space of each column she will list her sense as to the relative significance the category is having on her current symptoms. Her chart might look like this:

Cause of Jan's Symptoms 6 Months After the Onset of CFS

I: Biological	2: Environmental	3: Personal Choice	4: Spiritual
Altered H P A Axis	Job is only partially satisfactory	I am good and angry at my financial situation and job	I am mad at God for causing me all this suffering
Altered immune system	Doctor and family seem critical of me; think it's all my fault	I feel like telling my Doctor and family off and moving a long way away	I have stopped going to church
		I lie around most of my "free" time, eating junk food, watching junk on TV	
		I am gaining weight and refuse to exercise though I know I could do some exercise	
Moderate	Moderate	Moderate	Minimal to Moderate

Chart I

Having filled out the chart, Jan decides that she is going to deal with all the areas in her life over which she has some direct control. She has a heart-to-heart talk with her family and doctor and those relationships are markedly improved. Jan drastically decreases her TV-watching and in its place is reading some wholesome books. She has reconciled with God and is attending church again. Jan also started very gradually some aerobic exercise — it's not much, but a start. What has happened to her fatigue? Before she got ill she had about 75 units of energy a day (see Figure 2 on page 31). When she came down with her severe fatigue her energy level dropped to 35 units and stayed there for six months. She has now been working actively at regaining her strength for six months and now her energy level is at 55 units. What is the cause of her current symptoms? Primarily Biological. As she continues to work on the issues that are in her control, hopefully before too long her energy level will be within the normal range.

Where Are You?

You might want to pause and consider the symptoms with which *you* are wrestling. Then consider the four general causes of illnesses. Under each of these headings list all factors that may have caused or have contributed to the symptoms you *now* experience in the chart below (Chart 2). Finally, in the last horizontal row, come to a conclusion, crude as it might be, as to the relative significance of the column in producing your symptoms. List in that column the appropriate word: "Major," "Moderate," "Minimal," "Negligible." (Reproduce the chart into the size you need.)

I: Biological	2: Environmental	3: Personal Choice	4: Spiritual

Chart 2

This exercise can lay the groundwork as to how you might look at the current cause of your fatigue (or other disorder) and point the direction as to how to deal with it.

The Serenity Prayer is an appropriate response to the material in this chapter:

> God, grant me the serenity
> to accept the things I cannot change,
> Courage to change the things I can, and
> Wisdom to know the difference.[4]

SECTION FOUR

THE ENERGIZERS

Part Seven

Energize Your Life

CHAPTER 16

THE POWER OF CONTROL, ACCEPTANCE, AND CHOICE

The Power of Control

OUR ONLY DAUGHTER, 21, had just graduated from Occidental College, cap and gown, but no hair. She had completed her third round of toxic chemotherapy for Acute Myologenous Leukemia. Then the dreaded news came, the reoccurrence of leukemia. Back in the hospital for the fourth month-long treatment, her oncologist wanted to tell her she was going to die. We virtually forbad him from doing so. I had two reasons for this. First, initially she had been told the dreaded implications should the leukemia return – she already knew the prognosis.

But there was a second reason. The first few months after the diagnosis was made I wasn't able to read about the disease. When I tried, I cried, the statistics were just too grim. But I knew I had to get educated about the advances in treating the disease. I obtained several dozen articles about the various modes of treatment and found that a few centers were performing parent-child bone-marrow transplants. I made phone calls to verify my information. The prestigious medical center that was treating Susan had initially told us that since Susan was our only biological child, a transplant was out of the question. Armed with new information, I talked again to our oncologist who remained against even testing us to see if there was a match.

However, I persisted, we were tested, and Susan and I had a 1:20,000 match. Attribute this to prayer or persistence, or both – she is alive and free of leukemia 18 years later. Praise God!

I could tell you stories about my sinus surgery, nasal duct surgery, or a relative's cancer – to name a few medical contacts in which being educated on the issues changed the course and outcome of the illness for the better.

You might say, "You're a physician; it's easy for you to get the information and to talk to doctors." There is some truth in this, but I have seen others obtain information through the Internet and by consultations with other physicians; they have effectively and appropriately comanaged their treatment.

The medical literature is demonstrating the value of patients taking a significant amount of control of their treatment. For example, in one study carried out at Stanford Arthritis Center, a self-help program was devised for patients with arthritis. Patients were encouraged to take control of their lives and illnesses by making decisions about their treatment and designing exercise programs for themselves. Those who took part had a 35 percent reduction in their pain, a 20 percent reduction in swelling and an 18 percent decrease in depressive symptoms. Those who improved felt a sense of control regarding their arthritis. Those who did not feel they could take any control of their lives, either did not improve or got worse.[1]

As a physician, I am convinced, that it is incumbent on you to take a certain amount of control over your medical treatment. Whether we are talking about fatigue or any other medical problem, this is essential.

The Power of Acceptance

You may think that I am talking out of both sides of my mouth. I started this chapter talking about the importance and necessity of taking control of your life, especially in the area of the management of your health. Now I am saying that there comes a time to accept the illness, treatment, and outcome – even if it is not exactly the result that you desire. The facts are that there is a time and place for both.

In one study there were 116 patients who had a retinal detachment. They sought out excellent medical care and had surgery with varying degrees of recovery. How well these patients did depended, in part, on the degree of acceptance of their outcome. Those individuals who ultimately did the best were the ones that viewed their residual medical handicap as unfortunate but surmountable. They decided that the handicap would not interfere with their ongoing meaningful lives. When they had done all they could, they accepted the outcomes and with God's help made the very best of it. There is a time for both. We will return to this subject later when we discuss the "prayer of relinquishment" and address meaning and purpose in the latter chapters of this book.[2]

Note that acceptance is not helplessness. It is the awareness that any further fighting is counterproductive so that you are choosing an alternative approach. It is putting into practice the Serenity Prayer – having the serenity to accept the things that can't be changed.

If we try and control everything, we will be overstepping our prerogative of control. We will end up angry people trying to control others and make things worse for everyone, ourselves included. We will become uptight when we find we can't control everything. And no one, other than God can control everything.

The Power of Choice

The Choice is Yours

When God put Adam and Eve in the Garden of Eden, one of the most pivotal attributes that he gave them was choice. They could choose to be obedient to his explicit will or they could choose to defy it. Their decision set in motion the world as we know it today with its violence, evil, sickness, and death. Despite the barrage of pressures that tend to move us downward, God has also given us the ability to make numerous choices that will result in obedience to God and our temporal and eternal good. Fundamental to the direction that we take is choice.

Moses, speaking on behalf of God, told Israel, "See, I have set before you today life and prosperity, and death and adversity; . . . So choose life" (Deuteronomy 30:15, 19). The Bible is replete with instances of individuals or nations being given the opportunity to make choices; and we subsequently find many examples of good choices, fair choices, and terrible choices. The right choice can make the difference between life and death.

No matter what your situation may be, you have choices that *will* make a significant difference now, in the future, and throughout eternity for you; in addition, often they will affect those around you.

Viktor Frankl, a visiting professor to Harvard and known as "Europe's leading psychiatrist," described the universality of the laws of choice that God has established; he observed these in the crucible of a Nazi concentration camp. He stated:

> In the concentration camp every circumstance conspires to make the prisoner lose his hold . . . What alone remains is "the last of human freedoms" – the ability to "choose one's attitude in a given set of circumstances". . . The experiences of camp life show that man does have a choice of action. There were enough examples, often of a heroic nature, which proved that apathy could be overcome, irritability suppressed. Man *can* preserve a vestige of spiritual freedom, of independence of mind, even in such terrible conditions of psychic and physical stress . . . everything can be taken from a man but one thing: the last of the human freedoms – to choose one's attitude in any given set of circumstances, to choose one's own way . . . Every day, every hour, offered the opportunity to make a decision . . . in the final analysis it becomes clear that the sort of person the prisoner became was the result of an inner decision, and not the result of camp influences alone. Fundamentally, therefore, any man can, even under such circumstances, decide what shall become of him – mentally and spiritually.[3]

Personal Application

In the previous chapter we pointed out the four general areas that can cause illness. We also asked you to list possible specific items under each area that may be causing trouble and may need attention. You might want to add another row to Chart 2 and note in each category actions you might take to get help or to deal with the issue.

As stated earlier, if there is any possibility that the problem may be a physical one, by all means see a physician. If, after the physician has completed his evaluation, you are still not satisfied, request a consultation. But at some point, remember, there is the time to accept what you are being told. The very difficult part is to know when.

If your problem is spiritual, ask for the help of a pastor or other Christian leader whose life is yielded to Jesus Christ. If it is an emotional problem, you may want to seek appropriate professional help. If it is not clear what you can or should do, read on for we will be discussing many other things that you can do to increase energy and serenity.

Conclusion

The late Christian physician and counselor Paul Tournier reminds us that fatigue is a warning signal. He has written, "An illness must always be the occasion for a taking stock of oneself, for a growing awareness of unresolved problems, and for a revision of the values which few men undertake in full health . . . he [the doctor] must re-educate his patients, helping them to reform their lives. This is especially evident in the cases of overwork and fatigue." He goes on to say, "What does God think of my life? . . . What does God think of my activity, of my work, or of the way I organize it. . . For to live is to choose."[4]

CHAPTER 17

THE POWER OF PRUNING

ONE DAY I was driving in central California admiring a magnificent orchard. Several weeks later I was driving down the same highway, but this time I was startled by what I saw. The fruit trees had been pruned. It looked as though someone had butchered them. Most of the leaves and branches were gone. All that was left was the trunk and some of the main branches. As a novice in this sort of thing, it seemed that someone got carried away and didn't know when to stop. It looked like the trees had been damaged permanently. For many months the trees looked dead.

Then came spring. Numerous new branches and lush green leaves had grown and before long the trees had abundant fruit. It's counterintuitive, but that's the way it is. Pruning improves the quality and quantity of the fruit. It allows light to reach all parts of the tree and prevents limbs from breaking due to excessive fruit in the wrong places. Christ uses the same analogy with the vine and branches in John 15, saying that pruning is an essential part of a fruitful life.

And the pruning is not only of the "attractions of this world and the delights of wealth, and the search for success," but wonderful Christian pursuits (see Mark 4:19, TLB). In fact, if there is anything that we are not willing to submit to the Master's knife, it is probably an item of idolatry.

John Ortberg tells us about calling his spiritual mentor and telling him about his life. He then records this conversation:

"What did I need to do," I asked him, "to be spiritually healthy?"

Long pause.

"You must ruthlessly eliminate hurry from your life," he said at last.

Another long pause.

"Okay, I've written that one down," I told him, a little impatiently. "That's a good one. Now what else is there?" I had many things to do and this was a long-distance conversation, so I was anxious to cram as many units of spiritual wisdom into the least amount of time possible. Another long pause.

"There is nothing else," he said.[1]

We must ruthlessly prune anything in our lives that is an impediment to our walk with God. But it doesn't stop there. We also need to be willing to prune good productive activities, those that might not get done unless we do them.

John Eldredge approaches this from the vantage point of a necessary step to having the desire of our hearts. He writes:

> Those who have buried desire beneath years of duty and obligation may need to give all that a rest so that their hearts can come to the surface. Abandon all but the most essential duties for a while. You still have to pay the bills, but everything you can jettison, you should. Do nothing unless it reflects your true desire. . .You might even need to give up going to church for awhile . . . it was one of the most refreshing years of my life. I hadn't abandoned God and I very much sought out the company of my spiritual companions. What I gave up was the performance of having to show up every Sunday morning with my happy face on . . . I spent a year in the Psalms at the same time I was resting from the duty of Sunday morning. I wasn't studying them with my head; I was praying them from my heart.[2]

This is not a suggestion that you stop going to church, but it is a plea that you do whatever God might desire of you – that you be willing to prune ruthlessly no matter what that might involve.

In Chapter 7, I briefly told you about a situation at church in which I believed God would have me resign. The pruning meant that I had to be willing to sacrifice "what other people might think" and potential future leadership and ministry opportunities. Making the decision was part of the pruning process, and for a while it hurt; but then it was liberating in emotion, time, and energy. In fact it was exhilarating.

During an extremely busy time in my life, when I originally wrote this book, my wife and I went away for a few days of rest. While we were away I sat down and listed the activities in which I was involved. I was amazed to discover that I was involved in 26 specific responsibilities – committees, projects, and other endeavors. Many were work related, some in local hospitals. Over half were related to the church and other Christian organizations. Every one was good and worthwhile.

Although I could easily justify each activity, I was forced to admit that my life was suffering from a multiplicity of activities. So I determined that before I said yes to any activity in the future, three criteria would have to be met:

1. It must be worthy of my time on its own merits.
2. It must be worthy, not only in its own right, but more valuable than any other activity to which I would subsequently have to say "no". This meant evaluating all my other responsibilities and those I could anticipate for the future.
3. It must be God's will for me.

Then, still using pencil and paper, I grouped each of my 26 activities into four categories: *Prime importance, very crucial, important,* and *good.*

First, I listed those activities which were of *prime importance* – those responsibilities which I would have as long as I live – which would not change if I were flat on my back in a hospital bed. In this category I listed my relationship to God and my responsibilities as a husband and a father.

Second, I wrote down the *very crucial* things. They may not be lifelong commitments, but they were high-priority items. This list included my responsibilities as a physician and provider, the importance of Christian fellowship (including the church), continuing medical education, sharing Christ with others, and relaxation. Incidentally, relaxation was virtually nonexistent when I made this chart.

Prime Importance	Very Crucial	Important	Good
1) Relationship to God 2) Responsibility as a husband 3) Responsibility as a father	1) Responsibility to patients (and secondarily as a provider) 2) Christian Fellowship 3) Continuing medical education 4) Sharing my faith 5) Relaxation	1) Medical partnership responsibilities 2) Pulpit committee 3) Required hospital staff meetings 4) Paul Carlson Foundation Board 5) Conference evangelism meeting 6) Home Bible Study	1) Deacon 2) Sunday School Teacher 3) Writing personal tract 4) Friday prayer breakfast 5) Thursday doctor's fellowship 6) Office remodeling 7) Reading hospital EKG's 8) CCU committee chairman - hospital #1 9) Executive committee- hopsital #1 10) CCU committee - hospital #2 11) CCU committee - hospital #3 12) Bowling league

Chart 3

Third, on the page were the *important* activities which included some business and hospital responsibilities, church pulpit committee, board member of a foundation, conference evangelism committee, and our home Bible study.

In the fourth category were all kinds of great things, but considering their relationship to my other responsibilities, I could only give them a *good* rating. (Please note, however, this does not mean that these were not important, nor does it mean that anyone else should place them in this category, or for that matter, that I would always place them in this, fourth, category.)

My list looked like this – see Chart 3 above.

To my amazement, most of the items landed in Category Four. I could justify each activity with at least several important reasons why I should be doing that activity. Many of these tasks were receiving more emphasis than some of the items in the first three categories. After each item I graded myself. To some I was giving too much time and emphasis, others not enough, and some needed to be eliminated. Under the Holy Spirit's direction, I gradually weeded out virtually all of the items in Category Four.

What does your list look like? An important step in reducing stress and fatigue is to evaluate your involvement in activities and commitments. This can be the first step in taking appropriate control of your life. Below is an empty chart with the four columns in it (Chart 4). Please fill it out prayerfully. (If this is not large enough, use another piece of paper.) Now consider each item prayerfully. After each item put a plus (+) if it is getting too much emphasis, a minus (–) if it is not getting adequate attention, a zero (0) if it should be eliminated, and an OK if it is getting the proper attention. Which one or several items should you start working on first?

Prime Importance	Very Crucial	Important	Good
1)	1)	1)	1)
2)	2)	2)	2)
3)	3)	3)	3)
4)	4)	4)	4)
5)	5)	5)	5)

Chart 4

CHAPTER 18

THE POWER OF RESERVE

WHEN I WAS 14 years old, I talked my folks into allowing me to buy a used Harley Davidson motorcycle. I purchased it and learned how to drive it while heading home on the streets of Los Angeles. When I returned home, I proudly showed it to my brother, Paul, and took him for a ride.

Now that I was an expert, I showed Paul where the throttle, clutch, and brakes were located and suggested he take it for a spin. We went to a dead-end street far away from traffic where it would be safe, and off he went – that is, until he got half way down the block. At that point he wanted to slow down, but instead he turned the throttle the wrong way, quickly accelerating the cycle, heading for the house at the end of the block with its big bay window. I was running behind him yelling instructions, but they were useless. At the time I wasn't aware that the previous owner had modified the clutch so that it was now a "suicide clutch." I was terrified as he bounced over the curb heading straight for the bay window. Fortunately, the owners of the house had just watered their lawn and it was good and slippery, so the motorcycle flipped on its side. People hearing the commotion started to come out of their houses to see what was happening. Running up to the motorcycle, the motor still running and the back wheel spinning at what seemed like 40 miles an hour, I turned off the ignition.

I was greatly concerned about the extent of Paul's injuries. Fortunately, it was limited to a minor injury of his knee. As we were walking home I became concerned about the reaction of our parents. They might make me sell my Harley. So I asked Paul not to tell Mom and Dad and to try not to limp around them. As far as I know, they never found out about the incident.

It was with this Harley that I learned what reserve was all about. The motorcycle did not have a gas gauge on it; instead, it had a valve under the tank. I would drive the Harley with the valve in its "regular" position and when it would start to sputter, I would quickly reach down and turn the valve to "reserve", then I was driving on the reserve tank and had ample warning that I needed to fill up before the reserve ran out. Forgetting to switch the valve back to its "regular" position when I filled up the tank could end in disastrous consequences. I would ride merrily along, unaware of an impending problem, until all the gas was depleted and I stalled in the middle of traffic.

Running on Reserve

Let us now make an analogy to everyday life. Sometimes we carry on our activities, oblivious to the fact that we are on reserve, until our energy is depleted and we burn out as I did at age 19. Many of us in modern society are operating on "reserve" with more subtle but ultimately equally disastrous results. For some its first manifestation will be a heart attack or some other catastrophic event. We are stressed and it is affecting every area of our lives. It is causing us all the problems listed in earlier chapters.

Definition of Reserve and Its Synonyms

Let's define our terms. A *reserve* is something kept back or saved for future use. It is a buffer or cushion that is accessible to meet unexpected needs. It is a resource not normally called on but readily available. In the military the term is used to describe a force that is ready and available to augment the main force. In finances it is money set aside with no intent to use it. It is there only as a back-up for a "rainy day."

Richard Swenson refers to this as the need for "margin." He defines it as "*the amount allowed beyond that which is needed. It is something held in reserve for contingencies or unanticipated situations. Margin is the gap between rest and exhaustion, the space between breathing freely and suffocating. It is the leeway we once had between ourselves and our limits.*"[1]

You might ask, "What is the difference between pruning, that was discussed in the previous chapter, and reserve or margin?" In many ways they are similar. However, the idea of pruning is the *initial* drastic cutting back of one's excessively busy, fragmented life. It is also used appropriately to describe a periodic drastic cutting back when one has failed to keep an appropriate reserve or margin. On the other hand, the idea of reserve is the continuous, daily monitoring of one's activities and keeping them well below one's maximum capacity. If we carefully keep an adequate reserve, we seldom will have the need to do extensive pruning.

Using Your Units Wisely

Remember the Stress/Productivity/Satisfaction Response Curve in Chapter 1, page 27. You can increase your productivity up to about 125 percent, but over about 90 percent the amount of stress on the body increases exponentially and satisfaction drops drastically. Therefore the aim should be to live at 70 to 90 percent of your capacity. This will significantly decrease the amount of stress in your life. It will also allow for an unforeseen emergency with reserve energy, should that need occur. In later chapters we will discuss how to increase your efficient use of energy – but none of that is a substitute for keeping the demands on your system at a reasonable and manageable level.

God has given each of us a certain amount of energy. If you look at five-year-olds on the playground – they have energy to burn. They spontaneously skip and jump and run. Oh, to be young again! Even the college student can stay up most of the night and study for an exam, then function pretty well the next day. But what happens to that energy as we get older? It tends to decrease. If you visualize the senior citizen – what is your image? It's certainly not skipping and jumping and running, nor is it staying up all night. More likely you picture someone sitting in a chair reading a book or rocking on a front porch. With age, the available energy available to one does somewhat decrease. Furthermore, some people have innately more energy than others. In Figure 2, page 31, we suggested that most normal individuals have about 60 to 90 energy units. A rare person may have 100 units available to him each day. If I started out with 85 units a day at 19, I probably have 70 units a day now to utilize.

For a moment let's envision this like a charge account into which God is depositing energy units every morning. We'll arbitrarily suggest that God is giving you 64 units each day. If, on an average, you are awake 16 hours a day, that means that you have about four units available to you each waking hour. If you squander ten of those units by getting angry at a driver on the freeway, then you will have that many fewer units to use the rest of the day. If you exceed your daily limit, you will start the next day tired and stressed with fewer available units for that day.

What happens if you have been running a negative balance for months? Then chronic stress and fatigue set in. These can progress to exhaustion and potentially end up in burn-out. In time this cumulative stress load takes its toll on your body, mind, relationships, and spirituality.

Christ teaches in a parable about entrusting talents to his followers according to their abilities and desiring that they invest them wisely (see Matthew 25:14–30). Various translations refer to the talents as money, gold, goods, possessions, and property. Does it not follow that it could also refer to "energy"? So God has given each of us a certain amount of energy, and the question is how will we invest it – wisely or unwisely? The crux of the matter is not so much to wish for more energy, but to use the energy given to us wisely.

How Are You Now Using Your Units?

In Chapter 2 you were asked to think about your energy level. Now that you have read a good portion of this book, please consider this again. Do a brief inventory and evaluate, as best as you can, the question – how does your energy level compare with others? Are you a gifted person with 90 available units per day or an average person with about 75 units to work with each day? Perhaps you have marked fatigue and have to manage with 30 units per day. This may be a rough guess, but it illustrates the point. Hopefully you have done quite a bit of pruning already – if that is needed.

Now consider how you are investing the units God has given you. If you don't know where to start, you might write down how you use your time in the average week. Energy units are not the same as time (as we have previously discussed), for depending on the activity some things can consume two or three times the energy units in the same period of time as compared to another activity. But this is a starting point and you can refine it later.

Now look at the specific activities. Is every minute of your waking hours filled with some obligation or do you have some reserve? That is time that is not already obligated. Is it enough? Then consider your activities and obligations. Are there some activities that are especially draining?

How about people? Do you find that some seem to draw the energy right out of you? If so, they are using up your extra energy units. That doesn't necessarily mean you wouldn't continue a relationship with them, but you would need to consider the cost of being with those who drain your energy.

What about conflicts in your life, whether family, work, or church? Do you feel that you have many shoulds or oughts or musts? If so, add appropriate units to your load. Have there been many changes in your life? These will cause stress that utilizes energy as well.

Do you have appropriate control of your life? Are there people who are pressuring you to do things you would like to avoid, yet you yield to them? They may be wonderful things, even things for God, but if the main pressure is people pressure, be on guard.

Let's look at your finances. Do you have debts other then a home mortgage? Are your investments in risky assets? Do you have funds on hand that could carry you through a six-month period if you or your spouse lost his or her job? If you are in your 50s, are you set for retirement? If you answered "yes" to the first two questions or "no" to the second two questions, you are adding extra stress units to your life.

You may have a job where you have too little input; or at the other extreme, you may have responsibilities beyond your abilities in your job. Either extreme will add stress to your life and use up energy units.

From the questions posed above you have important clues as to where your energy might be wasted; in addition, your answers also suggest choices that you can make to decrease squandered energy units you are using each day and thereby to decrease your stress level.

This chapter addresses primarily external stresses. Internal drainers, or stresses, also affect the stress level, but we will focus primarily on these in subsequent chapters.

Decide How You Will Use Your Energy

Your energy is a valuable commodity. Jealously guard it. In doing that you are guarding your heart and your relationship to God. This will mean that you will monitor carefully the amount and kinds of activities in your life, thereby controlling your stress level. For most this will mean stress reduction. This requires courage, it means rearranging your life, and it may mean getting a different job, moving, or living with less income. It may mean saying "no" to some important friends. It will mean that you look at your total commitment, not only your time commitment but physical, psychological, and financial issues as well.

Remember that failure to decide how you will use your energy is, in fact, a choice. You will drift toward your weakness, whatever that may be. If your tendency is to say "yes" much of the time, you will be overcommitted. If your tendency is to avoid involvement, you will suffer from underactivity. Either way, you will sacrifice meaning in your life.

If your drift is toward excessive activity, like so many in this modern age, you are going to have to learn to say "no" to some very good and wonderful opportunities. Remember that we are in a spiritual battle and if the forces of evil can't tempt us with some of the crass sins, they will tempt us with good things that will rob us of God's best.

In Chapter 4 we discussed in some detail that the need is not the call and that Christ did not meet every need. Likewise the opportunity should not determine our action. The need or opportunity must be coupled with the fact that *God wants me* personally to pursue the particular activity. The person driven by needs or opportunities alone will be weary, frustrated, tired, and actually insensitive to God.

We, therefore, must learn to live with the needs and opportunities around us without feeling obligated or guilty if we cannot meet all of them. At the same time, we must not become indifferent to needs or opportunities. Satan would like us to fall into the trap of either extreme.

For some people the hardest words in the English language are "I'm sorry." For me it is the word "no." I would like to be able to say "yes" to everyone and everything, but obedience to Christ requires me at times to say "no."

Listen to God's Voice

The crucial aspect in all of this is, "In what activities would God have me involved?" When Christ was on the earth, he did not say "yes" to every request or opportunity. He was careful to do always those things that pleased his heavenly Father. He said, "I always do the things that are pleasing to Him [God]" (John 8:29). That is the one and only essential criterion – pleasing God in all that we do.

Paul Tournier sums it up well. He said:

> The more life is guided by God, the more it frees itself from fragmented toil. . . For this it is necessary to choose, to sacrifice a great many things. It is not necessary only to do what appears to be good, useful, or noble, but rather to do that which God wants. Remember David, when God kept him from building the Temple! It is a fine undertaking to want to build a temple for God, but to construct it when God does not want it, and when it is not God's chosen time, is time wasted. It is disobedience, not obedience. How many well-intentioned disobediences do our lives contain? That is the problem![2]

CHAPTER 19

THE POWER OF THOUGHTS

OUR MINDS ARE a stage with an endless stream of thoughts playing for our attention – some good, some bad, and often there are frequent reruns. Since the stage of our mind is a secret show (but not secret to God), we are tempted to indulge in many thoughts that we would never permit for general viewing. Nevertheless, on this stage the battles that shape our lives are fought. The kind of person we become is decided right here – in the thoughts that we choose to think. Our basic unregenerate nature is self-centered and coupled with this are the evil forces of darkness (see Ephesians 6:10–18), vying for every opportunity to steal the show. The longer we indulge in a performance the harder it becomes to change channels before a passing look develops into a full-length feature (see 2 Corinthians 10:5). Faulty thought patterns can easily become a way of life.

Invariably, the first step to getting ourselves in trouble, even sinning, is to indulge in thoughts that are not pleasing to God. David did not sin when, for a moment, he saw Bathsheba. But he undoubtedly sinned in his mind, even before he touched her, when he continued to "look upon" her. (The biblical account clearly outlines the steps leading to overt sin and its long-term results in 2 Samuel 11). Christ says that the indulgence of sin in our thought lives can be as sinful as the carrying out of the actual act (see Matthew 5:28).

So it is clear that thoughts are powerful. The world through radio, TV, billboards, our friends' comments or looks, sends us hundreds of messages each day. We interpret these messages and add to them our biases, thus sending ourselves thousands of messages every 24 hours. What we end up telling ourselves has a tremendous effect on our lives and well being. Some might contest these statements, saying, "Isn't this the power of positive thinking as advocated by Norman Vincent Peal or Robert E. Schuller?" Some would even associate giving any power to thoughts as a New Age phenomenon. It is true that some people may attribute almost infinite power to thoughts. Thoughts do not have unlimited power. We cannot do anything just because we want to or think we can.

Nevertheless, God has made our minds so that our thoughts have a real, albeit limited power. Proverbs tells us, "For as he thinketh in his heart, so is he" (23:7, KJV). Paul clearly appreciates this saying, "Meditate upon these things; give thyself wholly to them; that thy profiting may appear to all" (1 Timothy 4:15, KJV). The Scriptures are clear that what we think significantly affects our lives.

The Power of Thoughts

William Osler, often considered the founding father of American medicine, said over 100 years ago in reference to a tuberculosis patient, "It's just as important to know what's going on in the patient's mind as in his chest."[1] He was acutely aware of the tremendous power of the mind in healing the patient with tuberculosis.

Virtually everyone is aware of the placebo effect. If one wears a white coat and gives a person with, say arthritis, a little pink pill telling him or her it will do wonders for her pain – it will typically do wonders. In fact, you tell a person of the phenomenal success rate with two dozen others with pain worse then theirs, and presto, the little pink pill performs miracles in relieving the arthritic pain, even though it is only a colored sugar pill. This is a well-established scientific fact that operates around the world and there is evidence that it has worked throughout history.

Many frown on this and pass it off as "all in the head." It *is* all in the head, but it is nothing to be passed off. Facts are clear that our minds exercise a powerful influence over our bodies. This has often been referred to as the "Mind/Body Connection." Uncontroversial evidence exists that our minds do exercise a significant though limited influence on our bodies and our health. We may try to deny that fact, but it can be guaranteed that its effects will be operative in us – for better or for worse. If we don't understand it and use it to our advantage, it may well operate within us to our disadvantage.

If I cut myself, God has implanted within my body the ability to heal that cut. I don't understand much of the process, but it works anyway. This ability has limitations, but it nevertheless is present and performs a vital function. In the same fashion my mind contains certain self-healing mechanisms that affect my body. Essential is a positive belief that activates the healing processes in the system.[2]

Let's take a moment and look at the opposite of the placebo effect – *the nocebo effect*. The word "nocebo" comes from the Latin for "I will harm." In one study, residents who believed that they had been exposed to a toxic substance, had symptoms that they ascribed to the supposed exposure; when, in fact, there was absolutely no exposure to any hazardous material.

Some years ago when sarin and other deadly poisonous gases were released in Japanese subways, some passengers who were on trains where no such gas was present, became sick. In these situations the individuals heard of the traumatic situation and came down with symptoms that others had. Fortunately in this situation the symptoms were minor, such things as nausea, vomiting, and generally feeling ill. They were self-limiting and passed with time. But this phenomenon is not always so benign.[3]

In much of the western world there is the superstition that bad things happen on Friday the 13th. This self-fulfilling prophecy was verified in Finland where it was discovered that women had a 63 percent increase in traffic-related deaths on these "unlucky" days. Chinese and Japanese consider days that have the number "4" in them unlucky. Four is not used when numbering rooms in hotels and hospitals just like some of our western hotels don't have a 13th floor. In one study it was found that on those days there was a 13 percent increase in mortality, for all types of illnesses, over what would normally be expected. This was not true of Caucasians.[4]

In another study a group of women, "who believed that they were prone to heart disease, were nearly four times as likely to die as women with similar risk factors who didn't hold such fatalistic views. . . . Think sick – be sick! These people presume the worst, and that's just what they get. It is a self-fulfilling prophecy."[5]

It is now clear that our thoughts do affect bodily systems, including our nervous and hormonal system, blood pressure, pulse, platelet function, immune response, to name a few of the numerous effects our thoughts have on our bodily functions.[6]

No one can live unscathed from at least some traumatic events. Some people seem to have more then their share of such ordeals. But more important than the magnitude and number of such events is how we choose to deal with them. Studies of children, who have been traumatized due to a kidnaping, or adults, who have been exposed to the meltdown of a nuclear reactor, suggest that though damage is done by the original trauma, an important factor in the ultimate destructive influences on one's life is to what extent we replay the incident in our minds. With each rerun the incident and its resultant ill effects are indelibly etched a little deeper.

Even good or positive events can be viewed in a counterproductive fashion. Earlier in the book we discussed the fact that there has been a controversy in the field as to whether "good events" such as a promotion was an "uplifter" or added to one's cumulative stress load. We now have suggestive evidence that the answer to this depends on how a person views himself and the issue. If a "good" thing happens to a pessimist or to someone who thinks negatively about himself or herself, it adds to his or her stress load. If a "good" thing happens to someone who is optimistic about the issue and himself, it is much more likely to be an uplifter – that is, the issue adds energy and decreases the cumulative stress load. Thus, what we tell ourselves plays a crucial role in our lives and in our health.[7]

When we consider stress in our lives, we find three facets to consider. First, there is the stressor itself. Second, there is the reaction to the stress or activator. Third, there are the consequences of the reaction. In this section we are addressing the second facet – our reaction to the stress or activator. How we handle this makes a gigantic difference in the consequences that we reap. One study that evaluated how we respond to a given stress and its effect on Natural Killer Cell Activity concluded that "how one reacts to stress (coping) was thought to have more immunologic relevance than how much objective stress was experienced."[8]

How to Change Your Thoughts

The world saw the TV images of planes crashing into the World Trade Center on September 11, 2001. That was a stressor that most of us were exposed to. But those who chose to dwell on that stressor reaped the consequences. There is a direct correlation with the number of hours of TV that an individual watched of the disaster and the likelihood of a serious stress reaction. Those that watched 13 or more hours that day ultimately had a 58 percent probability of having a *substantial* stress reaction! What our minds dwell upon greatly affects our lives.[9]

Martin Luther once made a statement that you can't stop the birds from flying over your head, but you can keep them from building a nest in your hair. We do not have absolute control over our thoughts, nor does God hold us responsible for every deviant or destructive thought that comes to our minds. However, he certainly holds us responsible for what we dwell on and to some extent that will affect the frequency and strength of deviant thoughts that come to our minds.

Our Minds Are Not a Vacuum

Our minds and their thoughts can never be a vacuum. If we do not actively fill our minds with good constructive thoughts during all the free moments we have, the mind will take the course of least resistance and fill itself with self-centered thoughts, which often prove to be destructive (see Matthew 12:43–45). In a sense, our minds should be like a compass which, if working properly, always points north unless a magnet is brought close to it. As long as the magnet is within a few inches of the compass, it will point to the magnet, but as soon as the magnet is removed, the compass immediately returns to north. So we should apply our minds completely to the task at hand. But as soon as our minds are free, they should not spin aimlessly but return immediately to constructive pursuits and to God.

Displacement

Displacement is another important principle. I remember a little experiment in high school chemistry on displacement. If you turn an empty glass upside down and light a match at its mouth you fill it with smoke. Then you can turn it over and the smoke tends to stay in the glass. You can move it, try and pour it out, but, for the most part, the smoke remains in the glass. But if you fill the glass with water, presto, the smoke is gone. Thus, as our minds are filled with positive wholesome thoughts, negative, destructive thoughts will be displaced and less able to dominate our lives.

Thought Stopping

If, when a deviant thought comes to mind, an effective approach is "thought stopping;" that is, to the best of our ability, to stop thinking the counterproductive thought as soon as you are aware of it. Occasionally I will suggest to patients who are having trouble in this area, to wear a rubber band around their wrist. The moment they become aware that they are obsessing about something that is not helpful, they should pull slightly on the rubber band, allowing it to pop, and the moment it does so to think about something else. It is similar to the way we would discipline our children with regard to TV-watching. They may flip through the channels and be tempted to stop and watch some seductive junk. We would advise them just to change channels or turn off the TV. No ifs, ands, buts, or later; just do it now!

Another analogy is the question, "How do you get rid of a hot potato?" The answer is obvious – you just drop it. As soon as you sense that it is hot, you drop it. So it is with junk on TV or inappropriate thoughts. The moment we are aware that we are watching, listening, or thinking something that is unwholesome we need to develop a knee-jerk reaction to stop it, and focus on something of value. When this is a well-established habit, it will be easier to do; plus we will be less prone to think about unhealthy subjects in the first place.

Replace the Lies

Are you telling yourself lies? Unfortunately, most of us do: "I'm no good – I can't do anything right – I'll never amount to anything – that was a stupid thing that I said – God doesn't love me" are some of the lies that we often tell ourselves. The originator of lies is Satan, and it started in the Garden of Eden with Satan questioning the motives of God. Eve bought the lie, and it's all history since then. Satan remains the accuser of the brethren, accusing us continually (Revelation 12:10). It is crucial that we don't buy into these lies. So we need to evaluate the thoughts that come to mind as to whether they are truth, God's truth, or, in fact, Satan's lies. If we believe lies, they have the potential of being as powerful as if they were truth.

The Scriptures make a very strong point of this. Paul exhorts us to "set [our] minds on the things above" (Colossians 3:2) and tells us, "whatever is true, whatever is honorable, whatever is right, whatever is pure, whatever is lovely, whatever is of good repute . . . let your mind dwell on these things" (Philippians 4:8).

Constructive Reappraisal

Most situations or events can be viewed in several different ways. Some people see virtually everything through dark gray glasses. Every experience is negative. This is not to advise you to put on rose-colored glasses and glibly see everything as rosy. However, many things in our lives can appropriately be viewed in a negative or a positive light. In a book describing how individuals survived horrendous tragedies, an important tool used most successfully was "to redefine life's problems so that they don't seem as 'awful' or 'intolerable.'"[10]

During our daughter Susan's remission, her fiancé, John, had made arrangements to take her out for dinner and dancing at her college's "Vienna Night." But just before the evening arrived, the dreaded news of a recurrence of her leukemia necessitated that she return to the hospital. They could have moped and been discouraged. Instead, to make the very best of it, John brought in a meal, dimmed the lights in her room, lit some candles, and created "Vienna Night" in her hospital room. Due to the possibility of infection she was in isolation, so John had to wear a mask; Susan was hooked up to an IV for medications. However, if you had peeked into the room, you could have seen them dancing to Viennese music coming from a boom box. There was no denial of her medical condition, but they made the choice to make the most of the moment, to reappraise the situation, and to put it in the best possible light.

A Time to Change Your Environment

Sometimes we need to remove ourselves from situations where we are fed excessive negative thoughts. Certain relationships may continually pull us down. If that can't be appropriately changed, we may need to remove ourselves from that environment. Situations or relationships that were helpful at one point in life may change and become a destructive force. For example, a support group or educating ourselves about our illnesses can be very helpful. But in time this can change. One author writes:

> Some patients report that although some group interaction is helpful, too much contact or negative contact causes further preoccupation with CFIDS [Chronic Fatigue Immune Dysfunction Syndrome]. Bill says, "I have decided for the time being to divorce myself, where possible, from . . . support groups and reading the literature. I found that, after a while, these contacts were making me more obsessed with the illness." Such is often the case when complaining becomes the main focus of a group.[11]

Evaluate Your Thoughts

You may want to take a day or two and record each thought that you have. Do it confidentially and be ruthlessly honest. Many are amazed to see what they write and have been thinking for years. Then alongside each significant thought evaluate the validity of it. Where did I learn this thought? Is it a lie from Satan? Is the thought logical, helpful, or true? Is it pleasing to God? What are the potential positive and negative effects of the thought? How is this thought affecting my life? Would God have me change the thought; and if so, to what?

CHAPTER 20

THE POWER OF THE PRESENT MOMENT

My BROTHER, PAUL, was taken captive by Congolese rebels, beaten, and eventually killed. It all started in 1960 when the Congo obtained its independence from Belgium. As a result, virtually all the doctors left the country. Hearing of the desperate need there, my brother, a surgeon, went to the Congo for four months to help. At the end of his tour the Congolese people asked him to return. It was not an easy decision. But ultimately he returned to the northwest part of the country with his wife and two small children to serve 100,000 people who were without a single doctor.

He was there less than two years when warring factions among the Congolese started fighting for control of the nation and civil war followed. Rival forces were advancing on his area, so Paul took his nurse and family to safety and went back to his hospital to continue caring for numerous sick patients. He had planned an escape route, but it was unlikely that the rebel forces would come to that remote area and even if they did, it was not logical that they would hurt him. So he stayed and ministered to his patients.

But the rebel forces did come, took him captive, and beat him. He was able to write a couple of letters during his three months in captivity and we were able to talk to some fellow prisoners who later escaped. In one letter he wrote, "I was wrong to try to stay, but I feel I put it all into God's hands and must leave it there." He refused to speculate about the future or mope about the past. Instead, he actively engaged in helping other prisoners who were in need of his attention. He was literally living in "the moment," though he had ample opportunity to live in the past or future. Paul felt he had to live day-to-day. He had one assurance though: "Where I go to from here I know not, only that it will be with Him." His last entry in his New Testament, the night before he was killed, contained one word – "peace."

William Osler, a world-renowned physician at the turn of the 20th century, used to speak about living in "day-tight compartments."[1] By this he meant that most of one's energy and attention should be focused on the tasks that lie within the present 24-hour period. For me, living in "the present moment" means living and focusing primarily on the present – the task at hand. It is not criticizing myself for something I didn't do last night, or even focusing on what I am going to do tomorrow. It is primarily focusing on the job at hand, the situation in which I now find myself, or the people with whom I am right now.

The Scriptural Mandate

This is clearly a scriptural mandate. Christ included some beautiful exhortations along this line in the Sermon on the Mount when he said, "Therefore I bid you put away anxious thoughts . . . Instead, give first place to his Kingdom and to what he requires, and he will provide you with all these other things. So do not be anxious about tomorrow; tomorrow will look after itself. Each day has troubles enough of its own" (Matthew 6:25–34, NEB, TEV). In other words, we have our hands full living for the present without wasting precious energy on another segment of time for which we can do nothing at this moment. *In fact, today's neglect will be tomorrow's regret* and we will become weary in the process. *The Message* renders this passage like this: "Give your entire attention to what God is doing right now, and don't get worked up about what may or may not happen tomorrow. God will help you deal with whatever hard things come up when the time comes" (Matthew 6:34, MSG).

Solomon tells us, "Do not boast about tomorrow, for you do not know what a day may bring forth" (Proverbs 27:1). James picks up on this same theme, warning us that we don't know what a day will bring (see James 5:12–15). Regarding the past, Isaiah tells us, "Forget the former things; do not dwell on the past" (Isaiah 43:18, NIV). The Apostle Paul continues this focus, advising us to forget those things which are in the past (see Philippians 3:13).

The Present Moment Is the Only Moment We Have

In reality the present moment is the only one we have. We don't have tomorrow. Our lives may be snuffed out before it ever arrives. The past is gone. It is just a memory that cannot be relived or, in fact, changed. We only have today – this moment – now! So we should make the very most of it – live it to its fullest.

Results of Living in the Past or Future

When we live in the regrets of the past or the worries of the future, we neither help the past nor the future. In fact we burn up vital energy units that are totally wasted. Furthermore, our minds and thoughts are elsewhere and we have fewer energy units to use on the present. We are more likely then to blow the present and have new regrets tomorrow about what we messed up today. It can easily become a vicious, destructive cycle.

Even the faithful sufferer Job says, "For the thing that I fear comes upon me, and what I dread befalls me" (Job 3:25). Frequently the more anxious we become over the possibilities that a given undesirable event will occur, the greater is the likelihood that it will, in fact, occur. Self-fulfilling prophecies really do occur. All of this leads to internal stress and fatigue.

Why We Live in the Past or Future

Why do we live in the past? Certainly, if we conclude that the past was better than the present, we are prone to live in the past. This is especially true for senior citizens or those with terminal or chronic illness, including severe fatigue. This robs us of a meaningful life, happiness, and purpose. King Solomon said, "Do not say, 'Why is it that the former days were better than these?' For it is not from wisdom that you ask about this" (Ecclesiastes 7:10).

Still others nurse the past of "could-have-beens," reliving its regrets, disappointments, resentments, bitterness, and guilt. These acts may have been committed by the person or by someone else against him. Many resent what they think they may have missed in the past; this destroys any possibility of achieving meaningful life.

Living in the present does take some effort; new demands, issues, and battles have to be faced, and it requires becoming engaged in positive pursuits. It takes work. Unfortunately, some people would rather either live in the past or future than expend the effort necessary to live fully in the present. They may vacillate between living in the past and in the future, which is often done with much anger and resentment. One can almost see the energy units going up in smoke.

Living in the future can also be a problem to many, especially the younger generation. They often imagine what life will be like when they finish school, get married, become established in a job, and have their financial problems resolved. On and on the illusion goes. If this type of thinking persists, one day it will dawn on the person that "the future" was but a mirage. It is now past. Then, instead of hope and optimism, discouragement, despair, guilt, and the tendency to live in the regrets of the past often set in.

One's living in the future can be in anticipation of positive things that one doesn't appreciate in the now, or it can take the form of worry about the future – the "what ifs." This is primarily what Christ is addressing in the Sermon on the Mount when he admonishes us not to worry about having our needs met tomorrow (see Matthew 6:34).

When It Is Appropriate to *Think* About the Past or Future

It is always appropriate to *live* in the now, but it is clearly appropriate, at times and in the right ways, to *think* about the past or the future. In fact many passages in the Scriptures tell us to remember the great things God has done and to heed and learn from the mistakes and sins of bygone days. Certainly if we have sinned or owe someone an apology, dealing with that is crucial. But confess it, or in some situations make amends, learn from it, then *drop it.* Even if you have been wrong in a matter, deal with it appropriately, then let it go. Don't let Satan continue to use it against you. Learn from the past and move on.

Some planning is appropriate for the future, and as we will discuss in a later chapter, faith and hope are important ingredients in a healthy life. These involve some aspirations, plans, or looking into the future. But here again, take whatever time is necessary, but don't dwell on it so that you rob yourself of energy needed to live in the present moment.

Living in the Present Moment

The solution for living in the present involves learning to forget the past, trusting God for the future, and living each day to its fullest. It takes a firm decision to live fully in the present moment. A choice must be made. I will give my thoughts and energy to now. I will practice appreciating the richness of the present moment. I will endeavor to enjoy it. I will begin right where I find myself. Crucial to me as a Christian is to live in "now obedience," that is, I will not only live fully in the now but I will be careful to do that which God wants me to do – now. If I start to fail, I utilize the principles on handling my thoughts discussed in Chapter 19. The now contains all that is needed for a full and meaningful life. Thomas Kelly describes these things in his book, saying, "Past matters less and the future matters less, for the Now contains all that is needed for the absolute satisfaction of our deepest cravings. The present Now is not something from which we hurriedly escape . . . we stand erect, in the holy Now, joyous, serene, assured, unafraid."[2]

In the last few years I have had several friends with life-threatening illnesses. I have asked myself, "How would I live if I had six months to live? And, in fact, live that way?" I have been consciously practicing this philosophy and it does make a significant positive difference. Johann Christoph Arnold writes about a person who developed "hopeless" cancer, who said:

> Living with cancer, you begin to realize that you have to make use of every day; each minute becomes precious. You know, we spend a lot of our time dealing with petty problems and thinking petty thoughts, and I've come to see that that's a complete drain and has to go. There's anger, envy, every kind of emotion you have in a relationship with anybody. People hurt each other, and get hurt over little things. I've come to see that it's stupid—just plain stupid—to waste time on those things. Dale and I have talked about how we've probably wasted years of our lives carrying little grudges and things that we couldn't work out, or struggling to find enough humility to confront a problem, or apologize, or whatever.

The present moment — the time we have right now — is the same for you as it is for me or for anyone. It's all we have. We tend to think, "I'll do that tomorrow;" or, "I'll wait till I have time to follow through on that . . ." But we actually don't have tomorrow. None of us does. We only have today and we only have each other . . . I can remember yesterday, but I can't relive yesterday, and I have no idea what tomorrow will bring. All I have is just right now.[3]

As I contemplate living in the now, an example vividly comes to mind. One of the happiest days of my life was the day Susan was married. I don't think that one person in the church had a dry eye when Susan and John said their wedding vows "as long as we both shall live." Everyone knew that Susan had just gotten out of the hospital after a recurrence of her leukemia and there was little assurance that she would live very long. But this was a day to celebrate. We did not think about the future — oh yes, we knew all the facts — but we were focusing on the day. Though there were moments of tears, it was a wonderful, edifying day. We had decided to live in the present moment — to its fullest. It was one of the happiest days of my life.

CHAPTER 21

THE POWER OF RELATIONSHIPS

"FRIENDS MAKE GOOD medicine", said a slogan on a shopping bag in California and, "A friend, not an apple a day, will keep the doctor away," reported an editorial in *The Journal of the American Medical Association*.[1]

King Solomon appreciated this in antiquity. He advised, "Two people can accomplish more than twice as much as one . . . If one person falls, the other can reach out and help. But people who are alone when they fall are in real trouble" (Ecclesiastes 4:9–10, NLT). The biblical writer said, "Not forsaking our own assembling together" and James urged us to confess our faults one to another, and to pray one for another, that we may be healed (Hebrews 10:25, James 5:16). These are just a few of many passages in the Scriptures that emphasize the importance of people, relationships, and, at times, confession.

So what are the benefits of meaningful relationships? Social people tend to be happier. Social support is a buffer against stressful life events. Asthma, ulcers, hypertension, upper respiratory infections, immune response, anxiety, and depression are all helped by social or confiding relationships with others. Patients with various cancers survived longer with good support systems. Failure to confide after a traumatic event increases the incidence of stress-related disease and long-term health problems, including cancer and heart disease. When stress levels are high, individuals without emotional support suffer as much as ten times the incidence of physical and emotional illness, and mortality is 2 ½ times higher when compared with those with good social support systems.[2]

Individuals who are not married have a higher mortality rate for virtually all types of diseases. Widows have a significantly increased mortality rate up to ten years after the death of their spouses. The death rate for widowers is three to five times higher than that of married men. All of this data reveals the importance of close relationships. Furthermore, widows and widowers who did not have supportive relationships report more physical symptoms such as arthralgias, panic, sweating, weight loss, depression, increased use of alcohol and tranquilizers, diminished work capacity, and tiredness. Those that had two or more individuals giving emotional and practical assistance resolved their grief process faster, felt better, made new friends, and began new activities. All of this further substantiates the importance of relationships in our lives, especially in times of stress.[3]

To date there are no completed studies on socializing and confiding with patients with Chronic Fatigue Syndrome, Fibromyalgia, and related illnesses. However, the evidence is so strong for so many other illnesses that it is reasonable to extrapolate that individuals with these illnesses would in fact be helped as well.

What Types of Relationships Are Helpful?

Social. One study noted 12 types of social networks. These were relationships with one's spouse, parents, parents-in-law, children, other close family members, close neighbors, friends, workmates, schoolmates, fellow volunteers, members of groups without religious affiliations, and members of religious groups. The researchers found that those with three or less of these relationships had four times the risk of infection as compared to those with six or more different relationships. It was the diversity of the network that mattered, not the sheer number of network members. The greater the number of different social ties the better the individuals did. Other studies have shown that the greater the number of social affiliations people had, actually lowered their mortality rates.[4]

Prayer. In other sections of this book we have noted in detail the importance and value of our relationship with God. One aspect of that relationship is prayer. There are numerous passages and examples throughout the Scriptures of the Lord relating to us and answering our prayers to him. For example, the Psalmist petitioned God saying, "In my anguish I cried to the LORD, and he answered by setting me free" (Psalm 118:5, NIV). James tells us, "The prayer of a righteous man is powerful and effective" (James 5:16, NIV). Of interest is that medical science is starting to verify the fact that prayer is indeed effective in decreasing illness and increasing one's sense of well being.[5]

Other Types of Relationships. The presence of pets in a home repeatedly has been noted to be helpful. Watching fish in an aquarium or petting animals lowers the pulse rate and one's blood pressure. Involvement with pets decreases depression, and has been found to significantly decrease mortality after heart attacks. In fact, individuals who owned a pet were six times more likely to be alive one year after hospitalization as compared to those who did not own a pet.[6]

Alternate Ways of Confiding

Just the process of communicating significant events and the feelings associated with those events can be therapeutic. Journaling or writing about significant events, especially traumatic events, has been shown to decrease symptoms of asthma, increase mobility in arthritic patients, improve immune response, and decrease the need of health care. It is interesting to note that handwritten journaling was more helpful than typing a diary entry on a computer. Even talking to a tape recorder or sitting in a dark room with an imaginary confessor behind a curtain has been shown to benefit the individual.[7]

Criteria

Thus a good friend is invaluable. This does not necessarily mean one who advises or who has had professional training. But it must be a person who is objective, a good listener, and able to draw you out, thus helping you clarify tangled thoughts without condoning or condemning you.

The ability to confide honestly in others without fear of criticism or reprisal is an important ingredient. For instance, women with breast cancer survive longer if they are able to share their negative feelings and distress with others. However, not everyone is able to handle such feelings.[8]

Conclusion

One scientific writer has said, "Happiness is related to sharing one's life circumstances through close personal relationships. . . It seems that one of the basic laws of the emotions is that if you share joy, it increases, and if you share pain, it decreases."[9] The author of *Winning Life's Toughest Battles* has written, "Navy Lieutenant-Commander John S. McCain, III concluded that, 'The most important thing for survival as a POW was communication with someone, even if it was only a wave or a wink, a tap on a wall, or to have a guy put his thumb up. It made all the difference.'"[10]

Investigators are now talking not just about the Mind/Body connection in disease and health, but are now talking about the Mind/Social/Body connection. That is, each of these plays a vital role in contributing either to illness or to health. So to be able to share your life with others is invaluable. This is especially true of individuals with Chronic Fatigue Syndrome, Fibromyalgia, and related disorders as they are prone to isolate themselves – which generally aggravates the situation. It can be healing to verbalize your situation to others. It will often lead to the awareness that others struggle with comparable problems. Few of us are unique in that with which we have to deal.

CHAPTER 22

THE POWER OF UPLIFTS

IN EARLIER CHAPTERS we talked about "drainers" – illnesses, thoughts, and activities that can and do drain us of vital energy. In subsequent chapters we have discussed thoughts and behavior that can enhance our energy. In the scientific literature these are often referred to as "uplifts." As the name implies, these can give you a lift, energize you, and enable you to cope better with difficulties and problems. They are your positive experiences that serve as buffers against stress and its disorders. They are sustainers and restorers that prevent or attenuate the effects of stress. They can improve your feelings, enhance your peace, satisfaction, happiness, joy, and help the immune system. They have been shown to minimize the effects of illness whether one has work-related stress, Coronary Artery Disease, AIDS, or Chronic Fatigue Syndrome, to name a few of the illnesses shown to be helped by uplifts.[1]

What are some examples of specific uplifts? They are such things as enjoying a good night's sleep, eliminating resentment, having appropriate control of your life, maintaining a reserve, using various types of stress management, reframing thoughts to view them in constructive ways, living in the present, and continuing helpful relationships. In this chapter and throughout this entire section of the book on "The Energizers" we are elaborating on a number of specific uplifts.[2]

The Power of Exercise

Exercise is a powerful uplifter. The Scriptures support this saying, "Physical exercise has some value" (1 Timothy 4:8, NLT). Studies have shown numerous benefits, such as: reducing fatal myocardial infarctions by up to 25 percent; lowering blood pressure, enhancing sleep; improving moods; especially in depressed or anxious individuals; decreasing anger and distrust; lessening feelings of stress and the consequences of it; increasing life expectancy; improving thinking; reducing fatigue; and improving feelings of overall well-being.[3]

Though it might seem counterintuitive, individuals with illnesses such as Chronic Fatigue Syndrome or Fibromyalgia have been shown to benefit from an appropriate exercise program. Though workers in the field differ in their opinion on these matters, avoidance of exercise in Chronic Fatigue Syndrome patients has been associated with a worse prognosis.[4]

How much exercise is appropriate? For the physically healthy individual you can find recommendations varying from ten minutes a day of aerobic exercise, increasing one's heart rate to at least 60 percent of one's maximum, to other studies that recommend 30 minutes or more daily, working up to 80 percent of one's capacity. However, the preponderance of these studies encourages 30 minutes three times a week. For people with physical limitations the exercise program must be individualized. In individuals with Chronic Fatigue Syndrome it is recommended that they start very very slowly and gradually increase the amount of exercise. It is always preferable to be cleared for exercise by an appropriate physician. Generally it is recommended that a person exercise earlier in the day and avoid exercise several hours before bedtime.[5]

The Power of Relaxation

The Psalmist advises us to, "Be still, and know that I am God." Other translations render it: "Cease striving," or "Be silent, and know that I am God!" (Psalm 46:10, KJV, NAS, NLT). How do you do that? How do you disengage from the hurry and worry pace where most of us find ourselves? One possible approach has been advocated by Dr. Herbert Benson and his colleagues from the Mind/Body Medical Institute and Harvard Medical School. They have investigated extensively what he refers to as "the relaxation response." He describes this as the opposite of the "fight-or-flight response." Chronic hurry and stress are destructive. On the other hand, slowing everything down and relaxing, in a sense, "wiping the slate clean" of the input overload, has been shown to lower blood pressure, heart rate, breathing, and metabolic rate. Furthermore, it has been demonstrated that relaxation decreases muscle tension, pain, insomnia, cardiac arrhythmias, anxiety, depression, headaches, and hostility. It has helped infertile women become pregnant, decrease PMS symptoms, and cancer patients have noted fewer symptoms as a result of relaxation. It counters the tendency toward hypertension, heart attacks, and strokes.[6]

The technique Dr. Benson recommends is simple. Find a comfortable quiet place and dismiss all the extraneous external and internal "noise." To assist in this exercise, Dr Benson recommends focusing on a word or phrase. An example would be a phrase from the Lord's prayer such as "Our Father who art in heaven," or from the 23rd Psalm focusing on the clause "The Lord is my Shepherd," or from the 46th Psalm on the clause "Be still, and know that I am God." If, at this point your mind wanders, just dismiss the intrusive thought without making a big deal out of it; then return to slow breathing, thinking or saying the word or phrase each time you exhale. Usually it's preferable to close your eyes, although that is not necessary. Continue in a relaxed state, focusing on a single thought and disregard all other thoughts. As the mind quiets down, the body follows suit. For maximum benefit Dr. Benson recommends doing this exercise 20 minutes twice a day.

Many authors recommend a sort of mini-relaxation that can be utilized almost anywhere when you need to slow down and relax. You can just sit quietly with arms and hands in a comfortable position, possibly with your hands resting in your lap. Breathe with your diaphragm, taking slow breaths, focusing on your breathing, or on "nothing," or on a single positive thought as you would in the relaxation response. A few minutes of this can be helpful.

This is not meditation, which we will discuss in Chapter 26, but it is reducing the constant bombardment of external and internal thoughts and ideas that stimulate our minds and thus our bodies. We will take this one step further in Chapter 25 where we discuss "Focusing."

The Power of Humor

The book of Proverbs is as contemporary today as when it was originally written. Its sage advice for us today is: "When a man is gloomy, everything seems to go wrong; when he is cheerful, everything seems right! . . . A cheerful heart is good medicine, but a broken spirit saps a person's strength" (Proverbs 15:15, TLB; 17:22, NLT).

You might argue that if you are ill, suffering from fatigue or stress, you won't feel like or want to be around humor. It is true that if we are around someone struggling with symptoms or an illness, we must be sensitive to that person. But sometimes in the seemingly worst situations humor can be appropriate and helpful. Viktor Frankl, writing about his prison camp experience, says, "Humor was another of the soul's weapons in the fight for self-preservation."[7]

During my daughter's struggle with leukemia we not only cried together, but we laughed together. We hooked up a VCR to the hospital TV and watched movies together, sometimes of a humorous nature. One of Susan's isolation rooms did not have a bath or shower and she couldn't leave the room. After a while she began to detest the bed baths. So one evening two of her friends sneaked up the back stairs of the hospital with a child's wading pool and put it in her room. Now she could take warm tap water from the sink and fill up the wading pool and take a bath. Needless to say we all had a good laugh over this one. Norman Cousins in the 1970s and 80s promoted the role humor has as a treatment for illness.

Other Uplifts

Variety, Diversion, Hobbies

Almost 30 years ago I wrote the following paragraph: "Recently I made a list of exciting things I would like to do. I found, somewhat to my surprise, that the list included not only some things that particularly interested me but good constructive activities for God's work, my family, and society at large. One of the items on the list was to learn how to ski. So this winter our entire family took beginning skiing lessons and had a great time in the process. This might seem like a small thing, but out of such small things are the spice of life. Although I will be 40 this year, I have decided that no matter how old I get, this is one dog, as the saying goes, who will be endeavoring to learn new tricks the rest of his life – the Lord willing."

Today I am still skiing and enjoying it. The point is to try some new things. Experiment with some new hobbies. Set aside some days where the screen is off – that is, the TV and the computer. If you are very busy, stay home if at all possible. Develop a sense of play and an attitude of wonder in your life.

Diet and Nutrition

Our bodies are the temple of the Holy Spirit; therefore it is incumbent upon us that we take care of them as stewards of God (1 Corinthians 3:16). Clearly diet and nutrition are an extremely important facet of this. Poor dietary habits are rampant in our fast-food world and these need to be avoided. As we discussed in Chapter 10, a well balanced diet, eating from the basic food groups is vital; a multivitamin is valuable. Beyond this it becomes difficult to make recommendations based on good scientific information. The bottom line would be to follow basic sound food recommendations and avoid expensive or unusual dietary regimes. Of course, if you have a diagnosed medical disorder that requires special dietary regimes, such as diabetes, follow your doctor's advice.

CHAPTER 23

THE POWER OF HOPE AND OPTIMISM

WHEN YOU TALK to survivors of horrendous ordeals, such as prisoners of war or those who survived Nazi concentration camps, a crucial ingredient to survival is always hope. One psychiatrist found that the most important ingredient needed to survive the Nazi death camps was "blind, naked hope," which he defined as being the kind of hope a person has to have when, humanly speaking, he can see no reason to hope. If hope was lost, seldom did the prisoner survive. In concentration camps there was always uncertainty – "Would I live another day, would I be beat, how cold would it be, would there be any food, and will I ultimately survive anyway?" When the prisoner was unwilling to deal with these uncertainties, he typically traded his ration of a few spoonfuls of soup for a cigarette. He would get a fleeting puff of satisfaction before his certain demise.[1]

When we are confronted with any chronic form of illness – its daily discomfort and its uncertain outcome – we face similar struggles. We can obtain a fleeting, morbid satisfaction from pessimism and bitterness, which is sure to seal a fatalistic consequence.

In fact it takes little effort to despair. Even if you think the outcome will be catastrophic, at least there is certainty. Being hopeless carries the idea of being helpless, having lost control, then yielding to that loss of control and a more predictable, albeit, negative outcome. You won't have any surprises, nor will you be disappointed. You expect a negative outcome and regardless of what might otherwise occur, the negative outcome is now virtually assured. It becomes a self-fulfilling prophecy. The pessimist will become resigned, negative, trapped, introspective, and often hostile and blaming. All of this further complicates his or her predicament. But it seems to be an easier approach to the problem.

On the other hand, hope requires effort. It is a choice, a decision, a commitment. Hope always implies a certain level of uncertainty. As humans we find uncertainty uncomfortable. Hope requires a risk that what we are hoping for may not be realized. Hope forces one to envision the future and take action that runs the risk of failing. After all, if it is certain, it is no longer hope.

The Scriptures attest to this saying, "But hope that is seen is no hope at all. Who hopes for what he already has?" (Romans 8:24-25, NIV). Fortunately, God has given us the ability to hope which is vital if we are going to solve many of the problems of life.[2]

Definition

Hope is the belief that what is wanted can be had, or that events will turn out for the best. It includes a look forward to something that is desired and about which one has reasonable confidence that it will, in fact, take place. Optimism is the tendency to look on the more favorable side of the potential outcome; it is the belief that good will predominate.

In this chapter the concept of hope is used in a broad sense and not limited to a religious connotation. We are looking at how hopeful or optimistic thinking positively affects the mind and body. In a later chapter we will talk about faith and focus on hope or faith that has as its object the Person of God.

Consequences of Pessimism

Before we turn our attention to hope or optimism, let us first look at some of the results of pessimism:[3]

- Pessimists report more illnesses and rate their health more poorly.
- Pessimists followed 20-35 years were found to have a higher incidence of poor health.
- Elderly pessimistic men showed a significant increase in mortality.

Benefits of Optimism

On the other hand hopefulness and optimism result in:[4]

- A greater sense of wellbeing.
- A greater ability to cope with stressful life events.
- A greater satisfaction from relationships.
- Fewer physical symptoms and faster healing after surgery.
- Improved survival in burn, renal transplant, and cardiac patients.
- Increased survival in natural disasters and concentration camps.
- A 50 percent reduction of death over a 30-year period.
- Positive changes in body chemistry and immune function. In fact, "thoughts, expectations and hopes affect the body's stress reactions more than the actual stressful experience itself."

This does not purport to be an exhaustive study on the benefits of hope. We could add numerous additional research findings; however, we have listed enough benefits so that you can get a sense of how crucial hope is. For many, it literally can make the difference between getting well or remaining ill. E. Stanley Jones was a well-known evangelist whose very life was a demonstration of hope – which he called the "Divine Yes" – saying "Yes" to God and "Yes" to life. In his last book, written at 88 years of age, despite a crippling stroke, he gave one of the secrets of his life of hope: "I have learned that if you are blocked on one road in life, you can always find another that will open up for you." God gave a similar reason for hope to the nation of Israel when he promised he would transform her "Valley of Troubles into a Door of Hope" (Hosea 2:15, TLB).[5]

How to Become More Hopeful

How do you nurture hope in your life? Probably the best starting place is to envision, with God's help, one or several possible optimistic scenarios for your future. Pray about it and dream. Stress expert Shlomo Bresnitz wrote that hope takes energy: "It means finding something to build on – an unthinkable task if your energies are consumed by remorse. 'One has to . . . tell oneself some stories with happy endings.'"[6] At the same time it is important that you stop dwelling on negative scenarios. One author affirms that to be more hopeful means "ceasing to dwell on your fears or dreary prognoses or feelings that you can never again be happy or well. And in their place you find reasons for hope."[7]

Other things you can do to foster hope are:[8]

- Foster the spiritual side to your life, as studies have shown that people with a spiritual belief are both more optimistic and happier than those that do not encourage spirituality.
- Decide that you will be honest and look at all sides of a situation, but then you will embrace the hopeful/optimistic perspective.
- Associate with hopeful, optimistic people.
- List things for which you are grateful. Studies have found that people who wrote down five things for which they were grateful in weekly or daily journals were not only more joyful, but they were healthier, less stressed, and more optimistic.
- Embrace the fact that God has created you for a particular purpose; look for and be open to what that might be (see 2 Timothy 1:9). Consider how God might use you in your current situation.
- Choose to view life from God's perspective. When you do this and are personally aligned to his will in your life, you cannot help but be hopeful. This principle is exemplified in the Scriptures: "I would have despaired unless I had believed that I would see the goodness of the Lord in the land of the living" (Psalm 40:5; 27:13).

Studies have shown that individuals may have a genetic tendency toward either pessimism and despair, or optimism and hope; fortunately these tendencies are not fixed. Your hopefulness can be increased to an extent that makes a significant difference in your life. You can make changes in how you choose to view yourself and the world around you.

It is interesting to note that individuals who eventually develop significant fatigue, on the average, tended to have higher scores on pessimism before they came down with their symptoms. No one knows if this was a factor in their developing fatigue. Regardless, it is a fact that being hopeful about your future is an important step toward your recovery.[9]

So if you are struggling with fatigue or other stresses and if you feel at the end of your rope with personal resources exhausted, that is the opportune time to start, with God's help, to be hopeful. A choice is involved.

CHAPTER 24

THE POWER OF FAITH

CHARLES DARWIN IN the 19th century and Sigmund Freud in the early 20th century catalyzed an anti-faith environment throughout much of the scientific world. Freud termed the religiously committed individual as a "neurotic" and his followers developed the tendency to equate religion with pathologic religiosity or even emotional disturbance. They concluded that religion or faith was bad for one's health but never scientifically studied it. The voices in the academic wilderness such as Dr. William Osler, who wrote about "the faith that heals," in 1910, and the Philosopher and Psychologist William James of Harvard, who dealt with faith and religious experience, were largely ignored. Though we were moving into the scientific age, no one was studying faith in a scientific way. But that is not surprising.

At about the time Darwin was writing *On the Origin of Species* and Freud was born, Ignaz Philipp Semmelweis was doing his own scientific experiment. In 1846 the Vienna physician noticed that a particular maternity ward in the city had a high mortality rate. In fact this ward had developed such a dreadful reputation that women begged with tears not to be taken into it. Semmelweis noticed that the hospital was located next to a morgue that medical students used for dissection and would go between the two buildings without washing their hands. His detective work led him to the conclusion that Puerperal Fever was caused by blood poisoning due to bacteria. By instituting the simple experiment of having the students wash their hands in an antiseptic solution before going into the hospital, the death rate on this ward decreased from almost 10 percent to 1 percent.

Despite such impressive results, society and the medical community were not willing to accept his conclusions as to the cause and treatment of this illness. He was ridiculed for his ideas until his death in 1865; Dr. Semmelweis, being a very sensitive individual, died an "insane" man. He is considered one of medicine's martyrs; today every mother shares in the benefits of his discovery. Though we, in the scientific and medical communities, pride ourselves with the scientific model and objectivity, sometimes we frankly ignore the facts.[1]

Relative to faith, we now have solid evidence that it has an objective, measurable influence on our health. But faith, like bacteria, can't be seen with the naked eye. Thus we can either deny its existence or we can look at the results. In the past 100 years, well over 1,200 articles on religion and health have been written, many involving scientifically conducted experiments that demonstrate the value of faith. Of the studies performed, 80 to 92 percent demonstrate the positive effects of faith on our health.

Dr. Harold G. Koenig, founder and director of the widely respected Duke University Center for the Study of Religious/ Spiritual Health, has written 13 books and over 150 professional papers on the subject. He says, "Much of this research flies in the face of what Freud thought about religion and what generations of his followers have been taught ever since. The truth is that we now have enormous, credible scientific evidence that shows a connection between faith and better mental health."[2]

In 1997 *The Journal of the American Medical Association* reported, "Statistically significant associations between religious belief and health measures . . . pointing to differences in morbidity or mortality among religious groups have appeared in studies of many diseases (e.g., heart disease, hypertension, stroke, cancer, and gastrointestinal disease)."[3]

Specifically, what are some of the benefits that scientific studies have demonstrated that faith can do for you?

What Faith Will Do For You

Faith has been demonstrated to:[4]
- Improve immune function.
- Enhance the body's ability to fend off infections.

- Lower stress level.
- Decrease the incidence of cancer, hypertension, stroke, and gastrointestinal disease.
- Improve healing in burn patients.
- Foster faster recovery from surgery.
- Decrease the incidence of infertility.
- Improve general health status.
- Decrease the incidence of depression and if one is depressed it improves recovery time.
- Lower the risk of mental illness and promotes positive mental health.
- Assist overcoming addictions quicker.
- Decrease anger, anxiety, and fear.
- Decrease the incidence of suicide and use of illicit drugs and alcohol.
- Promote increased hope, optimism, purpose, and meaning in life.
- Decrease the likelihood that one's children will abuse drugs or commit suicide.
- Foster joy in life.
- Increase job satisfaction.
- Promote one's happiness.
- Double satisfaction with life.
- Increase one's sense of wellbeing.
- Foster black males' ability to leave the ghetto.
- Equip one to handle difficult situations better and to improve one's ability to cope.
- Promote a healthier life and increase longevity.

Hard Wired For God

One week after the September 11th attack on the World Trade Center in New York, the *New England Journal of Medicine* reported that the most common way individuals coped with the tragedy was to talk to others about it. The second most common means used by 90 percent of individuals was to turn to religious faith. Herbert Benson, researcher from Harvard, says that just like we are hard wired to fear snakes and heights, he believes humans are "wired for God."

This is another way of expressing Pascal's comment, which I quoted in Chapter 14, "There is a God-shaped vacuum in the heart of every man which only God can fill through His Son, Jesus Christ." Hope can be in virtually anything and can yield considerable, yet limited, positive benefits. However, faith must have an object. It is not faith in faith. It is faith in God. This faith in God is objectified in the person of Jesus Christ.[5]

God placed within each of us this vacuum, or the hard wiring, because he wants to draw us to himself. We have been told, "Long ago the LORD said . . . , 'I have loved you, my people, with an everlasting love. With unfailing love I have drawn you to myself'" (Jeremiah 31:3, NLT).

Initial Faith

The first step of faith is believing God. It is initially coming to him by faith. We discussed this to some extent in Chapter 14. The familiar passage in John 3:16–17 expresses it so well: "For God so loved the world that he gave his only Son, so that everyone who believes in him will not perish but have eternal life. God did not send his Son into the world to condemn it, but to save it" (NLT). Later on in his ministry Christ says, "Yes, I am the gate. Those who come in through me will be saved. Wherever they go, they will find green pastures. The thief's purpose is to steal and kill and destroy. My purpose is to give life in all its fullness" (John 10:9-10, NLT).

God's love and grace are available to us through confidence in what Christ has done for us, believing what he did for us and receiving him into our lives. This is faith – the first step in activating the power of faith.

Healing Faith

The second step of faith is to facilitate God's giving us life in "all its fullness." On one occasion when Christ's followers healed a lame man, they commented on the means of the healing saying, "And on the basis of faith in His name, it is the name of Jesus which has strengthened this man . . . and the faith which comes through Him has given him this perfect health in the presence of you all" (Acts 3:16).

The great faith chapter in the Bible says, "Without faith it is impossible to please Him, for he who comes to God must believe that He is, and that He is a rewarder of those who seek Him" (Hebrews 11:6). Taking this a step further, James tells us that "you do not have because you do not ask" (James 4:2). Thus, it is appropriate to ask God, in faith, for our healing. The Scriptures are replete with examples and promises that often he is pleased to give us our request.

Here are a few apropos verses from the Bible that summarize this chapter:

- "The fear [or trust] of the LORD prolongs life" (Proverbs 10:27).
- "Reverence for God adds hours to each day" (Proverbs 10:27, TLB).
- "Trust and reverence the Lord . . . then you will be given renewed health and vitality" (Proverbs 3:7–8 , TLB).
- "Reverence for God gives a man deep strength" (Proverbs 14:26, TLB).
- "Reverence for the Lord is a fountain of life" (Proverbs 14:27, TLB).

CHAPTER 25

THE POWER OF FOCUSING

MOST OF US live fragmented lives. Our lives are interrupted by the ringing of cell phones, unwanted e-mails, and the booming radio from the car next to us as we wait at a stop light. Then we are deluged by the "oughts" and "shoulds" and "musts" of family, church, or work. All of these are amplified by any internal disquiet destroying any semblance of serenity and undermining our ability to be "focused."

So the first question that we must ask ourselves is: "Are we fragmented or focused?" If one is fragmented, there are pulls in all directions with resultant turmoil.

If we are focused, then all the pulls and pushes are in one direction; for example: toward a career, making money, climbing the corporate ladder, or having a bigger church. If we are focused, we will accomplish more toward the unified goal for which we are striving, whatever that might be. We need focus to be successful. But all of these focal points will ultimately leave us empty, often with stress and fatigue.

Isaiah 26:3 says: "Thou wilt keep him in perfect peace, whose mind is stayed on thee: because he trusteth in thee" (KJV). Only the life that is focused on Christ will find peace, satisfaction, and fulfillment. So the question is: first, are you fragmented or focused; and second, what/who are you focused on?

Christ Our Model

In a far simpler day we find Christ addressing this very problem:

As Jesus and the disciples continued on their way to Jerusalem, they came to a village where a woman named Martha welcomed them into her home. Her sister, Mary, sat at the Lord's feet, listening to what he taught. But Martha was worrying over the big dinner she was preparing. She came to Jesus and said, "Lord, doesn't it seem unfair to you that my sister just sits here while I do all the work? Tell her to come and help me."

But the Lord said to her, "My dear Martha, you are so upset over all these details! There is really only one thing worth being concerned about. Mary has discovered it – and I won't take it away from her" (Luke 10:38–11:1, NLT).

Here is Martha frantically trying to tidy up the house and doing her utmost to prepare a Martha Stewart meal for the Lord. Her motive was right, but she ended up missing the main act and frustrating the Lord, herself, and her sister. We also see Mary, seated at Christ's feet, intently gazing into his face, drinking in every word that he was saying; she was probably oblivious to Martha's frantic preparations. One might be prone to criticize Mary, but she was focused on Christ.

As we look at the life of Christ we see one who is unhurried by the pressures of the world, his own disciples, or his close friends. He makes time to be alone with God. He certainly lives in "the present moment." He is focused on the Father. The epitome of his relationship with God was: "I always do the things that are pleasing to Him" (John 8:29).

Personal Pilgrimage

I started this book by telling you about my trying to do so many good things: things for God and for people. But I ended up totally exhausted and eventually I had to stop work altogether and rest. At the time I didn't have any real insight into the basic problem I was facing. Maybe someone was trying to help me, but I didn't appreciate it if he was.

Now, half a century later, it seems so clear. I was listening to all the voices around me, well-meaning spiritually influenced voices, but, at the same time, I was trying to cram into my life far more than God intended. I didn't really understand that "His commandments are not burdensome" and that "unless the Lord builds the house, They labor in vain who build it; Unless the Lord guards the city, The watchman keeps awake in vain" (1 John 5:3; Psalm 127:1–2).

During those early years of my life my primary focus was, as I now refer to it, the "to know" and "to do" phase of my Christian life. It was to gain as much knowledge of the Bible as possible and to strive putting what it told me into practice – especially Bible study, witnessing, and discipling. These are essential, but God had more for me to learn.

Focusing

Like the story of Mary and Martha, Martha was doing many good things for her Master, but she hadn't found his peace. Mary, on the other hand, found tranquility by being focused on Christ.

During the middle years of my life I tried to achieve this quality of a relationship with Christ. I followed Brother Lawrence's admonition to endeavor to practice the presence of God. He recommended "that we should establish ourselves in a sense of God's presence by continually conversing with Him." I sincerely tried to practice this, but in all honesty, most of the time I failed.[1]

Four decades ago I read *Hudson Taylor's Spiritual Secret,* but didn't really grasp what he was saying until I reread it within the last decade. Hudson Taylor was a 19th century missionary to China. Only after striving to please God for many years did he discover his "spiritual secret." He states that in the past he had struggled with a . . .

> constant falling short of that which I felt should be aimed at; an unrest; a perpetual striving to find some way by which one might continually enjoy that communion, that fellowship, at times so real but more often so visionary, so far off! . . . But how to get faith strengthened? Not by striving after faith, but by resting on the Faithful One. . . I have striven in vain to rest in Him. I'll strive no more. For has not *He* promised to abide with me – never to leave me, never to fail me? . . . I used to try to think very much and very often about Jesus, but I often forgot Him. Now I trust Jesus to keep my heart remembering Him, and He does so. . . Abiding, not striving nor struggling; looking off unto Him; trusting Him for present power . . . resting in the love of almighty Saviour, in the joy of a complete salvation . . . this is not new, and yet 'tis *new to me.*

... How then to have our faith increased? . . . Not a striving to have faith . . . but a looking off to the Faithful One. . .[Another individual observing him said] "He was a joyous man now."[2]

How to Focus on Christ

It must all start, of course, with the initial commitment of our lives to God and the desire to put him first in our lives. Not to do this makes us the center of our lives and our little universe, and that is precisely what has gotten the entire world into so much trouble. Contrary to our natural inclination, putting God first rights our upside-down-world and our own lives. It is interesting to note that the words *whole, heal*, and *holy* are derived from the same root word. If we are going to be healed and be whole, we are going to have to be holy. Likewise, if we are going to be focused, he will have to be pre-eminent in our lives. The first of all the commandments is, "thou shalt love the Lord thy God with all thy heart, and with all thy soul, and with all thy mind, and with all thy strength" (Mark 12:29-30, KJV). The number one thing is to want God and his will in my life and to maintain a focus on Christ and his desires for my life during the present moment. Then, periodically throughout the day, we will have moments of looking toward heaven, touching base, so to speak, with God. These may take the form of thoughts, prayers, or praise. In addition, even as Christ had the need for more extended times alone with his Father, so we will find ourselves with him.[3]

Meditation

Meditation can help decrease stress, fragmentation of our lives, and fatigue. Furthermore, it is a tool in helping us be focused on Christ. The late Swiss physician and counselor Paul Tournier says in *Fatigue in Modern Society*:

A man who meditates, who tries to place his life under the attention of God, finds a life infinitely more fruitful, infinitely more harmonious, much less fatiguing and more profound. . . . The more life is guided by God, the more it frees itself from fragmented toil . . . But the true meaning of meditation is to deepen our intimacy with God; it is to learn to live in constant communion with Jesus Christ, to share everything with him. . . The more life is guided by God, the more it frees itself from fragmented toil. [4]

I am talking about a very specific type of meditation – one that focuses on God and listens to God. God's Word can be an eminent help in this process. The aim should be to focus on God, his attributes, or a few truths from the Bible. It is not primarily Bible study, albeit as important as that is in our overall walk with God. Its aim is not head knowledge but alignment of our hearts with God's heart. Tournier elaborates: "To meditate is to listen to God . . . it [is] a question of encountering God and not of exposing ideas about God."[5] This kind of meditation causes us to have our life focused on God, allowing him to work out his will in our lives. Paul puts it this way: "Meditate upon these things; give thyself wholly to them; that thy profiting may appear to all" (1 Timothy 4:15, KJV).

How do you do this? As much as possible get away from all the external noise of the world. Turn off the cell phone, stroll quietly on the beach, walk in the mountains, or sit quietly in a chair. Turn off the internal noise of the world. Choose not to think about the pressures at work or church, political events, the economy, or the things that people want you to do. Then, actively focus on God, his Word, and listen to what he might want to communicate to you. This will assist your meditating and focusing on Christ.

Rest

On the seventh day of Creation God rested from his work. For many of us Sunday is the busiest day of the week. God does not intend for us to refrain from all activity on Sunday as a legalistic demand, but he is trying to teach us an important spiritual principle which has physical implications. To maintain a healthy body, mind, and soul, you need, on a fairly regular basis, to have a change of pace, a time to reflect, to rest, and to worship God. Part of this is just a physical or mental change of pace or activity. Christ clearly modeled this by getting away from the hustle and bustle of the crowds and being alone to pray (Mark 1:35; 6:31). All of us, like so many in this fast food, microwave, cell-phone society, are prone to forget this and suffer the consequences. It may mean turning off the TV or letting the answer-machine take all the phone calls.

Numerous scientific and medical studies show that the uplifter of rest, or relaxation, has numerous positive benefits, such as, decreasing anxiety and depression and rejuvenating and improving the immune function.[6]

Dr. Siang-Yang Tan, in his book *Rest: Experiencing God's Peace in a Restless World*, says: "Rest is not meant to be a luxury, but rather a *necessity*. The world and the church need genuinely *rested* Christians." He explains three words in the Old Testament that describe rest. Their descriptions are: "To stop or cease from work and activity . . . .inner ease or security," and "tranquility and absence of inner anxiety and external pressure." He goes on to say that we "must regularly cease from our work and become still before God to gain a sense of tranquility and to loose the shackles of stress."[7]

We need to work at resting. The writer to the Hebrews says, "There remaineth therefore a rest to the people of God. For he that is entered into his rest, he also hath ceased from his own works, as God did from his. Let us labour therefore to enter into that rest" (Hebrews 4:9–11, KJV). On the surface it would seem that working at resting is an oxymoron. The facts are, however, that it takes work – the right kind of work – to truly rest. The best analogy that comes to mind is floating in a pool or the ocean. It takes a deliberate stilling yourself and giving yourself to the water. As you lie back quietly in the water with arms outstretched, suddenly you are afloat. It is the same in our resting in God. It takes a quiet giving of yourself to the process, focusing attention on God.

The authors of *The Sacred Romance* ask, "How do we go about 'doing' rest?" They answer the question by saying, "The first thing we encounter is not rest but fear and a compulsion to return to activity . . . [The distraction] diverts us aside from the one thing that can help us to begin our ascent to truth . . . the sense of our own emptiness." They are addressing the fact that often our own internal struggles and emptiness propel us toward busyness and make it difficult to slow down enough to participate in rest or solitude. All of this is part of the internal noise that we must face and turn off to find true rest and focus in God. The authors go on to say, "Resting in Jesus is not applying a spiritual formula to ourselves as a kind of fix-it. . . When we give up everything else but him, we experience the freedom of knowing that he simply loves us where we are. We begin just to *be*."[8]

This deep rest certainly can be restorative emotionally, physically, mentally, and spiritually. It can combat much of the stress and fatigue that is so characteristic of this 21st century.

Relinquishment

Some of you who are reading these pages are either struggling with stress, fatigue, illness, or some other problem; you won't be able to rest or focus on Christ until you relinquish – that's right, relinquish your right to whatever it is that you are striving for. Rest requires relinquishment.

In the previous chapter we talked about "healing faith," that is, asking God for his healing of your body. This is Scriptural and hopefully God has healed/will heal your body. But there is another side to this. Paul apparently had some physical ailment and he prayed and wasn't healed. After the third time he yielded this to God, aware that his grace was sufficient for such a situation (see 2 Corthinans 12:7–10). In the great chapter on faith in the book of Hebrews we find numerous examples of God performing miracles through faith. Nevertheless, in the last 10 percent of the chapter we are told about a number of people who had an identical faith, but God did not intervene in a miraculous way. Christ wanted the agony of the cross to be circumvented but yielded to the will of the Father. Sometimes we demand certain things from God like a child making demands on his parents. Sometimes God's answer is "No, yield that to me."

Catherine Marshall, author, and wife of the late Peter Marshall, Chaplain of the U.S. Senate, tells about her struggle with relinquishment. She developed tuberculosis in 1943, before antibiotics were available and was ordered to bed 24 hours a day for an indefinite period. She prayed, but wasn't healed. She read about a missionary who had been an invalid for eight years, worn out with futile petitions and finally gave up saying, "If You want me to be an invalid for the rest of my days, that's Your business. Anyway, I've discovered that I want You even more than I want health. You decide." In two weeks she was completely well. Catherine struggled with this for some time and then says, "I came to the same point of abject acceptance. 'I'm tired of asking' was the burden of my prayer. 'I'm beaten, finished. God, You decide what you want for me for the rest of my life' . . . The result was as if windows had opened in heaven; as if some dynamo of heavenly power had begun flowing, flowing into me. From that moment my recovery began." She goes on to say, "I saw that the demanding spirit – 'God, I must have thus and so; God, this is what I want you to do for me – ' is not real prayer and hence receives no answer." If our lives are fixated on our health and what we want, we may not get it. Catherine quotes Elisabeth Elliot saying, "Only in acceptance lies peace. . . there is a difference between acceptance and resignation. One is positive; the other negative. . . Acceptance says, 'I trust the good will, the love of my God . . . I consent to this present situation with hope for what the future will bring.' Thus acceptance leaves the door of Hope wide open to God's creative plan." If, like Abraham, we are willing to yield our most precious possession, whatever that might be, God *may* ultimately give us what we desire. But that is not part of the deal. The deal is that we relinquish all our *demands,* yield it all to him, focus on him and not on our self or our problems or illness. For some, this is the necessary step; this will put you into a position to start really focusing on him.[9]

Results of a Life Focused on Christ

As you align your will with God's will, your life and the work you do will be his and not yours. This can give you a new freedom and will make whatever you can do into an *exciting adventure.* The gigantic fear of failure will no longer hang like a black cloud over your head. Any demanding or bitter attitude will be gone.

You will find a life focused on Christ a simpler life, unhurried, and a serene life. It will be radiant, sensitive to the prompting of the Holy Spirit. It will make saying "yes," or "no," easier, as it will be the result of what God wants and not the numerous divergent pulls of the world.

To a person who is focused on Christ there is no such thing as failure. Even if at times you seem to fail, you aren't a failure. The yoke of having to succeed is a heavy one. The person truly committed to Jesus Christ never does anything that eternally fails. Solomon stated, "Commit thy works unto the Lord and thy thoughts shall be established" (Proverbs 16:3, KJV).

Conclusion

Isaiah 26:3 is so powerful, let me quote it again: "[God] will keep in perfect peace all who trust in you, whose thoughts are fixed on you!" (NLT).

Paul puts it this way:

> And I pray that Christ will be more and more at home in your hearts, living within you as you trust in him. May your roots go down deep into the soil of God's marvelous love; and may you be able to feel and understand, as all God's children should, how long, how wide, how deep, and how high his love really is; and to experience this love for yourselves, though it is so great that you will never see the end of it or fully know or understand it. And so at last you will be filled up with God himself (Ephesians 3:17–18, TLB).

CHAPTER 26

THE POWER OF JOY

FOR ALMOST 500 years the nations of Israel and Judah had been repeatedly plundered and eventually taken into captivity by their enemies. They had suffered because of their ongoing disobedience of God's laws. Then, at the time of their restoration, several key individuals encouraged the rebuilding of the Temple and the wall around Jerusalem (445 BC). At its completion, Ezra, the scribe, read God's Word. This touched a sensitive nerve in the people and they started worshiping and weeping. Then he advised: "Don't weep on such a day as this! . . . Go and celebrate with a feast of choice foods and sweet drinks, and share gifts of food with people who have nothing prepared. This is a sacred day before our Lord. Don't be dejected and sad, for *the joy of the LORD is your strength!*" (Nehemiah 8:8–12, NLT, *italics* added). They owned up to their shortcomings, therefore God wanted them to find strength through joy.

Solomon tells us, "When a man is gloomy, everything seems to go wrong; when he is cheerful, everything seems right! . . . A joyful heart is good medicine, But a broken spirit dries up the bones" (Proverbs 15:15, TLB; 17:22).

What Joy Will Do for You

We learn from the passages above that joy is good medicine, it helps make things go right, and it gives energy and strength. Contemporary studies have shown that it also leads to better health, decreases stress, and fosters optimism. Thus a joyful attitude is an important uplifter – it will help abolish fatigue and give additional energy.[1]

Joy Versus Happiness

Joy can be defined as a feeling or state of great delight. The term has numerous synonyms and the more appropriate ones are "delight, enjoyment, gladness," and "jubilation." Joy is primarily based on what is inside of us. It depends on our internal emotional and spiritual state. It is not dependent on our environment. Even our physical or financial state should have little bearing on joy. Understandably, external things have some impact on our moods, but hopefully internal choices and our faith and hope in a sovereign God help us rise above environmental factors. Joy is a noun, a state that depends on the choices and allegiances of our hearts, minds, and spirits. Other synonyms that the dictionary gives are "cheer, pleasure, bliss, fun, merriment," and "thrill," but these better describe *happiness*. They describe a state derived more from the external environment, which puts us at its mercy.

In this book the focus is on *joy*, that quality of well-being that does not depend on the external, other than the Person of God. It primarily depends on the choices that we make.

Additionally, joy tends to connote a connection with God and a hope-filled view of eternity. In the book *The Door to Joy* the author says, "Joy is a confidence that operates irrespective of our moods. Joy is the certainty that all is well, however we feel." To that we can add, all is well now and for eternity.[2]

Another difference between joy and happiness is that joy is compatible with suffering, pain, and dying. We find numerous examples of that in Scripture, such as, Habakkuk, Paul, and Christ, who expressed joy in the midst of sorrow, pain, and suffering (see Habakkuk 3:16–19; 2 Corinthians 6:10; 1 Thessalonians 1:5–6; Hebrews 12:2).

What Robs Us of Our Joy?

First and foremost, we will need to deal with any persisting anger, bitterness, resentment, or unforgiveness. These are totally incompatible with joy. Joe Aldrich says in his article, "Joy: The Illusive Fruit":

It takes time, diligence, patience and hard work to make an apple tree productive. Fruit is not instantaneous! It is a victory over weather, bugs, weeds, poor soil and neglect. If the Spirit's indwelling presence guaranteed the presence of joy, every believer would be rejoicing all the time. We're not. Joy, as a way of living, is a hard-won victory over entrenched attitudes of apathy, pessimism, doubt, unbelief and despair.[3]

Second, expecting an external environment to supply us with a sense of internal satisfaction is sure to destroy any possibility of joy. The facts are that the external environment doesn't make people happier, to say nothing of joy, once basic needs are met. In fact, striving to be happy will rob you of joy. An article in the *American Psychologist* stated, "The more people strive for extrinsic goals such as money, the more numerous their problems and the less robust their well-being."[4]

In previous chapters we discussed some of the bigger stresses, both internal and external, that can steal our joy. But sometimes seemingly little things, like hassles, can play havoc with a sensitive commodity like joy. In the Song of Solomon we read about the little foxes spoiling the vines that have tender grapes on them (Song of Solomon 2:15). In our lives, sometimes the seemingly little things can be the biggest robbers of our joy.

Failing To Do the Hard Things First

In my daily life I just don't like to do certain things or chores. For example, I don't like to write reports to insurance companies because I feel they unnecessarily intrude into my work and my patients' private affairs. Furthermore, they often want to get information to deny a payment. My tendency is to open such a request from an insurance company, feel annoyed, and put the request in my "To Do" box for another day. Every few days I may notice the request, but shove it aside to do another day. Two or three weeks later I may get a "second request" for the report, or, worse yet, a phone call inquiring about the status of the report. Now I am more annoyed at the insurance company *and myself* for not expediting the matter in the beginning. All of this uses energy units and siphons off some joy — and I haven't even written the report yet! I am far better off if I deal with my own inertia and write the report within a couple of days of receiving the request.

Most every day I make up a "To Do" list. Generally this includes items that are not related to a specific appointment. My list generally includes five to ten items. If I don't get them all completed that day, they are included in tomorrow's list. Items that I don't like to do often end up on the bottom of the list. In fact, they may end up on the bottom of the list many days running. It's another way I tend to avoid the hard things. This is another way energy and joy get siphoned off if I am not careful. So, when I am aware that this is happening, I put the item at the top of the list with the note "do first." When it is finished, it feels like a weight is taken off my shoulders, or should I say energy is restored.

Allowing External Influences to Destroy a Joyful Walk with God

It seems like on at least a weekly basis something comes along that is prone to rob me of my joy of living focused on Christ. It could be a ding in the fender, my computer crashing, or an annoying telemarketer. In Chapter 3, I described one such situation where I was trying to understand charges on my phone bill, and in the process was given multiple phone menus, and ultimately, hung up on by a national phone company without ever being given the option of talking to a live person. The seven-minute phone conservation with no listening session was draining me of the day's energy units and stealing my joy. No, that is not quite true. I was engaged in frustrated and angry emotions and in the process was voluntarily giving up my joy and energy.

So I had a little internal board meeting and decided that investing more time and energy trying to get my question answered would most likely lead to further frustrations. Trying to find someone at the company to express my aggravation to was unlikely to yield any positive results. So I called another company and had them take over the service; in that process they would notify my current carrier that their services were no longer desired. Then I made a conscious effort to drop the whole issue "like a hot potato." That's right, I decided just to stop thinking about it. When it would crop back up in my mind later in the day, I would just drop the hot potato again. It quickly became a non-issue.

This is basically the way to deal with negative thoughts. Evaluate the legitimacy of the thoughts. Consider if there is some positive action that you should take, and if so, take it. But if you are ruminating on stuff that is not leading to some constructive end, drop it. If there is something you should do two weeks from now that tends to keep the issue on your mind and steal your joy, write down what you need to do on a calendar pad or in your notebook; include the day you should do it and work at forgetting it until then. Choose to ignore the negative stuff that is not in some way beneficial.

"Sweating the Small Stuff"

A popular saying promoted by a number of books is "Don't sweat the small stuff – it's *all* small stuff." Typically when I hear a statement like this my mind works in such a way that I think about the exceptions to the statement, then sometimes lose the power and significance of the point being made. For instance, in typing this, my mind jumps to a wonderful Christian professional couple in their prime of life. They were driving a small car to northern California for their daughter to use in college. They were abiding by the law, out to do a nice thing for their daughter, when a young man in a large SUV, who had stayed up most of the previous night, fell asleep at the wheel, veered across the double white line right into the oncoming traffic, and killed the couple in the smaller vehicle.

Is this small stuff? I think not. Oh, someone might say that this was "God's will" and in the perspective of eternity this is not a very big deal. My view, however, would have to come down on the other side. This *is* big stuff: two lives were snuffed out in their prime, and the trauma and loss to the families. So there is some big stuff out there to which we must give appropriate attention. Having said that, the facts are that probably 99 percent of the stuff that most of us worry about is "small stuff." I think it is Walt Whitman who said, "Most of the things I worry about never come to pass."

The Scriptures are clear on this issue. Christ says, "Do not be anxious for your life" (see Matthew 6:25–34). Paul picks up on this theme and states, "Be anxious for nothing," then he exhorts us to focus our attention on positive things with the promise that we will then have God's peace (see Philippians 4:6–8). Therefore, we should not sweat most stuff. Often a good question to ask ourselves is this: "Will the issue that now vies for my energy make any difference no matter how it turns out 20 years from now? How about 100 years from now?" The facts are that most of the things that occupy most of our thoughts are really not that important.

If there is some action that needs to be taken, do it. But otherwise leave the matter in God's hands. If you have made a mistake, confess it and go on. Worrying about it helps no one. You need to make it a constant practice of not allowing your mind to become focused on issues and worries about which you can do nothing. "Commit thy works unto the Lord, and thy thoughts shall be established" (Proverbs 16:3, KJV). "A relaxed attitude lengthens a man's life" (Proverbs 14:30, TLB).

Another very recent example comes to mind that illustrates several of these points. I find this one much harder to share with you because it involves my capability as well as my friends. The incident occurred at a time when the Lord's presence and the joy of the Lord was more real than at any time of my life. In the midst of this I received a phone call from a patient of mine who was not doing as well as we both wished. He moved out of the area but was very reticent to transfer care to another psychiatrist. Struggling, he made a number of phone calls to me complaining that he was not doing well. I really wanted to help him, so I gradually raised his medications over the phone and in retrospect overmedicated him. This caused him a week or so of feeling worse than he otherwise might have felt.

No permanent damage was done, but I felt awful. Self-recrimination took over; I worried about what he, his family, and our many mutual friends might think of me. I berated myself for several days and some nights. If I rated feelings on a scale of +10 to −10, one phone call resulted in their changing from a +9 to a −4. As I continued to think about it, I was aware the problem had been rectified and there was absolutely nothing I could do to alter the past. Whatever people chose to think of me, my worrying about it wouldn't change their thoughts one iota. But, and most importantly, continuing with my anxious thoughts was disobedience to God. The stark change in my feelings pressed home the issue: am I going to allow this to rob me of the joy of the Lord and my relationship with him? To which I responded in my head, "No, it's not!" So I decided not to allow myself to think about how I should have treated the situation or what others would think of me, and to stop berating myself. I finally dropped it like a hot potato. Then I actively engaged my mind to focus on God and his wonderful love and grace to me. Within a day my feelings went back up to a +8.

Fostering Joy

Pascal said, "Happiness can be found neither in ourselves nor in external things, but in God and in ourselves as united to him."[5] I would probably change that statement to read, "True happiness or joy can be found neither in ourselves nor in external things, but in God, as a direct result of my choosing to be in relationship with him." We need to recognize that God is the only true source of joy.

The Bible tells us that love, joy, peace, longsuffering, gentleness, goodness, faith, meekness, and temperance are a direct result of God's Spirit dwelling in us (Galatians 5:22–23, KJV). Another passage amplifies this, saying: "Thou wilt make known to me the path of life; In Thy presence is fulness of joy; In Thy right hand there are pleasures forever" (Psalm 16:11).

Choose to Be a Joyful Person

Make joy a definitive choice in your life. Decide that you are going to be a joyful person. That does not mean that you have your head in the clouds or that you deny reality; it means that you will choose to view life and all of its uncertain circumstances from a joyful perspective. You will focus on joy rather than doom. You will choose to view the glass of your life as at least half-full. To facilitate this process you will need to look for things for which to be thankful.

John Ortberg, in *The Life You've Always Wanted* says, "I think the time has come, strange as it sounds, for us to take joy seriously. You can become a joyful person. With God's help, it really is possible. . joyfullness is a learned skill. You must take responsibility for your joy."[6]

Express Gratefulness

The next step is to express joy or gratefulness actively and honestly. The Scriptures are filled with examples and admonitions to praise God, express thanksgiving, and to rejoice. These are all actions in which you can deliberately engage and they will lead to a joyful state of being. Engaging in these activities is an act of obedience. In fact, sometimes this may be hard. The writer of the book of Hebrews even calls it a sacrifice, saying, "Through Him then, let us continually offer up a sacrifice of praise to God, that is, the fruit of lips that give thanks to His name" (Hebrews 13:15).

Look for things to be joyful about and find ways to express it, whether it's in prayer, in song, or verbally to another person. Treasure your life right now.

In one study participants wrote down five things, on at least a weekly basis, for which they were grateful. The results were that the individuals were less stressed, healthier, more optimistic, and more joyful.[7]

Conclusion

Understandably there is a great tendency for people with a chronic illness to focus on the illness, or what they feel they are missing in life as a result of the infirmity. But this is highly destructive and greatly aggravates the problem. There comes a time when it is crucial that we relinquish our demands, foster joy, and as we shall see in the next chapter, discover God's meaning for our life in the present moment – today.

Robert Veninga, in his book *A Gift of Hope: How We Survive Our Tragedies,* speaks about individuals living out their last days in a hospice. On one occasion he asked a lady if she had any regrets? She said, "I wish I would have slowed down; I wish I would have *consciously* decided to enjoy each day." He goes on to tell us, "No matter how difficult the situation, life can be celebrated. . . Most people do not give up on life because of a catastrophe. They give up because they *no longer see the small joys worthy of celebration*."[8]

So celebrate and be joyful; it's essential for life.

CHAPTER 27

THE POWER OF MEANING

PEOPLE FROM DIVERGENT backgrounds, disciplines, and faiths agree on few things; but there is one that they do agree on – that meaning in life is fundamental to our existence. Let us take a look at a few examples.

A representative from the scientific community says that a fundamental sense of purpose is "the most essential and encompassing stress-resistance resource."[1]

The philosopher Nietzsche, addressing the existential vacuum, says, "He who has a *why* to live can bear with almost any *how*."[2]

Viktor Frankl, the Jewish psychiatrist and Auschwitz survivor, says, "The striving to find a meaning in one's life is the primary motivational force in man. . . Suffering ceases to be suffering in some way at the moment it finds a meaning."[3]

Psychiatrist Carl Jung says, "About a third of my cases are not suffering from any clinical definable neurosis but from the senselessness and aimlessness of their lives. . . Meaning makes a great many things endurable – perhaps everything."[4]

Nobel prize novelist Albert Camus says, "Life's meaning is the most urgent question of all."[5]

Rabbi Harold Kushner says, "Our souls are not hungry for fame, comfort, wealth, or power. Those rewards create almost as many problems as they solve. Our souls are hungry for meaning, for the sense that we have figured out how to live so that our lives matter."[6]

So discovering the meaning of our lives, including the circumstances in which we now find ourselves, whether sickness or health, is fundamental to our very existence.

What Meaning Will Do for You

What are some of the scientific proven benefits when there is meaning or purpose in one's life?   Meaning in our lives will . . . [7]

• Reduce stress.
• Help one bear almost anything.
• Buffer adversity.
• Increase hardiness.
• Facilitate constructive coping strategies.
• Facilitate positive reappraisal as discussed in Chapter 19.
• Facilitate planning for life's goals.
• Improve physical and emotional health.
• Foster a sense of control.
• Give suffering purpose.
• Give a sense of control and accomplishment even in the final stages of dying.

Important as these benefits are, the global rewards far overshadow these. Meaning in life is what your life is all about – period. It's the beginning, the middle, and the end. No matter what your station in life or your health, with your life having meaning it all comes together. On the other hand, if you are the richest person in the world with perfect health and your life doesn't have a clear, God-motivated purpose, it *will* all fall apart; it's just a matter of time.

The Source of Meaning in Your Life

Viktor Frankl is right on target when he says, "The meaning of our existence is not invented by ourselves, but rather detected."[8] Likewise Harold Kushner says, "The need for meaning is not a biological need like the need for food and air. Neither is it a psychological need like the need for acceptance and self-esteem. It is a religious need, an ultimate thirst of our souls."[9]

Numerous studies reveal the powerful influence of religion in crystallizing meaning and purpose in our lives; this becomes especially apparent in serious illness.[10]

This is really what Pascal was addressing when he said, "There is a God-shaped vacuum in the heart of every man which only God can fill through His Son, Jesus Christ."

Christ addressed this need repeatedly while he was on earth. In a significant encounter with the Samaritan woman at the well he said, "Whoever drinks of the water that I shall give him shall never thirst; but the water that I shall give him shall become in him a well of water springing up to eternal life" (John 4:14).

What Is God's Purpose for Your Life?

God wants to give you an overflowing life that has purpose; the crucial issue is to discover and live out that purpose. If you don't know God's purpose, you will be pulled by external or internal forces you don't understand and they will take you to a disappointing place. Seeking the traditional things that most of the world pursues – fame, wealth, power, sex , or the overt pursuit of happiness – will be short-lived at best.

A Right Relationship with God – God's Universal Purpose

God's initial calling on our lives is our putting our faith and trust in him, which we discussed in Chapters 14 and 24. Second, he wants us to live a life that is in harmony with his general will for mankind as revealed in the Scripture. Then comes learning how to make God the center of our lives. He will transform us as we focus on our relationship with him more than on our accomplishments, health status, or anything else. This is precisely what Christ is talking about when he says, "But seek first his kingdom and his righteousness; and all these things shall be added to you" (Matthew 6:33).

It is crucial that we keep the primary focus on God. Only after that decision does it become important to seek to understand God's purpose for us now in our current situation. If that doesn't take place, there will be a tragic disconnection.

God has known us from eternity past. He has created us with a plan and purpose in mind. The Scriptures teach us that "It is he who saved us and chose us for his holy work not because we deserved it but because that was his plan long before the world began – to show his love and kindness to us through Christ" (2 Timothy 1: 9, TLB).

God's Specific and Individual Purpose for Your Life Now

But more specifically, God has a calling on our lives and a purpose for us *right now*. This is true whether we have everything going just the way we want it, or if we have tremendous problems: major illness, severe fatigue, or some other problem.

Seek to understand and live out the purpose for which God has created you. Ask him in prayer, seek his understanding in the Bible, meditate on it, and pursue input from spiritual friends. How would God have you redeem your situation so that you live out God's purpose for your life – in the present moment?

Try and envision yourself as God sees you. If you could visualize your true potential as God does, you would probably be astounded by what you would see. His love for you would take on a new dimension as you realize that you are of vital importance to the Master.

I am reminded of my brother, Paul, who avidly enjoyed living. Yet, while a prisoner of the rebels, he wrote, "Pray not for deliverance but for my testimony." God's will became more important to him than his own life. He died at 36 years of age in a hail of bullets, but he died with purpose. The Congolese Church grew as a direct result of Paul's death. Numerous individuals have gone overseas to minister to others as a result of Paul's example. His wife recently said that probably more good came from his life as a result of his death, than if he had lived.

My daughter didn't know if she would live or die and endured tremendous suffering over a two-year period. She spent eight months as an in-patient in the hospital, often with nausea, chills, high fevers, and numerous days where the only thing she could do was to feed herself and bathe. She says, "During my slow recovery from the transplant I began to put into practice my belief that ultimately the meaning of a situation comes from God, not from the useful things I did myself. I had to learn experientially that there can be meaning even when I couldn't *do* anything."[11] She had several very difficult years before her strength and stamina returned.

No wonder Brother Lawrence, a monk in the 17th century, said, "The sorest afflictions never appear intolerable, except when we see them in the wrong light."[12] Three centuries later, Victor Frankl concurred, "Suffering ceases to be suffering in some way at the moment it finds a meaning . . . man is even ready to suffer, on the condition, to be sure, that his suffering has a meaning."[13]

Bad things do happen to good people. God created the world so that we would have the choice to love and follow him or to reject him and go our own ways. A certain amount of illness and suffering is due to mankind's bad choices and God allows the consequences to affect all of us. But God has promised that he would take whatever "bad" thing might be happening in our lives, sometimes to change it, but always to redeem it. A familiar passage is Romans 8:28, which says, "And we know that all that happens to us is working for our good if we love God and are fitting into his plans" (TLB).

As you live out your life with the meaning that God intended, God will work it all together for good – his good and your good. It will be a tremendous uplifter that will empower you, not only giving you purpose, but in most instances added energy, and in many situations actual healing.

Conclusion

Let us summarize this book with two appropriate passages of Scripture:

> "Don't you yet understand? . . . God . . . gives power to the tired and worn out, and strength to the weak. Even the youths shall be exhausted, and the young men will all give up. But they that wait upon the Lord shall renew their strength. They shall mount up with wings like eagles; they shall run and not be weary; they shall walk and not faint" (Isaiah 40:28-31, TLB).

Christ proclaimed: "I came that they might have life, and might have it abundantly" (John 10:10).

Endnotes

Chapter One

1. Story adapted from Francisco A. Tausk, editorial, "Skin and the Skin," *Archives of Dermatology,* January 2001, 137: 78-82.

2. G. P. Chrousos, "III. Therapeutic and Clinical Implications of Systemic Allergic Inflammation; Stress, Chronic Inflammation, and Emotional and Physical Well-being: Concurrent Effects and Chronic Sequelae," *Journal of Allergy and Clinical Immunology,* November 2000, 106(5): S275–91.

3. Chrousos, "The Stress Response and Immune Function: Clinical Implications," *Annals of the New York Academy of Sciences,* 2000, pp. 38–67.

L. J. Crofford, et al., "Hypothalamic-pituitary-adrenal Axis Perturbations in Patients with Fibromyalgia," *Arthritis and Rheumatism,* 1994, 37: 1583–92.

E. A. Mayer, "Review: The Neurobiology of Stress and Gastrointestinal Disease," *Gut,* December 2000, 47(6): 861–69.

Seija Sandberg, et al., "The Role of Acute and Chronic Stress in Asthma Attacks in Children," *The Lancet,* September 16, 2000, 356: 982–87.

"Correspondence, Stress and Asthma," *The Lancet,* December 2, 2000, 356: 1932.

Wolfgang Linden, et al., "Individualized Stress Management for Primary Hypertension," *Archives of Internal Medicine,* April 23, 2001, 161: 1071–80.

D. N. Brindley, et al., "Possible Connections Between Stress, Diabetes, Obesity, Hypertension and Altered Lipoprotein Metabolism That May Result in Atherosclerosis," *Clinical Science,* 1989, 77: 453–61.

Garg Amit, et al., "Psychological Stress Perturbs Epidermal Permeability Barrier Homeostasis," *Research in Dermatology,* January 2001, 137: 53–59.

Joachim Fischer, et al., "Experience and Endocrine Stress Responses in Neonatal and Pediatric Critical Care Nurses and Physicians," *Critical Care Medicine,* 2000, 28(9): 3281–88.

R. M. Sapolsky, "Why Stress Is Bad for Your Brain," *Science,* 1996, 273: 749–50.

Bruce S. McEwen, "Protective and Damaging Effects of Stress Mediators," *New England Journal of Medicine,* 1998, 338: 171–79.

D. Spiegel, "Healing Words: Emotional Expression and Disease Outcome," *The Journal of the American Medical Association*, 1999, 81: 1328–29 (Editorial).

Kathleen Brady, "PTSD," *Audio-Digest Psychiatry,* February 7, 2001, 30(3).

Selye, p. 94.

Jan Yeaman, "Stress & Coping Outline," 1998, Spring Arbor College.

B. S. McEwen, et al., "Stress and the Individual Mechanisms Leading to Disease." *Archives of Internal Medicine,* 1993, 153: 2093–101.

Richard A. Swenson, *Margin: How to Create the Emotional, Physical, Financial, and Time Reserves You Need* (NavPress, Colorado Springs, Colorado 1992), p. 122.

4. Mayer, "Review: The Neurobiology of Stress . . . ," 47(6): 861–69.

Regina Pally, "The Mind/Body Connection: The Neurobiology of Emotion," Conference given at Harbor General Hospital, Torrance, California, February 12, 2002.

5. Technically this has been called Allostatic Load. See McEwen, "Protective and Damaging Effects . . . ," 338: 171–79.

McEwen, et al., "Stress and the Individual Mechanisms . . . ," 153: 2093–101.

T. E. Seeman, et al., "Price of Adaptation–Allostatic Load and Its Health Consequences, MacArthur Studies of Successful Aging," *Archives of Internal Medicine,* 1997, 157: 2259–68.

G. P. Chrousos, & P. W. Gold, "The Concepts of Stress and Stress System Disorders: Overview of Physical and Behavioral Homeostasis," *The Journal of the American Medical Association,* 1992, 267:1244–52.

6. Selley E. Taylor & Rena L. Repetti, "Health Psychology: What Is an Unhealthy Environment and How Does It Get Under the Skin?" *Annual Review of Psychology,* 1997, 48: 411–17.

Psychiatric News, "Sleep Experts Ring Alarm On Sleep-Related Problems" reported by Lynne Lamberg, June 1, 2001, p.13.

7. D. G. Myers, "The Funds, Friends, and Faith of Happy People," *American Psychologist,* January 2000, 55(1): 56–67.

8. D. M. Buss, "The Evolution of Happiness," *American Psychologist,* January 2000, 55(1): 15–23.

Mark A. Schuster, MD, et al., "A National Survey of Stress Reactions After the September 11, 2001, Terrorist Attacks," *New England Journal of Medicine,* Nov 15, 2001, 345(20): 1507–12.

American Journal of Public Health; Association News, "2000, 18: Public Health Impacts of Job Stress," March 2001, 91(3): 502–503.

Swenson, p. 148.

M. A. Miller & R. H. Rahe, "Life Changes Scaling for the 1990's," *Journal of Psychosomatic Research,* 1997, 43: 279–92.

Christine Webber, as reported in the *London Daily Telegraph* by Sally Pook, October 16, 2000.

9. *U.S. News & World Report,* "Happiness Explained: New Science Shows How to Inject Real Joy into Your Life," September 3, 2001, pp. 46–54.

10. *The Lancet,* "Feature: Work-related Stress: Can It Be a Thing of the Past?" January 2000, 355: 124.

11. Selye, pp. 26–27, 60.

12. Seeman, et al., "Price of adaptation . . . ," 157: 2259–68.

Chrousos, "The Stress Response and Immune . . . ," pp. 38–67.

13. McEwen, "Protective and Damaging Effects . . . ," 338: 171–79.

14. Mayer, "Review: The Neurobiology of Stress . . . ," 47(6): 861–69.

Tausk, editoral, "Skin to Skin," 137: 78–82.

15. M cEwen, "Protective and Damaging Effects . . . ," 338: 171–79.

Taylor & Repetti, "Health Psychology: What Is an Unhealthy . . . ," 48: 411–47.

Angelique E. de Rijk, et al., "Complaints of Fatigue: Related to Too Much as Well as Too Little External Stimulation?" *Journal of Behavioral Medicine,* 1999, 22: 549–73.

16. Miller & Rahe, "Life Changes Scaling . . . ," 43: 279–92.

R. H. Rahe, "The More Things Change . . . ," *Psychosomatic Medicine,* 1994, 56: 306–507.

A. D. Kanner, et al., "Comparison of Two Modes of Stress Measurement: Daily Hassles and Uplifts Versus Major Life Events," *Journal of Behavioral Medicine,* 1981, 4: 1–39.

17. Selye, pp. 31, 70, 73.

18. Ronald N. Hoffman, *Tired All the Time: How to Regain our Lost Energy* (Poseidon Press, New York, 1993), p. 26.

J. E. Fischer, et al., Experience and endocrine stress responses in neonatal and pediatric critical care nurses and physicians," *Critical Care Medicine,* 28(9): 3281–88.

19.Shauna L. Shapiro, et al., "Stress Management in Medical Education: A Review of the Literature," *Academic Medicine,* July 2000, 75(7): 784–859.

Selye, p. 85.

20.Quoted by Myers, "The Funds, Friends . . .," 55(1): 56–67.

Chapter Two

1.Hans Selye, *Stress without Distress* (J. B. Lippincott Co., Philadelphia & New York, 1974), pp. 38–39.

2.A.Appels, et al., "Vital Exhaustion as a Risk Indicator for Myocardial Infarction in Women," *Journal of Psychosomatic Research*, 1993, 37: 881–90.

A. Appels & P. Mulder, "Fatigue and Heart Disease. The Association Between Vital Exhaustion and Past, Present and Future Coronary Heart Disease," *Journal of Psychosomatic Research*, 1989, 33: 727–38.

3.Selye, p. 94.

4. Debra Buchwald, et al., "Functional Status in Patients with Chronic Fatigue Syndrome, Other Fatiguing Illnesses, and Healthy Individuals," *The American Journal of Medicine*, October 1996, 101: 364–70.

Debra Buchwald & Deborah Garrity, "Comparison of Patients with Chronic Fatigue Syndrome, Fibromyalgia, and Multiple Chemical Sensitivities," *Archives of Internal Medicine,* 1994, 154: 2049–53.

5.J. B. Wright & D. W. Beverley, "Chronic Fatigue Syndrome," *Archives of Disease in Childhood,* October 1998, 79(4): 368–74.

Harrison's Principles of Internal Medicine; 15th Edition (McGraw-Hill, New York, 2001) p. 2541.

6.*Conn's Current Therapy* (W. B. Saunders Company, Philadelphia, 2001), pp. 109–11.

D. W. Bates, et al., "Prevalence of fatigue and chronic fatigue syndrome in a primary care practice," *Archives of Internal Medicine,* 1993, 153: 272–75.

Petros Skapinakis, et al., "Clarifying the Relationship Between Unexplained Chronic Fatigue and Psychiatric Morbidity: Results From a Community Survey in Great Britain," *The American Journal of Psychiatry,* 2000, 157: 1492–98.

David L. Stevens, "Chronic Fatigue," *Western Journal of Medicine,* November 2001, 175:315-19.

Niloofar Afri, PhD, and Dedra Buchwald, MD, "Chronic Fatigue Syndrome: A Review," *The American Journal of Psychiatry*, Feb 2003, 160: 221–236.

7.M. Sharp, et al., "A Report – Chronic Fatigue Syndrome: Guidelines for Research," *Journal of the Royal Society of Medicine,* 1991, 84: 118–21.

8.*Harrison's Principles of Internal Medicine* as quoted in Dwight L. Carlson, MD, *Run and not be weary,* (Fleming H. Revell, Old Tappan, N.J., 1974), p.17.

9.Paul Tournier, Editor, *Fatigues in Modern Society, Psychological, Medical, and Biblical Insights* (John Knox Press, Richmond, Virginia, 1965), pp. 24, 34.

Chapter Three

1. Miller & Rahe, "Life Changes Scaling . . . ," 43: 279–92.

2. McEwen, "Protective and Damaging Effects . . . ," 338: 171–79.

3. Skapinakis, "Clarifying the Relationship . . . ," 157: 1492–98.

4. Selye, p. 78.

5. A. Lyons & K. Chamberlain, "The Effects of Minor Events, Optimism and Self-esteem on Health," *British Journal of Clinical Psychology,* November 1994, 33(4): 559-70.

6. R. Williams, et al., "Life Events and Daily Hassles and Uplifts as Predictors of Hospitalization and Outpatient Visitation," *Social Science & Medicine,* April 1992, 34(7): 763-68.

J. F. Brosschot, et al., "Influence of Life Stress on Immunological Reactivity to Mild Psychological Stress," *Psychosomatic Medicine,* 1994, 56: 216–24.

7. Brosschot, et al., "Influence of Life Stress . . . ," 56: 216–24.

Lyons & Chamberlain, "The Effects of Minor Events . . . , " 33(4): 559-70.

8. L. J. Crofford, et al., "Hypothalamic-pituitary-adrenal Axis Perturbations in Patients with Fibromyalgia," *Arthritis and Rheumatism,* 1994, 37: 1583-92.

C. M. Ohannessian, et al., "Hassles and Uplifts and Generalized Outcome Expectancies as Moderators on the Relation Between a Family History of Alcoholism and Drinking Behaviors," *Journal of Studies on Alcohol,* November 1994, 55(6): 754-63.

L. Weller & O. Avinir, "Hassles, Uplifts, and Quality of Sleep," *Perceptual and Motor Skills,* April 1993, 76(2): 571-76.

T. M. Wolf, et al., "Relationship of Hassles, Uplifts, and Life Events to Psychological Well-being of Freshman Medical Students, *Behavioral Medicine,* Spring 1989, 15(1): 37-45.

J. J. Zarski, "Hassles and Health: A Replication," *Health Psychology,* 1984, 3(3): 243-51.

A. V. Ravindran, et al., "Primary Dysthymia: A Study of Several Psychosocial, Endocrine and Immune Correlates," *Journal of Affective Disorders,* September 1996, 40(1-2): 73-84.

A. V. Ravindran, et al., "Stressful Life Events and Coping Styles in Relation to Dysthymia and Major Depressive Disorder: Variations Associated with Alleviation of Symptoms Following Pharmacotherapy," *Progress in Neuro-psychopharmacology and Biological Psychiatry,* July 1995, 19(4): 637-53.

9. A. D. Kanner, et al., "Comparison of Two Modes of Stress Measurement: Daily Hassles and Uplifts Versus Major Life Events," *Journal of Behavioral Medicine,* 1981, 4: 1–39.

Chapter Four

1. F. Friedberg, & L. A. Jason, *Understanding Chronic Fatigue Syndrome: An Empirical Guide to Assessment and Treatment* (American Psychological Association, Washington, D.C. 1998), p. 114.

2. John Ortberg, *The Life You Always Wanted* (Zondervan, Grand Rapids, Michigan, 2002), p. 77.

3. Tournier, p. 27.

4. Brent Curtis and John Eldredge, *The Sacred Romance: Drawing Closer to the Heart of God* (Thomas Nelson Publishers, Nashville, Tennessee, 1997), pp. 2, 42, 169–70.

5. Alice Fryling, *Too Busy? Saying No Without Guilt* (InterVarsity Press, Downers Grove, Illinois, 2002), p. 7.

6. Henri Nouwen, *The Way of the Heart* (Ballantine Books, New York; 1981), pp. 10–11.

7. Michael J. Wilkins, *In His Image: Reflecting Christ in Everyday Life* (Navpress, Colorado

Springs, Colorado, 1997), pp. 53–54.

8. Eugene H. Peterson, *The Wisdom of Each Other: A Conversation Between Spiritual Friends* (Zondervan Publishing House, Grand Rapids, Michigan, 1998), p. 67.

9. John Eldredge, *The Journey of Desire: Searching for the Life We've Only Dreamed Of* (Thomas Nelson Publishers, Nashville, Tennessee, 2000), pp. 41, 80, 93.

10. G. Campbell Morgan, *Evangelism* (Fleming H. Revell, Rev. ed., Old Tappan, N.J., 1964), as quoted in Dwight L Carlson, MD, *Run and not be weary,* (Fleming H. Revell, Old Tappan, N.J., 1974), pp. 29–30.

11. Siang-Yang Tan, *Rest: Experiencing God's Peace in a Restless World* (Servant Publications, Ann Arbor, Michigan, 2000), p. 25.

12. de Rijk, et al., "Complaints of Fatigue . . . ," 22: 549–73.

13. J. B. Wright & D. W. Beverley, "Chronic fatigue syndrome, *Archives of Disease in Childhood,* October 1998, 79(4):368–74.

14. Dean Shea, "Clutter & Chaos," *Readers Digest,* May 2002.

Chapter Five

1. Simon Kemp & K. T. Strongman, "Anger Theory and Management: A Historical Analysis," *American Journal of Psychology*, 1995, 108(3): 397–417.

2. Redfords & Virginia Williams, *Anger Kills: 17 Strategies for Controlling the Hostility that Can Harm Your Health* (Harper Paperbacks, New York, 1998), p. 3.

3. Christopher I. Eckhardt, et al., "Anger and Hostility in Maritally Violent Men: Conceptual Distinctions, Measurement Issues, and Literature Review," *Clinical Psychology Review*, 1997, 17(4): 333–58.

Howard Kassinove, Editor, *Anger Disorders: Definition, Diagnosis, and Treatment* (Taylor & Francis, Publishers, Washington, DC, 1995), p. 28.

4. I. Kawachi, et al., "A Prospective Study of Anger and Coronary Heart Disease: The Normative Aging Study," *Circulation*, 1996, 94: 2090–95.

Taylor & Repetti, "Health Psychology: What Is an Unhealthy . . . ," 48: 411–47.

Ernest Harburg, et al., "Resentful and Reflective Coping with Arbitrary Authority and Blood Pressure: Detroit," *Psychosomatic Medicine,* May 1997, 41(3): 189–202.

Richard L. Verrier & Murray A. Mittelman, "Cardiovascular Consequences of Anger and Other Stress States," *Baillieres Clinical Neurology,* July 1997, 6(2): 245–59 .

M. Friedman, et al., "Alteration of Type A Behavior and Its Effects on Cardiac Recurrences in Post Myocardial Infarction Patients: Summary Results of the Recurrent Coronary Prevention Project." *American Heart Journal,* 1986, 112: 653–65.

P. Angerer, et al., "Impact of Social Support, Cynical Hostility and Anger Expression on Progression of Coronary Atherosclerosis," *Journal of the American College of Cardiology*, November 15, 2000, 36(6): 1781-88.

J. R. .Averill, "Studies of Anger and Aggression: Implications for Theories of Emotion," *American Psychologist*, 1983, 38: 1145–60.

5. J. M. Fernando Suman, "Hostility, Personality and Depression," *British Journal of Medical Psychology,* 1977, 50: 243–49.

Terry W. Moore & Joseph G. P. Paolillo, "Depression: Influence of Hopelessness, Locus of Control, Hostility, and Length of Treatment," *Psychological Reports*, 1982, 54: 875–81.

6. Margaret A. Chesney & Ray H. Rosenman, Editors, *Anger and Hostility in Cardiovascular*

and Behavoral Disorders (Hemisphere Publishing Corporation, Washington, D.C., 1985).

W. Doyle Gentry, et al., "Habitual Anger-Coping Styles: I. Effect on Mean Blood Pressure and Risk for Essential Hypertension," *Psychosomatic Medicine*, May 1982, 44(2): 195–201.

Kevin T. Larkin & Claudia Zayfert, "Anger Management Training with Mild Essential Hypertensive Patients," *Journal of Behavioral Medicine*, 1996, 19(5): 415–33.

David S. Krantz, et al., "Effects of Mental Stress in Patients with Coronary Artery Disease: Evidence and Clinical Implications," *The Journal of the American Medical Association*, April 12, 2000, 283(14): 1800–802.

Friedman, Thoresen, et al, "Alteration of type A . . . ," 112: 653–65.

W. Linden, et al., "Psychosocial Interventions for Patients with Coronary Artery Disease: A Meta-analysis," *Archives of Internal Medicine*, 1996, 156: 745–52.

Chapter Six

1. John T. Cunniff, "Americans Ask Where the Money Goes," *The Los Angeles Times*, February 11, 1972.

2. Myers, "The Funds, Friends. . . ," 55(1): 56–67.

3. Myers, "The Funds, Friends . . . ," 55(1): 56–67.

4. Ganzini, L., et al., "Prevalence of Mental Disorders After Catastrophic Financial Loss," *Journal of Nervous and Mental Diseases*, November 1990, 178: 680–85.

Chapter Seven

1. Nouwen, p. 11.

2. Alice Fryling, *Too Busy? Saying No Without Guilt* (InterVarsity Press, Downers Grove, Illinois, 2002), p. 17.

3. Nouwen, p. 21.

4. Brother Lawrence, *The Practice of the Presence of God* (Spire Books, Old Tappan, New Jersey, 1958), pp. 31, 14.

Chapter Nine

1. Abraham Lincoln (Source Unknown).

2. The monetary equivalents translate in many different ways in study Bibles, i.e., $10,000,000 versus 100 days' wages in the NASB and $100,000 versus $10 in THE MESSAGE; the NIV suggests "millions of dollars" versus "a few dollars" (so used here).

3. Gentry, "Habitual Anger-coping Styles . . . , 44(2): 195–201.

H. A. Kahn, et al., "The Incidence of Hypertension and Associated Factors: The Israel Ischemic Heart Disease Study," *American Heart Journal*, 1972, 84: 171–81.

4. *Multidimensional Measurement of Religiousness/Spirituality for Use in Health Research* (John E. Fetzer Institute, Kalamazoo, MI, October 1999), p. 36.

5. Keith Miller, *Habitation of Dragons* (Word Books, Waco, Texas, 1970), p. 161.

6. Lewis Smedes, *Forgive and Forget* (Pocket Books, New York, 1984), pp. 52–53.

7. Dallas Willard, *Renovation of the Heart* (NavPress, Colorado Springs, Colorado, 2002), p 60.

8. Bill Gothard, *BasicYouth Conflicts,* Section on a Clear Conscience (Oakbrook, Illinois), p. 24.

9.Smedes, p. 54.

10.Smedes, p. 141.

11.Goldie Bristol with Carol McGinnis, *When It's Hard to Forgive* (Victor Books, Wheaton, Illinois, 1982), p.116.

12.David Augsburger, *The Freedom of Forgiveness* (Moody Press, Chicago, Illinois, 1988), p. 39.

Chapter Ten

1.T. C. Friedman, et al., "Carbohydrate and Lipid Metabolism in Endogenous Hypercortisolism: Shared Features with Metabolic Syndrome X and Noninsulin-dependent Diabetes Mellitus," *Endocrine Journal*, 1996, 43:645–56.

K. Raikkonen, et al., "Psychosocial Stress and the Insulin Resistance Syndrome," *Metabolism*, 1996, 45:1533–38.

K. Raikkonen, et al., "Anger, Hostility, and Visceral Adipose Tissue in Healthy Postmenopausal Women," *Metabolism*, September 1999, 48(9): 1146-51.

G. M. Reaven, "Syndrome X: Is One Enough?" *American Heart Journal*, 1994, 127: 1439–42.

American Association of Clinical Endocrinologists, Findings and Recommendations from the American College of Endocrinology Conference on the Insulin Resistance Syndrome, Held August 25–26, 2002, Washington DC. [www.aace.com]

2.Penelope J. Hunt, et al., "Improvement in Mood and Fatigue after Dehydroepiandrosterone Replacement in Addison's Disease in a Randomized, Double Blind Trial," *The Journal of Clinical Endocrinology and Metabolism*, 2000, 85(12): 4650–56.

3. Lawrence M. Tierney, Jr., et al., Editors, *Current Medical Diagnosis & Treatment 2001* (Lang Medical Books, McGraw-Hill, New York, 2001), pp. 1404–11.

Medical Board of California, "An Update on the Epidemiology of Lyme Disease in California," *Action Report*, October 2001.

4 James Lane, et al., "Caffeine affects cardiovascular and neuroendocrine activation at work and home," *Psychosomatic Medicine*, July-Aug 2002, 64(4): 593–603.

Chapter Eleven

1.Colin Shapiro, MD, "Lecture on "Strategies to Manage the Sleepless Anxious Depressed Patient" given at Canadian Psychiatric Association meeting Banff, Alberta, November 1, 2002, quoting from the *British Medical Journal*.

2.Barbara Kantrowitz, "In Search of Sleep," *Newsweek*, July 15, 2001.

3.Benedict Carey, "Losing Sleep Over It," *The Los Angeles Times*, December 3, 2001.

American Family Physician, "Insomnia: Assessment and Management in Primary Care," June 1999, 59(11): 3029–38.

Stuart F. Quan, "Sleep Disorders Centers – Function, Structure, and Economics," *TEN:The Economics of Neuroscience*, September 2001, 3(9): 39.

4.Dolores Martinez-Gonzalez, et al., "Comorbidity of Insomnia with Medical and Psychiatric Disorders," *TEN:The Economics of Neuroscience*, September 2001, 3(9): 48.

5.Lynne Lamberg, "Sleep Experts Ring Alarm on Sleep-Related Problems," *Psychiatric News*, June 1, 2001, p.13.

6.Carey, "Losing Sleep Over It."

7.David A Katz, et al, "Insomnia Greatly Affects Quality of Life in Patients with Chronic Illness," *Journal of Family Practice,* 2002, 51: 229–35.

8.Mathew M. Clark, "Restless Legs Syndrome," *Journal American Board of Family Practice,* 2001, 14(5): 368–74.

9.J. L. Pike, et al., "Chronic Life Stress Alters Sympathetic, Neuroendocrine, and Immune Responsivity to an Acute Psychological Stressor in Humans," *Psychosomatic Medicine,* 1997, 59: 447–57.

10.Ronald D. Chervin, "Sleepiness, Fatigue, Tiredness, and Lack of Energy in Obstructive Sleep Apnea," *Chest,* August 2000, 118: 372–9.

Lyle D. Victor, "Obstructive Sleep Apnea," *American Family Physician,* November 15, 1999, 60(8): 2279–86.

11.Daniel F. Kripke, MD, et al., "Mortality Associated with Sleep Duration and Insomnia," *Archives of General Psychiatry,* February 2002, 59: 131–36.

E. Hartmann, et al., "Psychological Differences Between Long and Short Sleepers," *Archives of General Psychiatry,* 1972, 26: 463–68.

Chapter Twelve

1.As quoted by Mark A. Demitrack in *Audio-Digest Psychiatry,* March 22, 1993, 22, Side A.

2.Skapinakis, et al., "Clarifying the Relationship . . . ," 157: 1492–98.

J. B. Wright & D. W. Beverley, "Chronic Fatigue Syndrome," *Archives of Disease in Childhood,* October 1998, 79(4): 368–74.

3.Don L. Goldenberg, "Fibromyalgia Syndrome a Decade Later," *Archives of Internal Medicine,* April 26, 1999, 159: 777–85.

4.*Conn's Current Therapy 2001,* pp. 1030–32.

5.*Harrison's Principles of Internal Medicine,* pp. 2010–12.

Afri and Buchwald, "Chronic Fatigue Syndrome. . . ," 160:221–236

6.Multiple Chemical Sensitivities also goes by the name Idiopathic Environmental Intolerances (IEI), Environmental Sensitivities (ES), and lay people often refer to it as Environmental Illness.

Buchwald & Garrity, "Comparison of Patients . . . ," 154: 2049–53.

7.*Conn's Current Therapy 2001,* pp. 109–11.

Cecilia M. Jorge & Paul J. Goodnick, "Chronic Fatigue Syndrome and Depression: Biological Differentiation and Treatment," *Psychiatric Annals,* May 1997, 27(5): 365–71.

Benjamin J. Sadock & Virginia A. Sadock, Editors, *Kaplan and Sadock's Comprehensive Textbook of Psychiatry* (Lippincott, Williams, & Wilkins, Philadelphia, Pennsylvania, 2000), pp. 343–44, 1531–32, 1832–33.

Buchwald & Garrity, "Comparison of Patients . . . ," 154: 2049–53.

8.Andrew Stoll, "CFS and Fibromyalgia: True Disorders Coming of Age," *Psychiatric Medicine in Primary Care,* pp. 79–80.

9.Anthoney L. Komaroff, "The Biology of Chronic Fatigue Syndrome," *American Journal of Medicine,* 2000, 108: 169–71.

Afri and Buchwald, "Chronic Fatigue Syndrome. . . ," 160:221–236

10.The International Chronic Fatigue Syndrome Study Group and a number of experts on Chronic Fatigue Syndrome recommend the following evaluation: A good history and physical exam, including a mental status exam. Use of chemicals, alcohol, and other stimulants should be excluded as a cause of the fatigue. Laboratory tests should include a complete blood count with leukocyte differential, erythrocyte sedimentation rate, serum levels of alamine aminotransferase, total protein, albumin, globulin, alkaline phosphatase, calcium, phosphorus, glucose, blood urea nitrogen, electrolytes, creatinine, thyroid-stimulating hormone, and a urinalysis. If, on completing the above evaluation there is a suggestion of an abnormality, then appropriate tests should be performed to either verify or exclude another illness. "In clinical practice, no additional tests, including laboratory tests and neuroimaging studies, can be recommended for the specific purpose of diagnosing the chronic fatigue syndrome. . . Examples of specific tests that do not confirm or exclude the diagnosis of the chronic fatigue syndrome include serologic tests for Epstein-Barr virus, retroviruses, human herpes-virus 6, enteroviruses, and *Candida albicans;* tests of immunologic function, including cell population and function studies; and imaging studies, including magnetic resonance imaging scans and radionuclide scans (such as single-photon emission computed tomography and positron emission tomography) of the head." (See Keiji Fukuda, et al., "The Chronic Fatigue Syndrome: A Comprehensive Approach to Its Definition and Study," *Annals of Internal Medicine,* 1994, 121: 953–59).

11. Goldenberg, "Fibromyalgia Syndrome . . . ," 159: 777–85.

12. Robin McKenzie, "Low-Dose Hydrocortisone for Treatment of Chronic Fatigue Syndrome," *The Journal of the American Medical Association,* September 23/30, 1998, 280(12): 1061–66.

13. Michael Sharpe, et al., "Cognitive Behaviour Therapy for the Chronic Fatigue Syndrome: A Randomised Controlled Trial," *British Medical Journal,* 1996, 312: 22–26.

Pauline Powel, et al., "Randomised Controlled Trial of Patient Education to Encourage Graded Exercise in Chronic Fatigue Syndrome," *British Medical Journal,* February 17, 2001, 322: 387–90.

Wright & Beverley, "Chronic Fatigue Syndrome," 79(4): 368–74.

R. P. Bentall, et al., "Predictors of response to treatment for chronic fatigue syndrome," *British Journal of Psychiatry,* Sept 2002, 181: 248–52.

14. Penny Whiting, et al., "Interventions for the Treatment and Management of Chronic Fatigue Syndrome: A Systematic Review," *Journal of the American Medical Association,* September 19, 2001, 286: 1360–68.

15. Powel, et al., "Randomised Controlled Trial . . . ," 322: 387–90.

16. *British Medical Journal,* Letters to the Editor, 2001, 322: 1545; 1997, 315: 947, 1376.

17. *Current Medical Diagnosis and Treatment, 2001* (Lang Medical Books, McGraw-Hill, New York), pp. 30–31.

Chapter Thirteen

1. Randall D. Marshall, MD, "If We Had Known Then What We Know Now: A Review of Local and National Surveys Following September 11, 2001," *CNS Spectrums,* Sept 2002, 7(9): 645–49.

Terry W. Moore & Joseph G. P. Paolillo, "Depression: Influence of Hopelessness, Locus of Control, Hostility, and Length of Treatment," *Psychological Reports,* 1982, 54: 875–81.

Dan Blazer, et al., "Stressful Life Events and the Onset of a Generalized Anxiety Syndrome," *American Journal of Psychiatry,* September 1987, 144(9): 1178–83.

Clinical Psychiatric News, September 1990, "Life Stresses May Play a Role in Schizophrenia Onset."

Barry Glassner, & C. V. Haldipur, "Life Events and Early and Late Onset of Bipolar Disorder," *American Journal of Psychiatry*, February 1983, 140(2): 215–17.

A. Ellicott, et al., "Life Events and the Course of Bipolar Disorder," *American Journal of Psychiatry,* September 1990, 147(9): 1194–98.

Peter B. Roy-Byrne, et al., "Life Events and the Onset of Panic Disorder," *American Journal of Psychiatry*, November 1986, 143(11): 1424–27.

Carlo Faravelli, et al., "Prevalence of Traumatic Early Life Events in 31 Agoraphobic Patients With Panic Attacks," *American Journal of Psychiatry*, December 1985, 142(12): 1493–94.

Carlo Faravelli & Stefano Pallanti, "Recent Life Events and Panic Disorder," *American Journal of Psychiatry*, May 1989, 146(5): 622–26.

Clinical Psychiatric News, September 1990, "Life Stresses May Play . "

2. John M. Booker, & Carla J. Hellekson, "Prevalence of Seasonal Affective Disorder in Alaska," *American Journal of Psychiatry*, September 1992, 149(9): 1176–82.

Michael Terman, et al., "Chronic Fatigue Syndrome and Seasonal Affective Disorder: Comorbidity, Diagnostic Overlap, and Implications for Treatment," *American Journal of Medicine,* September 28, 1998, 105(3A): 115S–24S.

E. E. Michalak, et al., "Seasonal Affective Disorder: Prevalence, Detection and Current Treatment in North Wales," *British Journal of Psychiatry,* July 2001, 179: 31–34.

A. Magnusson, "An Overview of Epidemiologyical Studies on Seasonal Affective Disorder," *Acta Psychiatrica Scandinavica,* March 2000, 101(3): 176–84.

J. M. Haggarty, et al., "Seasonal Affective Disorder in an Arctic Community," *Acta Psychiatrica Scandinavica,* May 2002, 105(5): 378–84

3. This book was published by InterVarsity Press, Downers Grove, Illinois, 1994.

Chapter Fourteen

1. Cited in Chrousos, "The Stress Response and Immune . . . ," pp. 38–67.

2. A. W. Tozer, *The Pursuit of God* (Christian Publications, Inc., Harrisburg, Pennsylvania, 1948), pp. 110–12.

3. Harold G. Koenig with Gregg Lewis, *The Healing Connection* (Word Publishing, Nashville, Tennessee, 2000), pp. 9, 93–95.

D. B. Larson, et al., "Associations Between Dimensions of Religious Commitment and Mental Health Reported in *American Journal of Psychiatry* and *Archives of General Psychiatry*: 1978–1989," *American Journal of Psychiatry,* April 1992, 149(4): 557–59.

Dale A. Matthews, et al., "Religious Commitment and Health Status," *Archives of Family Medicine,* March/April 1998, 7: 118–24.

4. Generally ascribed to Augustine of Hippo a 4–5th Century theologian.

5. Attributed to Blaise Pascal a 17th Century French religious philosopher, mathematician, and scientist.

6. Dallas Willard, *The Divine Conspiracy, Rediscovering our Hidden Life in God* (Harper & Row, Publishers, New York, 1998), p. 360.

Chapter Fifteen

1. Cohen, "Psychological Stress and . . . ," 325: 606–12.

Mayer, "The neurobiology of stress . . . ," 47(6): 861–69.

Lyons & Chamberlain, "The Effects of Minor Events . . . ," 33(4): 559-70.

Michael Irwin, "Psychoneuroimmunology," Dr. Cousin's Center – UCLA Neuropsychiatric

Institute, Lecture given at Harbor General Hospital, Torrance, California, September 24, 2002.

Evans & Edgerton, " Life-events and . . . ," 64: 35-44.

2. For further information along this line see my book *Why Do Christians Shoot Their Wounded?*, Part II.

3. Cardno, et al., "Heritability Estimates for . . . ," 56: 162–68.

Brawman-Mintzer & Lydiard, "Biological Basis of. . . ," 57(Suppl. 3): 16–25.

4. Some discussion exists as to when and where this prayer originated. However, it is usually attributed to Reinhold Niebuhr, written in 1932.

Chapter Sixteen

1. Karen Gravelle, "Can a Feeling of Capability Reduce Arthritis Pain?" *Advances, Institute for the Advancement of Health,* Summer, 1985, 2(3): 8–13.

2. Randall Mason, et al, "Acceptance and Healing," *Journal of Religion and Health,* 1969, 8: 123–42.

3. Viktor E. Frankl, *Man's Search for* Meaning (Washington Square Press, Inc., New York, 1963), pp. xiii, 103–105.

4. Tournier, pp. 8–9, 21–22.

Chapter Seventeen

1. Ortberg, p. 76.

2. Eldredge, pp. 169, 178.

Chapter Eighteen

1. Swenson, pp. 91–92.

2. Tournier, p. 23.

Chapter Nineteen

1. Joe Wargo, "Psychoneuroimmunology: Mind-Body Medicine Merges into Mainstream," *GW Medicine,* Spring 1994, pp. 14–17.

2. Robert Ornstein and David Sobel, *The Healing Brain* (Simon & Schuster, New York., 1987), pp. 84, 87.

3. Herbert Benson, *Timeless Healing, The Power and Biology of Belief* (Fireside, New York, 1997), p. 267.

4. Simo Nayha, MD, PhD, "Traffic Deaths and Superstition on Friday the 13th," *The American Journal of Psychiatry,* Dec 2002, 159(12): 2110–11.

David Milne, "Can People Really Be Scared to Death?" *Psychiatric News*, June 7, 2002.

5. Arthur J. Barsky, et al., "Nonspecific Medication Side Effects and the Nocebo Phenomenon," *The Journal of the American Medical Association,* February 6, 2002, 287(5): 622–27.

Brian Reid, "The Down Side of Mind Over Matter," *Los Angeles Times*, May 27, 2002

6. A. Baum, et al, "Control and Intrusive Memories as Possible Determinants of Chronic Stress," *Psychosomatic Medicine*, 1993, 55: 274–86.

7. J. D. Brown & K. L. McGill, "The Cost of Good Fortune: When Positive Life Events Produce Negative Health Consequences," *Journal of Personality and Social Psychology,* 1998, 57: 1103–10.

8. Steven Locke, et al., "Life Change Stress, Psychiatric Symptoms, and Natural Killer Cell Activity," *Psychosomatic Medicine,* September/October 1984, 46(5): 441–53.

9. Schuster, MD, et al., "A National Survey of Stress . . . ," 345(20): 1507–12.

10. Robert L. Veninga, *A Gift of Hope: How We Survive Our Tragedies* (Ballantine Books, New York, 1985), p. 230.

S. Folkman, "Positive Psychological States and Coping with Severe Stress," *Social Science & Medicine,* 1997, 45: 1207–21.

11. Katrina H. Berne, *Running On Empty: Chronic Fatigue Immune Dysfunction Syndrome* (Hunter House Inc., Publishers, Alameda, California, 1992), p. 245.

Chapter Twenty

1. See book reviews in *New England Journal of Medicine,* Oct 30, 1997, 337: 1324–25.

2. Thomas Kelly, *A Testament of Devotion* (Harper & Row Publishers, New York, 1941), p. 95.

3. Johann Christoph Arnold, *Drained: Stories of People Who Wanted More* (The Plough Publishing House, Farmington, Pennsylvania, 1999), pp. 67–68.

Chapter Twenty-One

1. Berkman, "Assessing the Physical Health . . . ," 5: 413–32.

2. M. Cohen, "Happiness and Humour. A Medical Perspective," *Australian Family Physician,* January 2001, 30(1): 17–19.

J. W. Pennebaker & S. K. Beall, "Confronting a Traumatic Event: Toward an Understanding of Inhibition and Disease," *Journal of Abnormal Psychology,* 1986, 95: 274–81.

J. W. Pennebaker, et al., "The Psychophysiology of Confession: Linking Inhibitory and Psychosomatic Processes," *Journal of Personality and Social Psychology,* 1987, 52: 782–93.

S. Cohen, et al., "Social Ties and Susceptibility to the Common Cold," *The Journal of the American Medical Association,* 1997, 277: 1940–44.

S. Berkman, et al., "Social Networks, Host Resistance, and Mortality: A Nine-Year Follow-up of Alameda County Residents," *American Journal of Epidemiology,* 1979, 109(2): 186–204.

Berkman, "Assessing the Physical Health . . . ," 5: 413–32.

Eugene W. Broadhead, "The Epidemiologic Evidence for a Relationship Between Social Support and Health," *American Journal of Epidemiology,* May 1983, 117(5): 521–37.

Dr. Julius Segal, *Winning Life's Toughest Battles: Roots of Human Resilience* (Ivy Books, New York, 1986), p. 21.

Angerer, et al., "Impact of Social Support . . . ," 36(6): 1781-88.

Spiegel, Editorial: "Healing Words . . . , 281: 1328–29.

Janice Kiecolt-Glaser, et al., "Psychosocial Modifiers of Immunocompetence in Medical Students," *Psychosomatic Medicine,* January/February 1984, 46(1): 7–14.

3. Berkman, "Assessing the Physical Health . . . ," 5: 413–32.

John Cassel, "The Contribution of the Social Environment to Host Resistance," *American Journal of Epidemiology,* 1976, 4(2): 107–23.

Beverly Raphael MD, "Preventive Intervention with the Recently Bereaved," *Archives of General*

Psychiatry, December 1977, 34: 1450–54.

M. L. S. Vachon, et al., "A Controlled Study of Self-help Intervention For Widows," *The American Journal of Psychiatry,* November 1980, 137(11): 1380–84.

4. Cohen, et al., "Social ties and susceptibility . . . ," 277: 1940–44.

Berkman, et al., "Social Networks . . . ," 109(2): 186–204.

5. Randolph C. Byrd, MD, "Positive Therapeutic Effects of Intercessory Prayer in a Coronary Care Unit Population," *Southern Medical Journal,* July 1988, 81 (7): 826–29.

Philip R. Magaletta, et al., "Prayer in Office Practice: On the Threshold of Integration," *The Journal of Family Practice,* Mar, 1997, 44(3): 254–56.

Shimon Waldfogel, "Spirituality in Medicine," *Primary Care,* Dec 1997, 24(4): 963–67.

6. Faith Fitzgerald, "The Therapeutic Value of Pets (Commentary)," *Western Journal of Medicine,* January 1986, 144(1): 103–105.

Erika Friedmann, et al., "Animal Companions and One-year Survival of Patients after Discharge From a Coronary Care Unit," *Public Health Reports,* July/August 1980, 95(4): 307–12.

7. Pennebaker & Beall, "Confronting a traumatic event . . . ," 95: 274–81.

Pennebaker, et al., "The Psychophysiology of confession . . . ," 52: 782–93.

8. Leonard Derogatis, et al., "Psychological Coping Mechanisms and Survival Time in Metastatic Breast Cancer," *The Journal of the American Medical Association,* October 5, 1979, 242(14): 1504–508.

9. Cohen, "Happiness and humour . . . ," 30(1): 17–19.

10. Segal, p. 15.

Chapter Twenty-Two

1. Kanner, et al., "Comparison of Two Modes. . . ," 4: 1–39.

Michael H. Antoni, et al., "Stress Management and Immune System Reconstitution in Symptomatic HIV-Infected Gay Men Over Time: Effects on Transitional Naive T Cells (CD4+, CD45RA+, CD29+)," *The American Journal of Psychiatry,* 2002, 159: 143–45.

E. Diener, "Subjective Well-being. The Science of Happiness and a Proposal for a National Index," *American Psychologist,* January 2000, 55(1): 34–43.

Krantz, et al., "Effects of Mental Stress . . . ," 283(14): 1800–802.

Jac J. L. van der Klink, et al., "The Benefits of Interventions for Work-Related Stress," *American Journal of Public Health,* February 2001, 91(2): 270–76.

Whiting, et al., "Interventions for the Treatment . . . ," 286(11): 1360–68.

Alicia Deale, et al, "Long-term Outcome of Cognitive Behavior Therapy Versus Relaxation Therapy for Chronic Fatigue Syndrome: A 5-year Follow-up Study," *The American Journal of Psychiatry,* 2001, 158: 2038–42.

2. Kanner, et al., "Comparison of Two Modes . . . ," 4: 1–39.

3. James A. Blumenthal, et al., "Stress Management and Exercise Training in Cardiac Patients with Myocardial Ischemia," *Archives of Internal Medicine,* October 27, 1997, 157: 2213–23.

Dimen, et al., "Benefits From Aerobic Exercise . . . ," 35(2): 114–17.

P. Hassmen, et al., "Physical Exercise and Psychological Well-Being: Population Study in Finland," *Preventive Medicine,* January 2000, 30(1): 17–25.

B. W. Penninx, "A Happy Person, a Healthy Person?" *Journal of the American Geriatric Society,* May 2000, 48(5): 590–92.

Powel, et al., "Randomised Controlled Trial . . . ," 322: 387–90.

P. Salmon, "Effects of Physical Exercise on Anxiety, Depression, and Sensitivity to Stress: A Unifying Theory," *Clinical Psychology Review*, February 2001, 21(1): 33–61.

4. David L. Stevens, "Chronic Fatigue," *Western Journal of Medicine*, November 2001, 175: 315–19.

Powel, et al., "Randomised Controlled Trial . . . ," 322: 387–90.

Judith B. Prins, et al., "Cognitive Behaviour Therapy for Chronic Fatigue Syndrome: A Multicentre Randomised Controlled Trial," *The Lancet,* 2001, 357: 841–47.

Bentall, et al., "Predictors of response . . . ," 181: 248–52.

5. C. J. Hansen, et al., "Exercise Duration and Mood State: How Much is Enough to Feel Better?" *Health Psychology,* July 2001, 20(4): 267–75.

6. Herbert Benson MD, *The Relaxation Response* (Avon Books, New York, 1975), p. 141.

Herbert Benson MD, with Marg Stark, *Timeless Healing:The Power and Biology of Belief* (Fireside, New York, 1996), pp. 131–48.

Religion, Spirituality and Medicine: Research and Implications, Science and Mind/Body Medicine, Conference held May 2–4, 2002, Cambridge, Massachusetts.

7. Frankl, p. 68.

Chapter Twenty-Three

1. Steven Locke MD & Douglas Colligan, *The Healer Within* (A Mentor Book, New York, 1986), p. 220.

2. Ornstein & Sobel, p. 243.

Rose McGee, "Hope: A Factor Influencing Crisis Resolution," *Advances in Nursing Science,* July 1984, pp. 34–44.

3. E. H. Lin & C. Peterson, "Pessimistic Explanatory Style and Response to Illness," *Behavioural Research and Therapy,* 1990, 28: 243–48.

Kenneth I. Pargament PhD, "Religious Struggle as a Predictor of Mortality Among Medically Ill Elderly Patients,".*Archives of Internal Medicine*, August 13/27, 2001, 161: 1881–85.

C. Peterson, et al., "Pessimistic Explanatory Style Is a Risk Factor for Physical Illness: A 35-year Longitudinal Study," *Journal of Personality and Social Psychology,* 1988, 55: 23–27.

4. Judith Fitzgerald Miller, "Inspiring Hope," *American Journal of Nursing,* January 1985, pp. 22–25.

Fred Henker, "Hope and Recovery from Surgical Illness," *Comprehensive Therapy,* 1985, 11(11): 11–5.

John Bruhn, "Therapeutic Value of Hope," *Southern Medical Journal,* February 1984, 77(2): 215–19.

Daniel Goleman, "Denial and Hope (Denying The Worst and Hoping for the Best May Be Healthy, Not Unrealistic)," *American Health,* December 1984, pp. 54–9.

Locke & Colligan, pp.121–22.

M. F. Scheier & C. S. Carver, "Optimism, Coping and Health. Assessment and Implications of Generalized Outcome Expectancies," *Health Psychology,* 1985, 4: 219–47.

M. F. Scheier, et al., "Dispositional Optimism and Recovery from Coronary Artery Bypass Surgery: The Beneficial Effects on Physical and Psychological Well-being," *Journal of Personality and Social Psychology,* 1989, 57: 1024–40.

M. F. Scheier & C. S. Carver, "Effects of Optimism on Psychological and Physical Well-being: Theoretical Overview and Empirical Update," *Cognitive Therapy and*

Research, 1992, 16: 201–28.

Toshihiko Maruta, et al., "Pessimistic Outlook Linked to Poorer Health After 30 Years," *Mayo Clinical Proceedings,* 2002, 77: 748–53.

5. E. Stanley Jones, excerpt from the "Divine Yes," *Eternity Magazine*, February 1975.

6. Segal, p. 95.

7. Veninga, p. 88.

8. *U. S. News & World Report,* "Happiness Explained . . . ," pp. 46–54.

Locke & Colligan, p. 220.

Segal, p. 95.

Harold G Koenig, Religion, Spirituality and Medicine: Research and Implications, Science and Mind/Body Medicine, Conference held May 2–4, 2002, Cambridge, Massachusetts.

9. K. Kroene, et al., "Chronic Fatigue in Primary Care: Prevalence, Patient Characteristics, and Outcomes," *The Journal of the American Medical Association,* 1988, 260: 929–34.

Chapter Twenty-Four

1. Fielding H. Garrison, *An Introduction to the History of Medicine,* Fourth Edition (W.B. Saunders Company, Philadelphia, 1929), pp. 435–36.

2. Koenig with Lewis, pp. 9, 94, 125–26, 128.

Harold G. Koenig, "Religion, Spirituality and Medicine: Research and Implications, Science and Mind/Body Medicine", Conference held May 2–4, 2002, Cambridge, Massachusetts.

David B. Larson, et al., "Associations Between Dimensions of Religious Commitment and Mental Health Reported in the *American Journal of Psychiatry* and *Archives of General Psychiatry*: 1978–1989," *The American Journal of Psychiatry,* April 1992, 149(4): 557–59.

David. B. Larson, et al., "Clinical Religious Research," *CMDS Journal,* Summer 1992.

Jeffry S. Levin, et al., "Religion and Spirituality in Medicine: Research and Education," *The Journal of the American Medical Association*, September 3, 1997, 278(9): 792–93.

Mary A. Greenwold Milano & David B. Larson, "The Research Shows: Religion Is Healthy," *CMDS Journal,* Fall 1995, pp. 5–7.

3. Levin, et al., "Religion and Spirituality . . . ," 278, 9:792–93.

4. Of the 1,200 research studies and articles written, many different facets of faith have been examined. Some evaluate church membership, others church attendance; some evaluate religious activities, others spiritual commitment; and still others evaluate "religiosity," "spirituality," or prayer. Needless to say there is much overlap in these various groupings. Due to the limited space in one chapter I have combined the various studies and listed them all under the general heading of faith.

Harold G. Koenig, Conference held May 2–4, 2002.

Cohen, "Happiness and Humour . . . ," 30, 1: 17–19.

J. Gartner, et al., "Religious Commitment and Mental Health: A Review of the Empirical Literature," *Journal of Psychology and Theology,* 1991, 19: 6–25.

Harold G. Koenig, et al., "Religious Coping and Depression Among Elderly, Hospitalized Medically Ill Men," *The American Journal of Psychiatry,* December 1992, 149: 1693–700.

Larson, et al, "Associations Between Dimensions . . . ," 149(4): 557–59.

The American Journal of Psychiatry, "Letters to the Editor," May 1999, 156(5): 808–10.

S. M. Arnes, et al., "Religious Affiliation and Mental Health – Is There a Connection?

Health Survey in Finnmark 1990," *Tidsskrift For Den Norske Laegeforening*, December 1996, 116(30): 3598–601.

A. W. Braam, et al., "Religiosity as a Protective or Prognostic Factor of Depression in Later Life; Results from a Community Survey in The Netherlands," *Acta Psychiatrica Scandinavica*, 1997, 96: 199–205.

Koenig with Lewis, pp. 94, 125–26, 128.

Larson, et al., "Clinical Religious Research."

David B. Larson, "Religion Doesn't Harm, It Heals," *Physician*, November/December 1993, pp. 20–22.

Susan S. Larson & David B. Larson, "Clinical Religious Research: How to Enhance Risk of Disease (Don't Go to Church)," *CMDS Journal*, Fall 1992.

Levin, et al., "Religion and Spirituality . . . ," 278(9): 792–93.

Matthews, et al., "Religious Commitment . . . ," 7: 118–24.

Peter Pressman MA, et al., "Religious Belief, Depression, and Ambulation Status in Elderly Women with Broken Hips," *The American Journal of Psychiatry*, June 1990, 147(6): 758–60.

K. A. Sherrill and D. B. Larson, "Adult Burn Patients: the Role of Religion in Recovery," *Southern Medical Journal*, 1988, 81: 821–29.

Shimon Waldfogel, "Spirituality in Medicine," *Primary Care*, December 1997, 24(4): 963–7.

F. D. Willets & D. M. Crider, "Religion and Well-Being: Men and Women in the Middle Years," *Review of Religious Research*, 1988, 29: 281–92.

Benson with Stark, pp. 169–91.

Greenwold Milano & Larson, "Research Shows . . . ," pp. 5–7.

Lynn G. Underwood, PhD & Jeanne A. Teresi, EdD, PhD, "The Daily Spiritual Experience Scale: Development, Theoretical Description, Reliability, Exploratory Factor Analysis, and Preliminary Construct Validity Using Health-Related Data," *Annals of Behavioral Medicine*, 2002, 24(1): 22–33.

5. Schuster, et al., "A National Survey of Stress . . . ," 345(20): 1507–12.

Benson with Stark, pp. 197–8.

Chapter Twenty-five

1. Lawrence, p. 12.

2. Dr. & Mrs. Howard Taylor, *Hudson Taylor's Spiritual Secret* (Moody Press, Chicago, 1932), pp. 155, 161, 178, 156–57.

3. Ornstein & Sobel, p. 257.

4. Tournier, pp. 22, 29, 23.

5. Tournier, pp. 18, 20.

6. Janice Kiecolt-Glaser, et al., "Psychosocial Enhancement of Immunocompetence in a Geriatric Population," *Health Psychology*, 1985, 4(1): 25–41.

Janice Kiecolt-Glaser & Ronald Glasser, "Psychological Influences on Immunity," *Psychosomatics*, September 1986, 27(9): 621–24.

7. Tan, pp. 22–23.

8. Curtis & Eldredge, pp.1 71–72, 174–75.

9. Catherine Marshall, *Beyond Our Selves* (McGraw-Hill Book Company, Inc, N.Y. 1961), pp. 39, 82–83, 92–95.

Chapter Twenty-Six

1. *U.S. News & World Report,* "Happiness Explained . . . ," pp. 46–54.

2. Ken L. Williams & Gaylyn Williams Whalin, *The Door to Joy* (Broadman & Holman, Nashville, Tennessee, 1993), p. 10.

3. Joe Aldrich, "Joy: The Illusive Fruit," as quoted in Williams & Whalin, p. 10.

4. Myers, "The Funds, Friends . . . ," 55(1): 55–56.

U.S. News &World Report, "Happiness Explained . . . ," pp. 46–54.

5. Eldredge, p. 125.

6. as quoted in Ortberg, p. 66.

7. *U.S. News &World Report,* pp. 46–54, A Report on Robert Emmons of the University of California–Davis.

8. Veninga, pp. 271, 276, 278.

Chapter Twenty-Seven

1. A. Antonovsky, as quoted in Suzanne Kobasa, et al., "Hardiness And Health; a Prospective Study," *Journal of Personality and Social Psychology*; 1982, 42(1): 168–77.

2. Frankl, p. xiii.

3. Frankl, pp. 154, 179

4. Segal, p. 58.

5. Segal, p. 58

6. Harold Kushner, *When All You've Ever Wanted Isn't Enough,* (Pocket Books, N.Y., 1965), p. 18.

7. Suzanne C. Kobasa, "Stressful Life Events, Personality, and Health: An Inquiry into Hardiness," *Journal of Personality and Social Psychology*, January 1979, 37(1): 1–11.

Kobasa, et al., "Hardiness and Health . . . ," 42(1): 168–77.

Folkman, "Positive Psychological States . . . ," 45: 1207–21.

L. R. Peterson & A. Roy, "Religiosity, Anxiety, and Meaning and Purpose: Religion's Consequences for Psychological Well-Being," *Review of Religious Research,* September 1985, 27: 49–62.

Multidimensional Measurement of Religiousness / Spirituality for Use in Health Research, p. 36.

8. Frankl, p. 157.

9. Kushner, p. 29.

10. Harold G. Koenig MD, "Religion, Spirituality and Medicine: Research and Implications, Science and Mind/Body Medicine," Conference held May 2–4, 2002, Cambridge, Massachusetts.

Koenig with Lewis, p. 126.

Folkman, "Positive Psychological States . . . ," 45: 1207–21.

Peterson & Roy, "Religiosity, Anxiety, and Meaning . . . ," 27: 49–62.

11. Dwight Carlson & Susan Carlson Wood, *When Life Isn't Fair: Why We Suffer and How God Heals* (Harvest House Publishers, Eugene, Oregon, 1989), p. 172.

12. Lawrence, p. 62.

13. Frankl, p. 179.